First Overland

First Overland

LONDON-SINGAPORE BY LAND ROVER

Tim Slessor

Photographs *by*
Antony Barrington Brown

Signal Books
Oxford

Signal

This edition published in 2005 by
Signal Books Limited
36 Minster Road
Oxford
OX4 1LY
www.signalbooks.co.uk

First published in 1957 by George G. Harrap & Co. Ltd.
© Tim Slessor, 1957, 2005
Reprinted 2005
Reprinted 2006
Reprinted 2009

A catalogue record for this book is available from the British Library

ISBN 1-904955-14-2 Paper

Cover Design: Baseline Arts
Cover Images: Antony Barrington Brown

Printed in India

CONTENTS

✥

To all those who have helped me
with my spelling—
for without that help the reading of this book
would be almost impossible
T.S., May 1957

And to my wife, Janet.
We had not long met when I wrote
the dedication above—she was one of my 'helpers'.
Always supportive, now she is gone.
T.S., August 2005

FOREWORD

by Sir David Attenborough.

Today they are all into their seventies—grey-haired and grandfathers every one. But when I first met them they were mere undergraduates barely into their twenties. (Come to think of it, I was not *that* much older myself.) They wanted to know if, as the producer in charge of the BBC's Exploration Unit, I could be persuaded to back them in a seemingly madcap adventure. They suggested—with, I may say, no doubts or hesitations—that they could make some 'really good programmes' if only I would go along with their idea. So I took a risk—in those early TV days one sometimes did. They got £200 (with which to buy a clockwork camera) and enough film to start them down the road. I promised that there would be more film if, when they sent back the first batch, I liked what I saw. Well, I did. And a year later, when they got home, the end-result was just as they had predicted: three 'really good programmes' for a series called *Travellers' Tales*. And a book.

This *is* that book, reprinted after half a century. Over the years it has become something of an overlanders' bible. Indeed, one might reasonably claim that both the journey and its telling are now regarded as classics of their kind. Someone once put it rather well when they said that the only good reason for not buying a copy for your son's or husband's birthday is that "he will almost certainly then want a Land Rover for Christmas." An early critic (in *Motor* magazine) put it even more simply: "I think this is the best travel book I have ever read."

In many ways the world has shrunk since the mid-1950s, but that is primarily in terms of the many advances in air travel. The fact is that their own *landward* journey would be quite impossible today. Indeed, it has not been possible since about 1958—when it was reported that the Ledo/Stilwell Road had finally been washed away and gone back to the jungle. In any case, even if that road had survived, for the last three decades (or more) the totalitarian regime of Burma/Myanmar would never have granted visas for a land entry across the country's far northern frontier. The Indians too have long barred travellers from their side of the Assam/Myanmar border area. Further east, it would almost certainly be impossible to get permission to leave Burma across the Salween and over the Shan hills to Thailand; the Burmese army has been fighting the Shan independence movement for the last thirty years.

Elsewhere there are other problems. One thinks of the Middle East— Iraq, Iran, Baluchistan, Afghanistan... Members of the expedition are the first to point to their luck in having attempted their journey during a very short 'window of opportunity'. They also say that they were lucky in terms of the weather they arrived at the most problematic part of their route (the many-rivered eastern side of the Naga Ranges running down to the Chindwin and, eventually, to the Irrawaddy) in what was a particularly dry year.

The only part of their route which would now be easier is the leg from southern Thailand into northern Malaya. In 1956 there was a gap of more than 100 miles. There was no road, only a railway line. They planned to bump down the sleepers. But then they heard that only a few weeks earlier some bulldozers had made a surveyors' trace through the jungle— preparatory to the building of a proper road. In one very long day they were able to follow that trace. The road itself was built three years later.

So what, I think I hear you ask, have the six young men who made that long journey been doing for the last fifty years? I too was curious to find out. So I asked them...

Not too surprisingly, two of the six, Adrian Cowell and Tim Slessor, quickly found a home in documentary television. Adrian became, first, a director on an early ITN current affairs series called *Roving Report*; it took him from Tibet to Timbuktu, from New Guinea to the Andes. Later, he followed the freelance trail—with a particular penchant for films about the opium smugglers of the Burmese hill-country, and, on the other side of the world, about the remote tribes of the Amazon (which is where he is once again, even as I write). Many of his films—some of which have taken him two careful years to make—have been seen worldwide, and have won some of the highest awards in the business. Always a wanderer to the remotest corners, he still seems to have no fixed abode—just an e-mail address. Even then, as he says (if one can find him), "I'm not often within range of a cyber café."

Tim Slessor joined the BBC before he had even finished writing the expedition's book. He too became a traveller—making documentaries from the Outback to the Arctic. Over the years he developed a particular interest in the United States. Indeed, at one time he 'upped sticks' (with his wife and children) and went to work for a year in Wyoming—which, perhaps, is why he takes particular pride in an award from the Cowboy Hall of Fame for two films about The West made for Alistair Cooke's *America* series. Later, he became a London-based series editor. "That was mainly sending other people out to have the fun—interesting. But I much preferred to be out there myself." So, in the end, he too went freelance— more travelling. More recently, and now retired, he enjoys sailing his boat, from the Hebrides to Biscay. And he has just written another book: an investigation of the dissembling and half-truths coming out of Whitehall.

Antony Barrington Brown, (always known as BB) was the cameraman—for both film and stills. On getting home from the expedition, he ran his own photographic business in Cambridge until, he says, "a road-widening scheme saw my studio flattened." So, ever adaptable, he turned a hobby into a profession; he became an inventor. His designs ranged from a novel and very economic way of house building ('get the roof up first') to a quick way of erecting exhibition and industrial shelving. The latter is now in use all over the world, and had BB invented it on his own account rather than for his employer he would be a very rich man. As it is he had to be satisfied with a gold medal: "Nice, but it didn't pay the rent." So he went off to his beloved Wiltshire to start his own company—solving problems, building more 'inventive' houses, and making industrial furniture. Lately, now semi-retired, he works with and for his wife, an acclaimed sculptor. Last year, he was awarded the MBE for myriad services to his local community. And he has recently been elected a Fellow of the Royal Photographic Society—a life-long ambition.

Nigel Newbery was the youngest of the crew and the only one from Oxford. Indeed, unlike the others who were all fully-fledged graduates by the time the expedition set out, Nigel still had another year of studies to go. So, inevitably, (as this book explains) he took some stick from his Cambridge 'superiors'; indeed, it is said that they sometimes introduced him as "Our young undergraduate friend from Oxford". But he took it in good part and, anyway, as the others now acknowledge, "Nigel, even then the embryo wheeler-dealer, is probably worth as much as the rest of us put together." He first went into advertising, but became disenchanted working out "which balloon should go into which cereal packet". So, with a partner, he set up a company with (he decided) a novel twist to 'boil-in-a-bag' catering. All went well until a much bigger company saw profit in the self-same novel twist. So Nigel took off to build an abattoir in Bechuanaland. When he came home, he started in venture capital—which, as he says, "is mostly about risking other people's money." But then, as he goes on, it seemed simpler to get involved in actually managing some of the ventures himself. One thing led to another and, in time, he became the CEO or chairman of slew of successful companies, a director of others, and what he calls a 'consultant-handyman' to yet others. Now semi-retired in Cumbria, he can return to an earlier passion, the piano. And, between times, he goes trekking in the Himalayas with his wife.

By all accounts, as the expedition's linguist and visa campaigner, Pat Murphy developed into his own self-propelled, one-man diplomatic corps. Indeed, he evidently so impressed at least two British ambassadors along the way that, on the expedition's return, he was recruited by the Foreign Office. An early posting was to communist Poland where, as he tells it, he began a formative interest in the totalitarian regimes of eastern Europe and Russia—an interest which would, over the years, grow to a considerable expertise and, no doubt, play a part in his eventually being awarded the CMG. But, back in those early days, no sooner had he perfected his Polish than he was (typically?) posted to the other side of the world, to Cambodia. Later, as he ascended the diplomatic ladder, he served in Germany and Austria where, once again, the countries to the East engaged his attention. But when communism finally collapsed in the late 1980s, Pat was over the hills and far away; he had become a political advisor to the Sultan of Oman. Finally, since retiring from FO he has developed a whole new career. He works for a development agency (a sort of 'senior' VSO) which arranges for retired experts (in medicine, health, education, engineering, etc.) to help third-world countries and, also, to advise some of the emerging economies of eastern Europe. So nowadays Pat spends much of his time back in his beloved Poland. Indeed, he takes as much pride in the Officers' Cross of the Order of Merit, recently awarded him by the Polish President, as he does in that earlier CMG.

Once on the road (and quite often off it), the expedition was more dependent on Henry Nott than anyone else. He was the mechanic. The others say that no matter what the problem, he just quietly got on with it. 'No fuss' was his motto. So, I am told that in 32,000 miles the two cars hardly missed a beat. But Henry's practical skills were later to broaden well beyond the intricacies of carburettor adjustment, grease nipples and rear wheel-bearings. As a young man he bought a rundown farm near Rugby and, over the years, he and his wife turned it into a successful, indeed a model business. On the side, he converted derelict cowsheds into modern cottages, and rebuilt an old school. Later, he became chairman of the parish council, he served as a church warden, he got involved with the NFU. Between times he walked 600 miles on a pilgrimage to Santiago de Compostela, he sailed the Atlantic, and he went to Nepal to advise on cows and dairying. Then two years ago, quite unexpectedly, he died. After his memorial service—so crowded was the village church that people were standing in the doorway—one of his expedition friends (they were all there) said that Henry was "as modest a person as one could ever meet— a very quiet Englishman—a gentleman who just got on with it—no fuss." The expedition think that he would have been rather pleased with that epitaph.

Tim Slessor says that they are sometimes asked if they are all still friends and do they still see each other. He answers 'yes' to both questions. "But we become terrible bores when the talk gets 'expeditional'—which it does almost immediately. 'Do you remember this?' 'Do you remember that?' 'What about old So-and-So?' Our wives had heard it all before—many times. So they just smile in the way that wives do, and push off to make a pot of tea in the kitchen."

Perhaps understandably, their wives have had enough. But, for the rest of us, it seems to me that this tale of a most unusual adventure is just as fresh and just as much fun as in the year it was written.

David Attenborough
June 2005

PREFACE

I suppose that an author who has told his story well should not really need a preface. I need a preface.

On our journey we did so much, saw so many things, met so many people, and drove so far that I have found it impossible to include more than a thin part of the whole. My main problem has always been one of deciding what to leave out. Often I have just had to take pot luck and hope for the best; sometimes I have chosen wrongly—but it is too late to go back now. Nevertheless, the reader has some right to know what he will not find.

The most serious omission of all is the story of the second half of our journey, six months out of twelve. Those six months were the drive home from Singapore, and they included more than half of our field-work. But I have decided to leave them out (apart from a brief Appendix summary) because, although on reaching our outward destination *we* had to turn round and come back, it occurs to me that it is expecting too much of the reader to do likewise—even though the return was made by a different route. However, I take the chance to point out that our *complete* journey (London—Singapore—London) led across twenty-one countries, and covered 32,000 miles.

There are other omissions as well, and just because, for example, I do not catalogue our impressions of the New India, or discuss our field-work in more detail, or make more mention of the many friends who helped us on our way, it does not mean that we went about with our eyes shut or are ungrateful. It means that it has not been possible for me to include these various topics and, at the same time, combine brevity with reasonable continuity. My endeavour has not been to include something about everything, but to turn what for us was a wonderful journey into what for the reader will be—I hope—a passable story.

Why did we go? I am not going to be drawn into a discussion of whether we did anything useful. We went because, if I may coin a cliché, we wanted to. I will not try to explain our motives more deeply, but that does not mean that they were merely superficial. Nevertheless, perhaps I might make a point by mentioning a few random names: Baalbek, Baghdad, Katmandu, Ledo, Mandalay, Bangkok, and Trebizond. These, and a few hundred more, are no longer just names. To me they've become *places*—because I've been to them. That, then, is my own very brief philosophy of travel. I count myself very lucky, since, if I should never again travel farther afield than the ways London Transport can provide, I have enough recollections to make me a thundering bore for the rest of my life.

I must, of course, acknowledge the deep debt that we owe to all those who helped us, both before we left England and then all along our route. Particularly we thank our Home Team, for they did much of the work while we had all of the fun. Without their help we might be driving yet.

One more thing. Whatever else the reader is tempted to think that we did, there is one thing that we did not do. We did not 'gallivant' —please. The Expedition has a deep and particular aversion to that verb.

T.S.
May 23, 1957

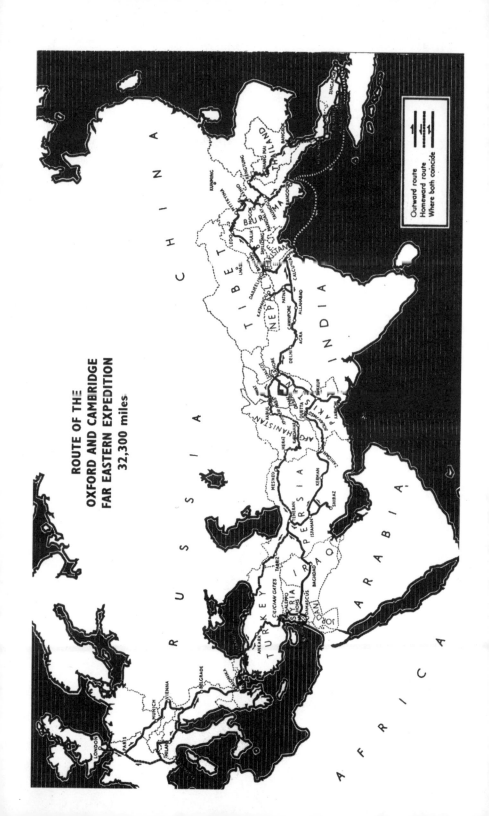

ROUTE OF THE
OXFORD AND CAMBRIDGE
FAR EASTERN EXPEDITION
32,300 miles

1.

The Idea

"YES, old boy," I said paternally, "a fine scheme, but the milk is boiling over."

It began, like almost everything else at Cambridge, late at night over gas-ring coffee. I lived on the same college staircase as Adrian Cowell, and I had gone up to his room one winter evening for a nightcap. He started talking of an idea he had for a combined Oxford and Cambridge overland expedition to Singapore.

"Well, no one else has ever done it—so why shouldn't we?"

"And you'll pay for it," I suggested heavily, "by digging a chutney mine somewhere in deepest Asia?"

But Adrian went on. He got out the atlas and talked more about the idea and its problems. When I left his room some hours later there were two of us with that idea. "The expedition was born." (These words are almost traditional to all expedition stories!)

Why Singapore? If one gets out an atlas, as we had done, one will see that the farthest point from London on the Eurasian land-mass is Malaya. One looks south-east over land for ten thousand miles, from the Atlantic to the Pacific.

Every year one reads of motorized parties leaving London for the Far East. Some, with a steaming radiator, or lack of funds, or both, get no farther than the Old Kent Road. Others, more fortunate, may reach the Middle East, and some, the organized few, eventually make the long and dusty road to Calcutta. But no one had ever gone on from there—though a few had tried.

Five hundred miles north-eastward from Calcutta, up beyond the tea-gardens of Assam, rise the tangled mountains of the Patkai and Naga Ranges. Jungle-covered offshoots of the Himalayas, they form one of the world's great natural barriers. No permanent road has ever crossed them. But in wartime 1944 two roads were cut and bulldozed through to Burma, and for a short time they were held open. Then, with the Japanese defeated, the need for these strategic supply-lines was gone.

During our inquiries we were told that neither road had been used since the War's end. It seemed that they would be overgrown and derelict, that their once graded surfaces would have been lashed by ten years of the heaviest monsoon rains in the world. But to go on by land from Calcutta there was no other way. This was the problem—and the reason to "why Singapore?"

I have written that in Adrian's room the expedition was 'born.' More accurately, I should have written that it was 'conceived,' for, as with most other ventures, an expedition does not just suddenly occur by some process of spontaneous generation. The gestation from obscure idea to illogical fact is a long and complicated one. No money, no equipment, no cars, no political permission, and the failure of all previous attempts to complete the overland drive—these were some of the pre-natal problems.

Sometimes, however, it does not pay to look too hard before one leaps. Rather, it seems better to have a little confidence and then look and leap simultaneously. Anyway, we had nothing to lose. We made inquiries; we started preparations.

The expedition, the two of us agreed, should consist of five or six people, but if Adrian and I had any pompous ideas about forming a two-man selection board to assess the worthiness of applicants they were quickly dispelled by "B.B." He had heard of our plans through the Cambridge grape-vine, and, having sought us out, announced that he was coming too.

His full name was Barrington Brown, but this was too long for any but the most formal use and, consequently, he is always called by his initials. Having graduated three years before, he had set up his own photographic business in Cambridge. The expedition had thus gained an expert cameraman, which, we reckoned, should somewhat raise its non-existent assets. Now there were three of us.

In the Royal Geographical Society's useful book *Hints to Travellers* one finds that "the only general principle is that the cost is enormously increased if the expedition requires a ship of its own." As our journey, with the exceptions of the Channel and the Bosporus, was intended to be entirely overland, the last thing we required was our own ship. But we did require two cars, for our chances of success would be greatly increased with two cars working in mutual support. Once these were in our possession we should really be able to call ourselves an Expedition—they formed the essential base on which to build. Much of the terrain east of Calcutta would be extremely difficult, and this was, in fact, one reason why no one else had ever made the journey—if it was possible at all. A tough four-wheel-drive vehicle with low-ratio gears was essential; relatively little discussion led to the conclusion that the cross-country Land Rover was the only car suitable. We needed two, and they cost £600 each. We had possibly £200 between us.

Adrian, looking as he leapt, opened up correspondence with the Rover Company. In this he was helped by the fact that in the previous year he had been the 'home representative' of the Oxford and Cambridge Trans-African Expedition. That party, using two Land Rovers of their own purchase, had driven to Capetown and back in the four months of the summer vacation. On their way they had created considerable interest in their vehicles, and we now hoped that from this example the Rover Company might recognize that undergraduates can—sometimes—have serious objectives, and the organization to carry them through. Perhaps they would lend us two Land Rovers? Maybe we could make a film for them? Perhaps and maybe. But we already knew that the Company received similar requests from almost every one who was going anywhere, and, as Rovers were clearly not in business for philanthropy, we waited pessimistically.

Meanwhile Adrian got in touch with various petrol companies. After an interview Mobilgas generously replied that if the Expedition could get the cars they would ask their associate companies along our route to help us with petrol supplies.

We called ourselves "The Oxford and Cambridge Far Eastern Expedition," though as yet there was no one from 'the other place' taking part.[1] [Endnotes are to be found on p.245] A network of contacts and undercover-men was alerted, and Adrian got in touch with all the Oxford colleges and relevant societies. While he was about it he also sent circulars to forty American universities. Why not an Oxford and Cambridge versus Harvard and Yale long-distance motor rally? To Adrian nothing was too obscure; he permanently wore a pair of long-range spectacles to bring far-fetched ideas a little closer.

B.B. was talking of films and photos. Why not a film of the journey for Television? He hurried off to London, and on returning announced—B.B. usually 'announces' rather than 'says' things—that the B.B.C. were interested. What about writing a book? Letters (on the Expedition's new headed notepaper) went off to various publishers. We were going from strength to strength, but were, to coin another cliché, building an Expedition without any foundations. We had no cars.

A few days after the beginning of the Easter vacation Adrian phoned me to say that a letter had arrived from the Rover Company. I saw him off for Birmingham a few days later.

Exactly how that vital interview went Adrian has never said. But he must have persuaded some one that we were capable of doing what we talked about, for, when he returned two days later and I met him in a London pub, he said, "Well, we've got them." Those were some of the best words that I have heard.

On returning to Cambridge for our final term, it was decided that the Expedition would not leave England until three months after we had graduated; until September. Thus time was allowed for exams *and* adequate expedition preparations. Departing in September also meant that we should not arrive on the Burmese frontier until the start of the dry season. This was essential if we were to stand a chance of getting into that country by land.

Now that the cars were certain, and our plans had some sense to them, another important object was added to that of 'overlanding' to Singapore. The Expedition would carry out some irrigation studies and research in Pakistan and India. The idea of some practical geographical field-work had been in our minds for some time, but until now—when it seemed that the Expedition would at least leave England—there had been little point in pursuing it.

One other matter was pressing. There were still only three of us, all from Cambridge. True, there had been faint inquiries from Oxford, as also from America, but they had all faded out. Meanwhile Henry Nott, the Secretary of the C.U. Auto Club, was keen to come, and by reputation he was a first-class mechanic. We went round to see him, and then there were four.

Just when all faith in Oxford had been lost a telegram arrived from some one who signed himself Newbery. He came over to Cambridge the following Sunday. Nigel was a second-year man at Worcester College, and thought it might be possible to obtain a year's leave to come with us—especially as our proposed fieldwork would be of some value to his course in Economics. He had the advantage of being a free-lance mechanic (i.e., he did not own a car), and, having explained our plans to him, we gave him a week to decide. At the same Sunday tea-party was a friend of mine, Pat Murphy. Pat and I both read Geography, and he was particularly interested in the intended irrigation work, for, as he put it, "I know about irrigation." He had spent the previous summer studying various French schemes in Morocco.

Nigel let us know two days later he could come. Pat was with us too. The 'team' was complete. Admittedly, Nigel was the only Oxford person, but when we suggested deleting 'Oxford' from our title he objected vehemently. So Oxford stayed.

For the next few weeks the tempo of things expeditional slackened while heads were bent to learn some of the facts necessary to satisfy the examiners. Even so, the Wool-trade of the Middle Ages and Erosion Cycle Theories rode uneasily in our minds alongside the Distances between Persian Petrol Points and How Much Water Six Men Drink in a Day.

Nevertheless, we managed to obtain reasonable degrees—though, long before the results came out, our preparations had begun in earnest again.

2.

Preparations

ACCORDING to his passport, Adrian was born in Tongshan (China) in 1934. This made him twenty-one, and the youngest member of the party. He had come straight up to St Catharine's College from school as a History Scholar. With his China coast connexions, he spent his first year organizing the Cowell Oriental Trading Agency, which imported Chinese porcelain figures, straw hats, and cheap ivory chopsticks from Hong Kong and sold them to undergraduates or shops in Chelsea. The energies he devoted to this enterprise rather affected his exam results. The consequence was that, at the end of his first year, his scholarship was reduced. So Adrian, taking on a partner, expanded the business and used the profits to make up the difference on his college fees.

Anything that smacked of commerce was an immediate attraction to him. Adrian was the only undergraduate I knew who could genuinely excuse himself from an engagement on the grounds that he had to see his accountant. It was natural that he should become the Expedition's Business Manager and Cashier. In addition to his 'long-range spectacles' he also had a very fertile imagination, and could write wonderful letters about the terrors of the 'burning sands and steaming jungles' that lay ahead. Many of these phrases found their way into our 'blurb sheets,' of which he was Editor-in-Chief. Blurb sheets were what one would expect them to be—roneoed sheets of blurb about the Expedition. There were 'academic blurb sheets' about our intended field-work which went to various learned bodies and societies; there were 'diplomatic blurb sheets,' which were sent to Embassies and Consulates along our route in order that they might make suggestions or comments on our plans; there were 'general-purpose blurb sheets'; 'commercial blurb sheets'; 'address-list blurb sheets'; and new editions of old blurb sheets. In fact, on more than one occasion the things got a bit out of control. In the commercial blurb sheet, for example, we said that "we shall be particularly happy to carry any product which, due to its distinctive shape or colour—such as an electric razor or a packet of soap-flakes—would be easy to incorporate and publicize in our T.V. film without actually mentioning its trade name." We were most concerned to discover that a 'distinctive shape' blurb had been erroneously dispatched to a well-known Trust Fund. No doubt the Trustees considered that there was nothing particularly distinctive about their shape or colour, and perhaps that is why we never had an answer.

In appearance Pat Murphy is rather of the crape-soled Latin co-respondent type. He says he was born in Ireland, and he speaks fluent French, good German, a little Spanish, can get by in Italian, and was educated in England. His vacation habitat was definitely Continental, usually Spanish. He claimed to be on first-name terms with the head waiters of almost every night club between Paris and Casablanca, he was a practising *toro aficionado*, and had mastered at least three major chords on the guitar. With this obviously international background, he was given the task of negotiating all our visas and passport endorsements. As our route was to cross twenty-seven international frontiers, Pat became a one-man Foreign Office and our No. 1 Form-filler. Armed with six passports, he campaigned with a dozen different Embassies for the next three months.

He had done his National Service with the R.A.F.; he never talked about it much—perhaps it was rather 'hush'? Perhaps that was the idea. Anyway, besides dealing with passports he was also the Navigator, and collected over fifty maps and followed every possible contact for information about the route. Although he was a pilot in the University Air Squadron, he was, strangely, the only person in our party who could not drive. Two of us used to take him out in a borrowed car to a disused air-field near Cambridge. He treated the car like an aircraft, and it was some time before we persuaded him that the gear lever was not, nor was worked like, a joy-stick. He also had trouble, he told us, in "getting used to this foot-throttle idea."

Pat and I were responsible for working out the Expedition's field-work programme. Irrigation was an obvious subject to choose, for, apart from Pat's previous experience, there were in our party two Geographers (Pat and myself), a Geologist (B.B.), an Economist (Nigel), an Agriculturalist (Henry), and a Historian (Adrian). Between us we covered quite a range of subjects, and would each, therefore, have something specific and different to contribute to the intended studies.

It was hoped that the Royal Geographical Society (to whom we were submitting our irrigation plans) would consider them worth while, and recognize us with a grant towards expenses incurred on the work. Pat and I had a sympathetic hearing from the Director of the Society, who forwarded our plans to the Awards Committee. They generously gave us £100.

B.B. was older than the rest of us. He had graduated in Natural Sciences three years earlier, and was, in fact, an M.A. This, he claimed, gave tone and respectability to the Expedition. His National Service in the Royal Armoured Corps was something he only vaguely remembered: "It was in the days when the War Office lived in a tent. This, he had us believe, was some time in the dim and dark middle 'forties. Since graduating he had taken up photographic journalism with a studio in Cambridge; his small flat became our H.Q. during the summer after the Colleges had closed.

He was—and is—not an easy person to know. He has an acid wit, and non-existent tact; if an idea does not meet with his approval it is "bloody awful." He was—and is—usually right, which sometimes does not please anybody. This take-it-or-leave-it-but-don't-push-me-around attitude is designed to intimidate. He would not agree that his bark is worse than his bite, and he will bark my head off when he sees this in print.

B.B. is one of the most practical and thorough persons I know; the sort of person who addresses and stamps an envelope before he has written the letter, and who can be absolutely relied on to get up in the morning an hour before anybody else. Besides being our "professional photographer and cameraman" (he likes the full title), we made him The Doctor. After all, it was reasoned, he had rows of antiseptic-looking flasks in his darkroom, and a degree in Natural Sciences. Obviously there was a connexion between drugs and developer. He saw it differently, and, in writing for advice to the University Health Service, began the letter with "Sir, I have been appointed to look after the medical side of this expedition solely by virtue of my chemical knowledge, which is, of course, quite irrelevant."

However, the job was tackled with characteristic thoroughness, and a comprehensive medical chest assembled. He 'clued up' in several books which, he morbidly announced, were of the opinion that for most tropical diseases we were liable to suffer "treatment is unavailing and the disease is almost invariably fatal."

For each of us he arranged a medical check, a visit to the dentist, and a course of twelve preventive injections. It was during a 'jabs week' that the Expedition, writing arms hanging useless, had to hire two shorthand typists in order that the 'secretarials' should continue uninterrupted. Planning, conferences, and arguments stopped for nothing,

Henry was the Chief Engineer. He had built several Austin Seven Specials, and raced them successfully at Silverstone Club Meetings. But, contrary to many of the sports-car set, he did not wear a flat cap, a bow tie, or cavalry trousers. In fact, Henry was very quiet—though he warmed considerably to the mention of king pins, gear ratios, or power drifts. In spite of being Secretary of the University Auto Club, he lavished his pride on a decrepit old van, about which the most satisfactory thing that could be said was that it sometimes started first time.

During the journey Henry's duties were obvious, but they began a long time before that. More thought and discussion centred on the cars than on anything else, for we were going to have to live in or around them for nearly a year. To pack twelve months' equipment into any car is a problem, but it was greatly increased for us by the variety of conditions we expected to meet, by limitations of space and pay-load, and by the multiplicity of functions the vehicles would have to perform. They had to be mobile cook-houses, workshops, camera tripods, pantechnicons, and even, if the need arose, ambulances. All this they had to be, and yet still remain capable of tackling some of the world's toughest terrain. They had to be warm in Persian frosts and cool in Indian heat, they had to get through mud or sand, and still be drivable at good speeds along the tarmac. Even Rovers were doubtful. "You don't want a cross-country vehicle; you want a cross-country miracle," they said.

Henry and Nigel (the second mechanic) went off to Rovers in Birmingham for a 'works course,' and to be present—like the skippers of new ships—at the fitting out of the cars. It was a great day three weeks later when the two cars, new, shiny, and with the Expedition's name painted on the doors, arrived in Cambridge. Everybody got in, out, under, and on top of them at least a dozen times, and then in turn drove them round and round the town until after midnight. We debated what to call them, but as one was painted dark blue and the other light blue they simply became known as "Oxford" and "Cambridge."

On each front bumper was a powerful drum winch (driven by the engine) and two jerry-cans for water. Inside was a heater, and, as well as the normal dials, oil-pressure and water-temperature gauges. Each car could carry fifty gallons of petrol in built-in tanks, which, at an average of twenty miles per gallon, would give us a range of one thousand miles. A sun-visor and roof-rack (which bolted right into the body) were fitted, and a sliding roof-hatch over the passenger's seat would keep the car cool or, with some one standing through it, it could be used for photography or guiding the driver below (when travelling across sand). A heavy tow bracket, a vice, and a quick-release fire-extinguisher were bolted to the rear of each car. For nearly all these modifications, and for many others, such as searchlights, oversize tyres, and high-frequency horns, we were drawing on the invaluable experience of our friends from the earlier Trans-African Expedition.

Nigel came in for a certain amount of harsh treatment when he first came to live in the H.Q. The rest of us—all Cambridge men in the first flush of our degree status—used to introduce him as "our young undergraduate friend from Oxford." But he gave as good as he got, and as an ex-Paratrooper he had plans for us all to learn judo. He was also the knowledgeable possessor of a book called *Mysteries of the Orient—Pagan Rites* (I think that was the title—anyway, it became compulsory Expedition reading!).

Besides being second mechanic, Nigel was the Quartermaster. This was one of the biggest single jobs of them all, and he took it on because, being the last to join us, he got no choice. He may have lacked choice, but the rest of us gave him no chance to lack advice. In conferences which lasted from early afternoon until midnight we would argue whether we should have paraffin or petrol stoves, whether space allowed a wireless, how much food and water should be carried at a time, what sort of clothes should be taken, whether sand mats (to stop the cars getting bogged) were a good idea, and how much they weighed, how many shovels should be carried, whether wool or cotton socks were best in the tropics—all these and dozens of other problems were finally hammered out. Then Adrian and Nigel would sit down and type letters of inquiry to various firms.

We had very little money, and could afford few items of equipment at retail prices. Why many firms to whom we wrote should have helped us with the reduced price, loan, or gift of their product one can only guess. I think there are three possible answers.

First, there were those concerns interested in the publicity that a 'first overland' might produce. This was probably true for most motor-accessory companies, or those with trade connexions in the Far East.

Second, there were those manufacturers who wished to know how their equipment stood up to the journey. It might be of interest to know, for example, that one component of an otherwise excellent article was very susceptible to dust or vibration, which could be easily remedied by firmer installation or packing. Another firm could make use of the information that in tropical heat and damp the lids of their containers warped, and therefore leaked.

A third motive was generosity. As they sometimes wrote, "We rather like the idea." But it is impossible to separate one motive from another. Generosity was clearly one reason for almost all our supplies. I take this opportunity to express our deep gratitude to those many, many firms that helped us. Without that help we could never have left England.

But ready cash was still a problem. Each person had placed what he had in the Expedition's account, and, between the six of us, this came to £600. In addition, we had grants from the R.G.S. and other bodies towards the field-work, and there was also the possibility of selling the advance rights for the book and film. We also hoped that during the journey it would be possible to make some pocket money through the sale of articles and photos. B.B. and I went down to London to negotiate over the book and film, and, after various discussions, sold the rights on both projects. It was good to know that other people were prepared to put some confidence in us. In the case of the film, the advance payment was immediately swallowed up in buying a cine camera with which to take the film for which we had just been paid!

Nigel was full of money-making ideas. He had heard of a film subsidiary which offered £25 for the best household tip of the week. Nigel's contribution to this organization was a method of toasting crumpets on a paper clip, but no acknowledgment, let alone £25, for this revolutionary device was ever received. So instead Pat and I went off and

\n

\ntook jobs for a part of the summer. Pat became a barman in a Cornish hotel, while I drove round the seaside resorts of England publicizing South African oranges!

\nMeanwhile work at the Cambridge H.Q. went on as usual. By this time over one thousand letters had been picked out on the typewriters, but it was to be nearer one thousand five hundred before we left. Parcels and crates were arriving every day, and B.B.'s work-shop looked like a contemporary Aladdin's Cave, with piles of everything from sulpha drugs to spark-plugs, toothpaste to a tape-recorder, medical kit to machete knives.

\nThe layout of the cars' interiors and the loading was worked out by a 'logistics sub-committee' of Henry and B.B., in close liaison with the Q.M. Some people might say that we were too military in our approach, but there were good reasons—although we did not take them all too seriously. Six people travelling self-sufficiently in equipment and belongings in two cars for a year cannot live in comfort without some organization. Any fool can be uncomfortable, and, as a result, ill-tempered—and a Land Rover is a very small place. But the details of loading will be explained later, for it was not until we had experimented under 'operational conditions' on the road that we came to the best and final arrangement.

\nBesides the Logistics Sub-committee, there were others to cope with the field-work plans, the design of the tent, and our route inquiries. The route as far as India seemed fairly straightforward—one drove down to the Bosporus, east through Turkey and Persia, then across Pakistan and into Delhi. Actually, we decided to diverge from this route and dip down into the Middle East in order to visit and film some of the historical sites in Syria, Lebanon, and Iraq. But the route eastward from Calcutta was almost as vague as ever. We had read all the Burma Campaign books, chased obscure wartime maps in Ministries and libraries, and written or talked to anyone who had ever been near Northern Burma. We had exchanged letters with tea-planters in Assam, with the High Commission in Delhi, with the Embassy in Rangoon, with people who had tried the journey before, and with every relevant motoring organization of which we had ever heard. But nowhere was there any reliable or modern information. Some people advised us to take a ship from Calcutta, which to us, with our

specifically overland intentions, seemed like telling a mountaineer to take
an aeroplane. By others we were condemned, and compared to people
who "go rock-climbing in sandals." Others were more encouraging, and,
thinking a route might be possible, gave hazy details and wished us luck.

Looking far ahead, our plan was to get up into Assam soon after the
end of the monsoon rains, and to try either of the old wartime roads from
India across the Naga Hills to Burma. If we failed to get through it was
intended to return to Calcutta and ship to Singapore in time to make an
overland attempt in the reverse direction before the end of that dry season.
But, in any event, it seemed that we should have to leave England in the
hope that, as we got nearer to the problem area, the information would
become more definite. Perhaps in Delhi or Calcutta we should find out
more than in London.

On the question of whether the Expedition should have a leader there
was some controversy. If it did then he would have to be elected, and this
would be rather invidious; besides, there was no one who stood out
beyond the rest in his display of 'officer-like qualities'! On the other hand,
without a leader there was no one to 'carry the can,' and before anything
could be done everybody had to be told about it. This would—and had
already—slowed us down considerably. But in the end the matter was
dropped; each person was responsible to the rest for his own department.
Therefore, we had no leader, or, alternatively, we were all leaders—
depending on which way one looked at our uniquely democratic system!

It was decided that B.B. and I would travel in the Oxford car with
Nigel, while the other three went in Cambridge. We did not intend to
stick too rigidly to this arrangement, but it was obviously better to have
one mechanic in each car, and it simplified loading if the rest of us did not
have to switch our personal kit (trunks and sleeping-bags) from one car to
the other any more than was necessary. Thus B.B. and I came to be Oxford
men by proxy.

One other facet of the planning has still to be mentioned—the Home
Team. It was essential to leave an 'administrative tail' (to use the Army
phrase) in England. Two or three friends were needed who were
thoroughly familiar with all our plans; who would forward and answer
mail; who would deal with inquiries and pass on our news to the firms and
individuals who had helped us; who would, in fact, act officially on our

behalf. Three people who had already given us much help, John Deuchars, Peter Wills, and Gethin Bradley, accepted the responsibility. No one at that stage realized how much work it would involve.

The only person who has not yet been introduced is myself, but, rather than risk inviting the written remarks of another member of the Expedition, I think it would be better to let this book speak for itself!

September 1st had been fixed as the starting-date a long time before, and in the last few weeks of August things became very busy. Nigel claimed to have developed a weal on his thumb from pressing piles of coins through the slots in phone-boxes while chasing last-minute items of equipment! (This is obviously an occupational disease, and might be known as "Expedition Thumb.") While the rest of us crossed our fingers, Pat took and passed his driving-test. If we lived anywhere in the last week it seemed to be in a fast train or car rushing up and down between London and Cambridge. There was even one occasion when Adrian typed urgent letters seated in the locked lavatory of the *Fenman Express*. But at last, with the cars run in, we optimistically decided we were ready—or as ready as we ever should be.

Our departure was hardly in the nonchalant tradition of most expeditions. During the morning we assembled at the Grenadier, a small mews pub just behind Hyde Park Corner. It would have been impossible for any onlooker to have claimed afterwards that "They took it all quite calmly." In fact, we flitted about in various stages of excitement while taxis were dispatched on important errands, urgent phone messages were taken or sent, and last-minute stores were packed into the cars.

The newsreel and photographic tribe arrived at opening time. Men wearing exposure meters and flat caps pulled yards of cable but from little black vans, and then crouched inside to tune our noises.

"Now tell me, Mr Nott, what gave you all the idea?"

"How long do you expect to be away, and what will be your route?"

"I wonder, Mr Cowell, if you would tell us in a few words what your main objectives are?"

Then we stood about in awkward groups or climbed aboard to lean out of windows and roof-hatches waving our synthetic good-byes to the cameras.

Friends and relatives arrived to peer anxiously inside the cars—"Oh, but how tiny! My dear, you will be careful, won't you?"—and to give us their good wishes, together with the innumerable names of god-daughters who had married Air Attachés in Kabul or brothers-in-law who were contractors in Baghdad. "You will look them up, won't you?" Eventually we went inside the pub for a drink and a Scotch Egg; some one already at the bar stood the round, and made the inevitable suggestion that it was "Just one for the road — to Singapore." B B replied that we did not know if one existed. Then we went outside, moved the still unpacked kit off the seats, climbed into the cars, shouted our goodbyes, and drove off.

In the lunch-hour traffic between Hyde Park Corner and Westminster we, in Oxford, lost the Cambridge car and stopped to wait for them in Parliament Square. There were maps aboard for every country from France to Malaya, but none, of course, for England. Cambridge failed to appear, and so, agreeing that the route to the Silver Cities aerodrome at Ferryfield was fairly straightforward, we went on without them.

On Westminster Bridge the milometer stood at 1844 miles; it would be reading something over 30,000 miles next time we crossed the Thames—if all went well. We bought an evening paper in Camberwell, and then went on through the North Downs and out into the country. Surely we had forgotten something?

It had clouded over by the time we wound across Romney Marsh and up to the terminal building at Ferryfield. Cambridge had not yet arrived, and we 'Oxford men' joked about our obvious superiority on this, the first leg of the journey. But there was a telephone message from the others to say that they would arrive shortly—they had delayed to get their car weighed for Dunlop's, who were concerned that the tyres ran at their recommended pressures to cope with the load.

Presently the three of us were joined by the Home Team, who had borrowed a car to come down to see the Expedition off. Then, a little later, Cambridge arrived with a story about a policeman of whom they had asked "the way to Singapore."

There were two impatient hours to wait for the plane, but there was the usual form-filling to keep us busy. Pat, the Documents King, padded gently from counter to counter dressed in sky-blue overalls, a Basque beret, and dark glasses. He had a marked foreign accent—"warming up my gutturals for the other side." This enthusiasm was catching, and the Customs, currency, passports, air-tickets, and A.A. were dealt with in high style.

B.B. left the reception hall quite early on in the proceedings to get his cameras and photographic equipment out of bond. Presently he reappeared across the main foyer with our new cine camera atop a long tripod; he had talked about this camera for months, and now it was held aloft for all to see, and the tripod legs, extended to the full, trailed noisily across the tiles behind him. For the next hour he roamed the airport buildings looking like a cross between a medicine man with a ju-ju stick and a child with a new toy. Meanwhile Adrian donned a large slouch hat, which at that stage did not suit him at all. But his serious and official manner completely behoved an Expedition Business Manager.

Eventually the loudspeakers asked the Oxford and Cambridge Far Eastern Expedition to proceed to their plane. It stood ready on the tarmac outside, doors swung open, and the ramp was put in place for the cars. B.B. never let his totem-pole camera out of his grasp; he set it up by the plane, and we paraded back and forth from the buildings a couple of times before he was satisfied.

The cars were driven up the ramp, where it was found that they were too high to fit into the plane. This last-minute panic—"Hey, you chaps, *une grande catastrophe*"—was averted by deflating the tyres and unloading the roof-rack. Then we climbed aboard, the door slammed shut, and we chattered about nothing at all. The plane taxied out to the end of the runway, revved her engines, and then, with a sudden roar, leapt forward. The tail lifted, the vibrations eased, the airport dropped away below, and, as Dungeness ran out into the Channel, we were on our way.

3.

Outward Bound

FIFTEEN minutes later we landed in France. Our new passports were stamped, and the Douane officials, after peering through the windows of the cars, gave an incredulous shrug of the shoulders and tore the first page from the *carnets*.

That night the Expedition made camp among the sand-dunes outside Le Touquet. But first we called at the local Mobilgas station to take *un fill-up*. The pump attendant was glad to see us, for his head office, having got our arrival times mixed up, had previously phoned him to be ready at six o'clock that morning. Accordingly, his wife had pushed him out of bed at 5.30 A.M. in order to greet "L'Expédition d'Oxford et de Cambridge à l'Extrême Orient," and he had been waiting ever since. "A l'Extrême Orient"—that sounded very good!

Among the dunes clumsy hands rigged the tent and put up the camp-beds while Pat, his vocal chords now tuned to their Continental perfection, conducted his first French lesson for the rest of us. Since his arrival in France a few hours earlier (and, in fact, considerably before) he had been shedding his English reserve, and was now in his element. He seemed to develop a typical Gallic after-shave shadow, and, while we had been at the petrol pump, he strode about purchasing *du pain, du vin, et du fromage*, and exchanging pleasantries with all and sundry. With a student bag over his shoulder, a beret on his head, and his blue trousers, he was the Englishman's idea of a Frenchman. That was, I suspect, his intention. Anyway, during the washing-up of our supper he told us that he had "worked out a few O.K. phrases for you chaps so you can know what it's all about and answer the stock questions!"

We learnt that in France one does not drive a car but 'conducts' it, and that the modifications to our *voitures* were better referred to as *quelques améliorations*. We were also told how many litres the cars did to 100 kilometres and what *vitesse* (*en kilomètres*) they were capable of doing. We listened with mock attention, and made a point of mispronouncing everything. There then followed a sharp discussion on the pros and cons of garlic. Pat maintained, despite fierce opposition, that it was an indispensable culinary aid, and he added strength to his argument by saying that it was also a gentle aphrodisiac. It was immediately banned from all future use on the grounds that we could ill afford its physiological properties.

The next day we drove through the rain to Paris. The occasional G.B. car on the road gave us a toot of recognition, and we cheerfully tooted back. In the capital we went straight to a small party arranged by the motoring Press, and, with champagne and sponge fingers, talked to the reporters, who, despite Pat's lessons, could all speak English anyway. Having encouraged our hosts to donate the surplus champagne to the Expedition, we drove round Paris for the benefit of Paris Television. This was an amusing and hectic half-hour following behind a genial French cameraman who exposed at us what must have been miles of film. He led us round the Etoile, and then to the Palais de Chaillot. There he parked his van and ran up the flight of steps on to the terrace, signalling us to follow—in the cars. We hesitated, but he insisted, and so, much to the amusement of the bystanders, we bumped our way up the steps in quite an impressive manner. At the top the cameraman demanded that we get out the cookers and billycans and *fait le brew-up*. Apparently the sight of six Englishmen brewing tea in the middle of this Trafalgar Square of Paris was just what the French viewers would expect. It was *vraiment les Anglais*. We complied rather self-consciously, but it was thoroughly worth while to see the cameraman so happy. He had, he told us, tapping his camera, "*fait un grand scoop.*"

The Expedition decided to spend a couple of days in Paris in order that it might get its breath back after the rushed and hurried last few weeks in England. Accordingly, it took itself off to the official *camping* in the Bois de Boulogne, and there, under the trees, pitched tent. It was discovered on registering at the near-by Bureau that the International Camping card issued to us in London was made out in Henry's name, while we were listed in alphabetical order as his children.

Pat's Gallic influence was spreading fast, for after only thirty-six hours east of Westminster he had fitted Henry up in a French mechanic's beret and blue overalls. B.B., on the other hand, remained quite unchanged; he was always cooking "a last meal before we leave civilization," and his main concern in *le camping* surrounded by 'foreigners' was that we should "impress these bods." This was difficult, for it seemed that on the Continent the prestige accorded by the other campers to one's nation is directly proportional to the cut and style of one's tent. As our tent depended on fittings and clips on the cars to hold it up, we must have ranked very low, for, with one or both the cars away on business, our daytime tent consisted of nothing more than a series of canvas strips draped over our stores and trunks in a system of odd poles, hooks, and guy-ropes. At night, however, the tent was properly pitched between the cars, and looked workman-like, even if rather ugly.

The other campers stood around and viewed us with curiosity. There was a map of Europe and Asia painted on the glass of the cars' back windows, and across it was marked our proposed route. "Here," one could almost hear them say, "are the mad English." We rather enjoyed it.

We left Paris one evening and, motoring across the dull plains of Northern France, reached the frontier city of Strasbourg the following afternoon. The French passport official apologized for his bad English, but, he explained, since the Liberation he had had few occasions to listen to the B.B.C. His wife, whom we also met, was much more fluent, as she had visited England on a number of occasions, and had even been, she said, "a spectacle" at the 1948 Olympic Games in London.

The cars ran across the bridge into Germany, and were soon speeding down the autobahn to Stuttgart. Germany's autobahns are ridiculous. One gets on to them and drives at full speed, uninterrupted, until one reaches the other end; to gear-weary drivers from England they are an unfair and slightly dishonest simplification of motoring.

We pulled off the autobahn and turned into Stuttgart, but in the evening light and thickening traffic we, in Oxford, lost the other car. As Pat had all the town maps, and was leading us to the "Kampingplatz," we had to stop in the hope that they would come back for us. After half an hour's wait we decided to find the Kampingplatz for ourselves. The only word of German we had between us happened to be the relevant one of Kampingplatz, and this, combined with a questioning inflexion, raised eyebrows, and a finger pointing in a vaguely interrogative direction, eventually brought us to our destination. Cambridge, of course, had arrived at least thirty minutes earlier, and had given us up. Pat was given every chance to be penitent, and all agreed that in future it was the leading car's responsibility to keep visual contact with the second. This was a principle that, with modifications, we were to stick to for the next year.

That night was somewhat disturbed, for at about 2 A.M. it started raining, and Henry and Nigel had to bring their beds inside the tent. Then, for reasons which did not bother the rest of us, the tent leaked on Henry's bed. As he had designed the tent he kept fairly quiet, and was tactfully left to sort out his problem.

The main reason for going through Germany was in order that B.B. might collect some camera equipment in Munich, and it was on arrival there that we saw a small but staggering example of German speed and efficiency. We had telegraphed ahead to the petrol station which handled Mobilgas to give them our estimated time of arrival.

We arrived on the dot, and the manager was already waiting on the pavement to greet us. Hands were shaken all round, and then both cars were ushered on to the ramps. Henry and Nigel leapt clear as four mechanics, led by a white-coated foreman, swept in. Bonnets were flung open, the sump, the transfer-box, the gear-box, and both front and rear differentials on each car were drained and refilled, the radiator water was changed, the batteries topped up, and all greasing-points attended to. Then the cars were rushed to the 'washbox,' where mackintoshed mechanics hosed and scrubbed the bodies with special grease-removing soap. They were then rubbed down, dried, and the windows polished. After this they returned to the ramps, where the undersides were sprayed with a fine protective oil. From there to the petrol-pump for a fill-up. The whole operation, from start to full tanks, had taken less than thirteen minutes! I could understand why the Germans have such a superlative reputation for their pit-work in motor-racing. If we had wished it those mechanics would have changed the air in our tyres—as it was, they checked the pressures. The fact that we had only asked for some petrol seemed irrelevant.

In the streets of Munich the evidence of the thousand-bomber raids of twelve years ago could be seen everywhere. The city received a greater plastering than any in Britain, but the evidence was not in the rubble but in the reconstruction. Where there were new buildings, striking in their clean simplicity, one assumed that the previous buildings had been bombed—and almost everywhere there were new buildings. Few cities in Britain could compare.

From Munich, over the Austrian frontier, and down to Vienna was a couple of days' easy driving. On the long, open stretches of road we compared the speeds of the two cars; both could reach an identical 62 m.p.h.

Just outside Vienna we were waved down by a motorcycle policeman. Guiltily thinking we must have been speeding, we slowed, stopped, and prepared to misunderstand every word. But the policeman pulled out in front and signalled us to follow—evidently it was more serious than we had imagined, to warrant this visit to the police station. But then it gradually dawned on us that we were being privileged with an escort. On entering the city the Expedition swept through the busy streets behind the policeman, who, switching on a screaming siren, waved other, lesser traffic out of the way. Outside the local Rover agent's showroom we halted triumphantly.

Our three days in Vienna were divided between sight-seeing and working on the cars. Our billet was a half-completed garage lent by the motor agent; the cars were driven right inside, and we could spread ourselves without bothering about the tent. Here Henry and B.B. finished making the interior fittings for the cars. For three days they worked with drills, hacksaws, pliers, and screwdrivers making clips and brackets to hold the Thermoses, first-aid boxes, lamps, cookers, and the tape-recorder. Henry even built, on Pat's suggestion, a small book-shelf inside Cambridge—"The Library," as it came to be known.

The garage in which we lived was most convenient, but it was far from completion, and had no electricity or lavatories. In the evenings, with our two lamps burning in the middle of the low basement, with gloomy, shadowed corners and piles of girders and builders' rubble lying about, it only needed a zither, and Harry Lime could have been standing in the doorway. This atmosphere was further enhanced by the city itself, for it was the weekend and all the streets were quiet and deserted except for the untidy autumn leaves. Perhaps the Russian occupation—ended only the previous month—had left its mark, but the once gay and important capital of the Austro-Hungarian Empire now seemed sad and wistful, struggling to recall her gaiety like a dowager wearing high-heeled shoes. By the

second evening this atmosphere was beginning to tell, and Nigel, no doubt
thinking of the Third Man, was all for organizing a sight-seeing party "to
take a dekko at the sewers." Anyway, we all trooped out—though for a
different reason.

Our garage had no lavatory, and, despite earlier searches, no public
facilities had been found either. By this time—the second day—the
problem was urgent, and accordingly search-parties set out. Pat and I
wandered into an ill-lit square and found a likely-looking public building,
but, on placing two schillings in the relevant slot, nothing happened.
Concluding that we must be in a bus shelter, and that the slot belonged to
an out-of-order cigarette machine, we hurried on, and eventually, after
another frustrating half-hour, found what we were looking for in a
tumble-down railway station.

On leaving Vienna the cars circled the square which, at the liberation
in 1945, had been renamed the Stalinplatz; we paused to admire the two
memorials left behind by the recently departed Russians. One, I thought,
was undoubtedly striking: atop a slim stone column stood a Red
infantryman leaning into the wind and holding a streaming banner of
triumph. Near by was a more functional memento of the Russians: a toad-
like black Joseph Stalin tank with a faded red star on the side of its squat
turret. Overlooking the scene, above a high public building of the late
'thirties, was a battered and headless Nazi eagle. My thoughts were as
mixed as were these emblems of recent history.

By the time we climbed over the pine-clad mountains of Southern
Austria and down towards the Yugoslav frontier the Expedition had been
on the road twelve days, and, having overcome various of its teething
troubles, was settling well into its stride. B.B. and Nigel had ten days' bristly
growth on their chins, a pin-up had glued herself inevitably to each car's
ceiling, and already we were able to recite "Yes, we're on our way to
Singapore" in three different languages.

By now there was more rhythm to the day, and less time was wasted
in making and breaking camp. In spite of what was felt about any
organization that was too military in method—all ex-National
Servicemen seem to feel this way—each person had a specific job once the
cars had left the road for a suitable camp-site. Two people, usually Pat and
B.B., lit the stoves, started the cooking, and set out the plates, cups, salt,

sugar, and all the other oddments which annoy in their absence while one's soup gets cold. Meanwhile Henry, Nigel, and I looked after the rest of the camp. We lit the lamps, rigged the tent, set up the beds, and arranged the personal trunks as seats and tables around the cooking. Adrian's job was the 'running' paper-work, and, setting up office under a lamp, he would enter the day's expenses and type any necessary 'thank-you' letters until supper was ready. After supper I wrote up the diary while the others did the washing-up. Then, unrolling the sleeping bags and turning out the lamps, our day ended.

B.B., having once been the youngest sergeant-major in the Armoured Corps, was always first up, and got the porridge under construction. During this time the breaking and repacking of camp began along the same lines as the night before, except, of course, in the reverse direction. When all was stowed away, and breakfast finished, the cars were driven off the site while a couple of us looked around for anything that might have been forgotten.

There were, naturally, many exceptions to the system. B.B. might break away from the cooking to take photographs; one of the 'tent party' might be conscripted by the kitchen section for 'spud-bashing,' while in the mornings the mechanics were excused washing up in order that they might check tyre-pressures, oil-levels, and attend to any other maintenance jobs that had to be done. Occasionally, too, the cry might go up from the cooks at night for some one to "Hurry up with those lamps," and, according to whom these instructions were yelled, the reply might come back, in measured civil servant tones, "Sorry, but that's not my department, old man." But, as time went on and the necessity arose, all the jobs became interchangeable.

This rough division of labour had already given us some amusement in Germany and Austria, where the Press reporters who caught up with us were much more specific and detailed in their questions than they had been in England or France. We were, they said, a *Mannschaft* (team), and therefore—with obvious Germanic reasoning—each person must have some special jobs. In addition, then, to telling them that Pat was the Navigator, Nigel the Q.M., and so on, we said that B.B. was our leading-petrol-cooker-expert and Adrian was our chief-letter-writing-man. The reporters scribbled seriously, and it was later reported that B.B. was Herr Oberbenzinkochenführer, while Adrian became Herr Hauptbriefschreibermann—or words to that effect!

A few miles before the Yugoslav frontier we stopped in Graz, and, for the first time, filled up with petrol to the full capacity of fifty gallons per car. The Austrian Mobilgas people had kindly suggested this in view of the fact that in Yugoslavia all petrol was nationalized, and, therefore, we should not be able to get free supplies again until we reached the first Mobilgas pump in Greece. In other words, we hoped to drive right through Yugoslavia—a distance of nearly 800 miles—without refuelling.

However, on driving the few miles down to the frontier it was found that, in our enthusiasm to take aboard every possible pint, we had over-filled. Our eyes had been too big for our tanks, and now petrol was dribbling around the floor and down on to the road. While Pat, the Expedition's Political Attaché, shuffled into the border-post and dealt with the formalities as if he had been at it all his life, the rest of us were forced to syphon the surplus petrol out of the tanks and then give it away to other motorists. The Austrians were incredulous. Here were these English busily and seriously engaged in taking petrol out of their own tanks and putting it into other people's!

The only other trouble was with a Yugoslav frontier guard, who—obviously promotion-conscious—proved difficult over our two red fire-extinguishers. But, with a great deal of sign language, it was eventually explained to him that they were for putting fires *out*, and not, as he seemed to think, incendiary bombs for *starting* them.

Soon after crossing the frontier I wedged myself up against the passengers' door and dozed off. I woke a little later to see B.B., who was driving, waving one arm out of his window. As this particular hand signal was new to me, and quite unrecognizable in the Highway Code, I asked him what it meant.

"Well," he replied seriously, "we've just passed a crowd of children, and that signal meant 'Greetings from the Youth of Cambridge to the People's Republic of Yugoslavia.'" Then, in further explanation, he added, "Got to have stacks of Youth Angle here."

It must have been school closing-time, for, as we drove through the late afternoon to Zagreb, we passed many straggles of children, walking home to their farms and villages. When we approached them on the road they would turn towards us and wave so seriously and solemnly that they seemed to be saying "Please wave back to us—no one ever does." So we waved back, and then they would jump up and down with pleasure, and the waving became even more vigorous. At first we were amused, and laughed to each other but the children were so sincere that laughing at them would not have been the right thing at all. They were giving us an unexpected and charming welcome to their country.

In the middle of a Zagreb street we noticed a small van with G.B. plates surrounded by a crowd of curious townsfolk. We stopped, and, having identified the three owners by their khaki shorts, inquired if they were in trouble. It seemed that something was wrong in the back axle—so wrong, in fact, was this 'something' that neither of the rear wheels would turn, but remained locked solid even when the van was pushed and manhandled off the road. There was little we could do to help, but, nevertheless, we felt concerned for our countrymen. They, however, were not the least perturbed, and when asked their destination gaily replied, "Singapore." We wished them well, and motored on rather thoughtfully.

Camp that night was in a pine-wood on the outskirts of Zagreb. As we had arranged to be in Belgrade, 240 miles away, by noon the following day we decided on a very early start the next morning. Accordingly B.B. was 'set' for 4 A.M.

Sure enough he 'sounded off' on the dot, and we crawled out into the dark to the hiss of our lamps, and to the incantations of B.B. over a new consignment of porridge—Yugoslav variety, bought the previous evening. In fact, this consignment took several more days of patient research before the exact recipe was discovered.

The *autoput* between Zagreb and Belgrade must be one of the fastest and dullest roads in Europe. For 240 miles the level concrete runs uninterrupted across an almost endless plain of green maize-fields and dark pine-woods. There is virtually no traffic, and in a journey of four and a half hours we passed only five other vehicles. But on entering Belgrade's backyard—an untidy and windswept area of marshalling yards, rubbish-tips, and enormous blocks of half-completed flats—we came upon twelve glorious red, double-decker London buses. They were destined for new work in one of Yugoslavia's growing industrial cities. With their advertisements still on their sides, exhorting us to 'Keep Britain Tidy,' and telling us which was the nation's favourite nightcap, they gave us a nostalgic glimpse of the King's Road and the Strand—now well over a thousand miles behind.

Belgrade is of the Balkans; the last of Western Europe had ended at Zagreb, only a morning's drive away to the north-west. Yugoslavia's capital seemed a spacious, sombre, and rather unimaginative city.

We found the British Embassy, and, while collecting our letters, were invited to meet the Ambassador that evening for a drink. The other call was a courtesy visit to the Yugoslav agency for Rovers.

We were shown straight in to the young, athletic-looking manager, who, having set us up with plum brandy and Yugoslav small talk which we did not understand, sent for his secretary to act as interpreter. She had never been out of the country, but had learnt quite good English at Belgrade University.

The manager would talk very seriously and earnestly to the girl for a few moments, and then she, staring at the light-bulb in concentration, would translate.

"Please, he is wishing to know why you make this travel."

One of us would answer—with the others butting in to muddle her— and then she would tell him our reply. He would nod and ask some more.

"He asks what you have taken at Universities."

"Where have you learn to drive; it is how long now you have driven?"

"Have students in your country their own motors?"

"The rich ones, you say. Are you rich . . .?"

"Then what motors you drive at your home?"

"Your families'. How many families got motors in England?"

I know nothing of the manager's relative views on capitalism and communism, but he was clearly perplexed by the fact that three of our families "got motors" while the other three had not. I thought that his questions—there were many others—were most interesting: probably much more interesting to us than our answers were to him. When he was satisfied we were solemnly introduced to almost the whole office staff, after which plum brandy and black coffee alternated until closing-time. As some one said, "These Communists are all right."

Back at the Embassy the Expedition endeavoured to tidy itself up in the bathroom, and then went across to the Residency. The Ambassador quickly put to rest the worries about our crumpled trousers, and introduced us to various of his staff who seemed to have turned up for the Expedition's benefit. We were very flattered. After having talked Ambassadorial and Expeditional 'shop' for a pleasant hour we returned to the bathroom and our operational clothing, then headed south from Belgrade to make camp.

As one drives through Southern Yugoslavia the road deteriorates, while the people and their hilly, wooded country become more picturesque. There is often such an inverse ratio of roads to surroundings, and it must be one of the reasons that makes it worth while to visit out-of-the-way places; the harder the going, the more pleasant the achievement. It was not that this stretch was hard, but rather that, softened by the smooth tarmac of Western Europe, we now had a foretaste of the pot-holes, dust, and corrugations which stretched for thousands of miles ahead.

The road ran up through the Morava valley and then to the town of Kumanovo, where, for the first time on the journey, we saw mosques and the Muslim tarboosh and skull-cap. The atmosphere of the countryside had been growing quickly more Eastern. But here, quite suddenly, was the clearly focused mark of the Ottoman rule and culture left behind by the Turks who, until a century ago, had held sway over this part of Europe for nearly five hundred years. It was market-day and, in the cattle souk, with its wailing Eastern music, dirt, and smell, the pedlars converged around and tried to sell us cheap fountain-pens, teapots, and rough blankets made of coloured wool. With horns tooting, we threaded the cars through crowds of peasants, laden ox-carts, and panniered mules and donkeys. Here in Kumanovo, with its mosques, flat roofs, and pumpkins drying in the autumn sun, we might already have been in the Levant.

But by the time the cars pulled up in Skopje, only twenty miles farther on, we were back again in Christian Europe. Pat went off to buy some cheese and bread for lunch, and then, anxious to reach Greece by dark, we hurried on.

The road became a rocky track as it curved along beside the Vardar river, and several times we had to leave it altogether and follow twisting diversions through the fields or across dried-out streams. Once the narrow way down into a rocky river-bed was blocked by a vastly overladen horse-cart which had got half-way up a steep slope and then could go no farther. The two farmers sat waiting for their horses to raise more steam. The horses stood waiting for their owners to unload a few of the huge sacks and make the task a little lighter. All three groups— the farmers, the horses, and ourselves—waited patiently on each other. Then, as the farmers and their horses clearly had more time to waste than we, Cambridge ran out the winch cable and pulled them to the top. The farmers climbed on to the cart and, without a word, went on their way.

In the evening the dry countryside became rougher and more desolate, the treeless limestone hills grew pale gold in the orange sun as slow, deep shadows drew across them. Well before dark we in Oxford had switched on the searchlight and closed the roof hatch because of the dust thrown up by the other car ahead.

Eventually, a mile in front of us, Cambridge's red brake lights flashed suddenly bright as whoever was driving slowed down. Then, as we drew nearer, our head-lamps lit up a slim pole barrier across the road, and a low concrete hut to one side. It was a frontier post in the best tradition. The Yugoslav guards sat by a table on the veranda and seemed to do everything with a minimum of movement. They shouted for us to come forward for scrutiny. Having no electric light, they peered short-sightedly at our documents in the glow of a paraffin lamp, and then, spitting on the pad, ostentatiously stamped and scribbled for twenty minutes. It was all done with such deliberation that we could not help comparing them with the French, who had gaily stamped at anything in sight. We lifted the barrier and drove into Greece.

Immediately the road surface changed to tarmac, and, a mile or two farther on, we passed a large electric sign saying *Hellas*. We drew up outside a streamlined Customs post with strip lighting, glass-topped tables, petrol-pumps, and a bar attached. In the car-park was a travel-tired Land Rover with "Cambridge Afghanistan Expedition" painted on the sides. I knew at least one of that Expedition quite well, and, having last seen him at a Cambridge farewell party before they set out three months before, I hurried inside to find him—at the bar.

"Hey, John," I said. He looked round.

"Well, so you boys finally got on the road! I thought it was all just a line-shoot!"

"How did you find Afghanistan?" I asked.

"Oh, not too bad—now we're back here. But it's pretty rugged. You wait till you get there!"

"We're not going that way—not on the way out, anyway. We're going through Southern Persia, Desert of Death, and all that sort of thing."

"Oh, hell, that's nothing. Anybody can do that."

John, the sunburnt, hardened expeditioner and I, the novice (as he pointed out), laughed and chattered on.

"Did you find that mystery mountain you were telling everybody about before you left?"

"Well, sort of—saw it from the plain. Only our measurements made it 35,000 feet high, so we reckon there must be something wrong somewhere!"

The "Afghan boys" came and talked to us as we dealt with our passports and the Customs forms. Then both Expeditions went outside to inspect and admire each other's vehicles. We asked them about the route and roads, and heard about their six weeks' field-work in Afghanistan, somewhere up near the Russian frontier. Then, full of vulgar advice and comments on the roads we should encounter, they said good-bye. We watched their tail-lights disappear up the road towards Yugoslavia—and Cambridge. They would be there in a week.

"I can smell the Med," said Pat, as we drove on to a village football pitch that night. "It never rains, so let's scrub round the tent." Actually, the tent was little trouble to put up, and the rest of us, looking up at a clouded night sky, overruled Pat. Perhaps it is time that I explained the tent, for it was of a novel design—it had to be, for it was built to a variety of requirements. It had to go up quickly, be waterproof in rain, cool in heat, and be divisible into two smaller tents when the cars were apart. In order to erect it, as on this particular night, the two cars were driven back to back, and each end of the tent roof threaded into a ∧-shaped metal track which was fixed above the cars' rear doors. The cars were then driven slowly apart until the roof was taut between them, after which the vertical sides were hooked on. Beyond this point description would become reminiscent of so many obscure 'do-it-yourself' kits. But suffice it to say that the tent, when properly rigged, did all that was asked of it.

The next day, after being woken by a crowd of curious small boys from the village who yelped "Eoka" and then giggled shyly, we drove down to Salonika and the Mediterranean. Our fuel-tanks were almost empty after the long drive from Austria, and two Greeks from Mobilgas took us under their wings, with more petrol and a wonderful lunch in a beach-side restaurant. We chose our fish and peaches, and then relaxed under the shady pines. Cyprus and Enosis need not have caused any doubts of Greek hospitality. It was not that this subject was tactfully skirted—on the contrary, it was seriously discussed—it was spoken of quietly and in good humour by our hosts. It seems a pity that by the time some men become their nation's statesmen they have so often lost the friendliness in which once they could have disagreed.

From Salonika the road turned east along the Ægean shore. In the hot sun we motored through a quiet countryside of Cyprus pines, barren hills, vineyards, and grey-green olive-groves. Along the road jogged strings of donkeys led by little boys, and in the rocky fields the men and women in wide straw hats looked up and shielded their eyes against the glare as we swirled by. Below and beyond the headlands stretched out the calm blue, twinkling sea, and far behind in the pale haze of distance rose Mount Olympus.

Sometimes the colours were so splashed that if one had seen them in a painting one would not have believed the artist. In Kavalla the white and pink-washed houses held back steeply from the sea, and below the ancient citadel the black-and-yellow caiques waited in the harbour while their nets hung drying in the bright sun. It is a warm and lovely coastline.

The Expedition thought that a couple of days by the sea would do it good, and so, conveniently deciding that it was well ahead of schedule, it unrolled the map. The Navigator, Pat, was instructed to lay off a course for the nearest suitable spot. He placed the chart on the ground, held it against the breeze with an elbow or knee at each corner, did some navigational calculations with the prongs of a fork, straightened up, and then, with the deliberation of an automatic pilot, said, "Peramos—thirty miles." We set off.

Peramos sounded an attractive name, but as I looked at other places on the Greek map I realized that it is to the towns and villages of the Ægean that the doctors and the dentists of this world owe so much. Polynos or Kalymnos—toothpastes? Asprovalta is presumably a sort of fruit-salts sedative. Piræus or Pelagonis might perhaps be diseases of the gums. Ysternia and Skantzoura are probably complaints for which a truss is necessary. But Ghioura is obviously something for which one should hasten to a specialist—if it is not already too late.

We drove down the street of Pelamos, and chose a perfect site on the headland a mile beyond. The tent had barely been erected when a fleet of small boys appeared from the village. They sucked their dirty thumbs and stared, then they took their thumbs out and meandered in among our kit, our cars, and ourselves. Subsequent events first began to take on a military tone when Nigel bad-temperedly suggested to the boys that they should "——off." They, however, did not understand. This was disturbing, and accordingly a rope was run round the camp perimeter, and the eldest boy was placed inside to keep the others out. We congratulated ourselves on this subtle 'man-management,' and at dusk, after no further trouble, the boys withdrew to their village.

A swim before breakfast, and all was set for an easy day of recuperation—though from exactly what I cannot remember. As on the previous evening, the rope barrier had been strung up, and, confident behind it, 'sorting out' had started. This process usually consisted of taking everything out of both vehicles, spreading it all on the ground, looking at it, discussing it—sometimes heatedly, sometimes apathetically—and then replacing it all just as it had started. But on this particular morning the discussion stage was hastily cancelled. It seemed that our security arrangements had been compromised. From the direction of the village the entire male population under twelve was now marching on the camp. By 10.00 hours the enemy—as he now became—judged that all his ranks were massed ready for the Big Push. At first we managed to hold the position, but after two hours of sporadic skirmishing the infiltration of small boys was becoming too much. Even B.B., who strode about swinging his tripod in lethal, scythe-like movements, admitted that the situation was grave. We had noted the disappearance of a number of stores: my gym shoes, two exposed films, a Land Rover maintenance manual, a roll of well-known British paper; and—the Q.M. suspected—our plastic tea-spoons were missing. A rapid reappraisal of strategy was necessary.

The Business Manager erected a wicked system of Dragon's Teeth with the trunks, and the Navigator rushed out of the position as a decoy, shouting "Cyprus! Enosis! Eoka!" and one or two other equally inflammatory phrases. This diversion worked splendidly, but even the Navigator had to stop running at some time, and, having completed several circuits, he returned to the lines exhausted. Both sides regrouped, and for several hours there was a comparative lull.

When the enemy returned we were ready. Each man was armed with a shovel, a jack-handle, an axe, or a tripod. As the first wave advanced we went forward to meet them, wielding our weapons as if we were film extras in a Cecil B. de Mille epic. The day was quickly won, and we drove them back almost to the village. But before honour was satisfied the tea-spoons had to be retaken—and we had an idea which of our tormentors had them. However, no action could be taken until he was seen to retrieve the loot from beneath some secret hillside bush. And return to retrieve them he surely would.

As the evening drew on the Business Manager seated himself, shooting-stick fashion, on a car starting-handle and peered through his binoculars. Then, at last light, the quarry was sighted low on the horizon. He came slowly on. All were tense, and the only sound came from the Business Manager, who, in approved gunnery manner, sat softly chanting the ever decreasing range of the target. He came to within two hundred yards, and then suddenly stooped under a bush, picked something up, and quickly started back to his village.

With a low curse the Expedition split into two groups and swept stealthily forward in a wide encircling movement. The quarry idled his way up among the boulders, serenely unaware of his immediate peril. Then he glanced round, and, horror-struck in realization, started clawing his frenzied way across the rocks. But our pursuit was too fast, and the sight of two echelons steadily gaining and closing numbed and paralysed him completely. Utterly demoralized, he lay down under a bush, and, with plastic tea-spoons lying all around him, he chattered feebly.

Retribution was a problem, but, magnanimous in our victory, even the kick-in-the-pants was scaled down appropriately. The prisoner was not more than eight years old.

The Expeditionary Force returned triumphant to its base and held a short and informal victory parade at open order with tea-spoons at the high port. Nevertheless, all ranks were exhausted, and had accomplished nothing all day. It was decided to give up the ideas of recuperation, and to evacuate to Turkey at first light the next morning.

Some have suggested that Greece has always regarded her eastern frontier with Turkey as a rather weak one, and for strategic motives, therefore, the road to this frontier has been purposely neglected. This may not be the whole reason, but an afternoon's crashing, bumping, and twisting drive made it a fairly convincing one.

The traditional enmity between Greece and Turkey had not been lessened by the series of sharp anti-Greek riots in Istanbul ten days earlier, and we were naturally concerned about our passage through the frontier. However, we arrived at the Turkish guard-post without, as yet, having officially left Greece. Reversing half a mile back down the road, we presented our apologies and passports to a group of somewhat perturbed Greek officials who did not see the joke.

There arrived shortly from Turkey a couple of wonderfully bearded Frenchmen who, travelling in a 2 C.V. Citroën, were returning from a 20,000-mile journey of filming in Afghanistan and thereabouts. They told, with graphic Gallic gestures, of *les voleurs* who, in the East, remove everything but the air in one's tyres—and, if given half a chance, will take even that if they think it worth while. The only solutions, the Frenchmen suggested, were to weld everything that could be moved; never to leave a vehicle without an occupant; and, if possible, to chain this guardian to a suitable ring-bolt, or else he might be removed too. We were most impressed.

Inside the Turkish border, on the way to Istanbul, there are a number of military zones through which one is only allowed to pass provided that one stays on the road and does not stop. We were awoken a little after midnight by a soldier with a long, droopy moustache, a rifle, and a torch. He made it plain that our camp was in a prohibited area. Expressing surprise—admittedly not altogether innocent—we invited him to have some rum. He became quite genial, and could even see our point of view, and when it was explained, pointing at a watch, that we should be gone by dawn he smiled sympathetically. His C.O. need never know. He signalled two other men out from the bushes—where they were presumably covering him—and sent them into a nearby field. They returned a minute later with two wonderful water-melons, which the guard had us understand were in exchange for the rum and our company. Then he left us to return to our sleeping-bags. This happened several other times in Turkey—our tactics were always the same, and they always seemed to work.

Istanbul was still recovering from the anti-Greek riots. Armed police patrolled in pairs, tanks were stationed on the outskirts, and there was a midnight curfew. This curfew meant that we could not camp, but, fortunately, accommodation was generously found for us in a petrol-filling station. In arranging this, and welcoming us, the American Mobilgas 'chief' wondered "if you gentlemen would care to take luncheon with me at the Hilton to-morrow?" We gentlemen hastily accepted this golden opportunity to avoid our own washing-up, and paraded promptly at noon the next day.

The Istanbul Hilton—one of a world-wide American chain—had been opened one month earlier by two Constellation-loads of film-stars who flew over from Hollywood for a two-day million-dollar house-warming, and then flew home again. It is a twelve-story building of glass and concrete, and is the last word in trans-Atlantic design. With sumptuous suites, penthouse cocktail bars, chrome kitchens, circular swimming-pools, and wind-screened loggias overlooking the Bosporus to Asia (only a mile away), there can be few hotels to compare with it. At lunch the Expedition quickly absorbed the American flavour, and, 'Times Squarewise,' captioned a photo taken of Pat standing in the canopied entrance thuswise: "Seen under a snap-brim fedora arriving at swank, plushy, exclusive Istanbul Hilton Hotel yesterday was stout, affable, balding, 20'ish Patrick J. Murphy, member of the globe-girdling troupe from Cambridge (England)."

Martial law made little difference to Istanbul. It is a wonderful city, one of the most cosmopolitan places in the world. In the narrow Bosporus lie craft from almost every country that ever flew an ensign; along the waterfront are mosques and churches; in the cafés one chooses between kebabs and hamburgers, while in the crowded streets the noise from hooters, horns, bells, and pedlars is only drowned by the pavement loudspeakers, which range from Anatolian love-lyrics to current 'bop.' In a half-hour's walk one can listen to Turkish, Arabic, French, Italian, Greek, and American. Every colour, every country, every creed—and Istanbul has a number of her own as well.

It is a city which goes back beyond the time when, as Constantinople, it ruled the Ottoman Empire, or when earlier, as Byzantium, it was the Christian centre of a sophisticated medieval culture. On this site has stood a city for nearly three thousand years.

We only stayed three days—we might have stayed three years, and not been bored. But our destination lay to the east, and so, looking out our sun-hats and dark glasses for the dust and heat ahead, we drove down to the quay and aboard a ferry.

As the ship cast off and nosed out into the blue Bosporus I looked back astern to the crowded, sunlit shore. It was much more than the end of Europe. It was a sweeping sight of time and history, so clear that one knew it then without reflection. I looked from the skylined Hilton, claimed as the most modern hotel of the twentieth century, over the Golden Horn to Santa Sophia, dedicated as a cathedral seven hundred years before the First Crusade. Byzantium, Constantinople, Istanbul—it must surely be one of the ageless cities of the world.

4.

Nearer East

TEN minutes later the cars drove on to the Asian shore, and behind us was, we hoped, our last sea-crossing before reaching Singapore.

It was at this precise moment that B.B.—the Doctor—issued an important edict. From here on all drinking-water would be boiled, and uncooked vegetables were banned. Both these measures became unwritten law, and were, without doubt, one of the major reasons for our continuous good health. "No lettuces beyond the Bosporus" evolved into an Expedition battle-cry, and has since been suggested several times as a title for this book.

The road ran out of Uskudar past the barracks of Scutari. Allegedly they are the largest barracks in the world, but our thoughts were more concerned with Florence Nightingale and that ill-managed war. We climbed away from the Mediterranean, up through the coastal hills, and then across the Turkish tableland towards Ankara.

The Expedition was now three weeks out from London (the nautical term has a satisfying ring)—long enough to have ironed out most of its household problems. Chief among these had been the ordered stowing of equipment. Space was very limited, and the final arrangement was the result of much thought before we left England, and then, subsequently, of practical experience as we drove across Europe. Some objects had built-in rattles (pots and pans), while others had to be packed firmly and yet be easy to remove (Thermoses and cookers). Sometimes there was a difficulty for almost every solution. "Yes, that's all right for the pressure-cooker, but you can't get it out without moving the typewriter." Or, "If you put the cameras there they'll get covered in dust." Or, "That's no good; the medical kit must go somewhere where one can get it quickly." But now, after three weeks of experiment, we had argued here, compromised there, and finally reached a working arrangement.

Everything lived in an allotted place. Thus each person would know where things were to be found, and there would be a minimum of scrummaging. That was the theory, anyway.

Small items were packed in a set of eight two-pound biscuit-tins stacked in a rattleproof rack behind the driver. The tins were marked: Film, Household Stores, Developer, Mechanical Spares, Electric Spares, Medical Spares, and Q.M. Spares. Thus a new lamp-mantle was found in Q.M. Spares, fresh soap in Household Stores, and a head-lamp bulb in Electric Spares, etcetera.

Along one side of the interior in each car was a strong shelf for the bigger things: built-in wireless, tape-recorder, typewriters, and the Business Manager's "Busyness" Box (most important, the latter: it was the Expedition's office). Around the metal walls of the car were clips, rubber pads, and elastic straps which firmly held the Thermoses, lamps, cookers, and a small 'ready-use' first-aid kit. All the tinned food went in a wooden Food Box; the cutlery, plastic crockery, tea, sugar, salt, and jam lived in a rattleproof (almost) Cook Box; and the car's tools were, of course, in a Tool Box. All these boxes fitted snugly into appropriate spaces. The crew's three small trunks lived on top of the extra petrol tanks, while elsewhere 'in the back' went sleeping-bags, billycans, a pressure-cooker, a plastic bucket, and everything else that Nigel referred to as "general mundungus." In a bolted locker under one of the passengers' seats was each car's Strong Box, containing passports, inoculation certificates, car documents, compasses, and cash. On the bonnet was the spare tyre, and under it, around the engine, were clipped the jack, wheelbrace, and a tin of oil. On the front bumper was the winch and two 4½-gallon jerry-cans of water. Lastly, if the reader is still with me on this conducted tour, the roof-rack carried the tent (split between the cars), camp-beds, spare inner tubes, shovels, and axes. Not for nothing were the cars sometimes known as the "Flying Bedsteads."

Normally we travelled with only two, out of five, petrol-tanks full—this was a considerable saving of weight. The full tankage was intended for later stages in the journey when petrol points might be few and far between. Nevertheless, when each car was 'fully operational,' all tanks full, and 'crew' aboard, it weighed two tons. In fact, each Land Rover was expected to carry nearly its own weight in equipment and stores.

"Well, our first night in Asia," said Pat, as we stopped late that night some way short of Ankara. "I wonder how many more there'll be before we get to the other end."

"Much more to the point to know how many more there'll be before our *last* night in Asia—we've got to come back, y'know," was B.B.'s typical reply.

"What do you reckon?" I asked. "Eight months?"

"Haven't a clue, but it won't be much less before we reach the Bosporus again."

Ankara was surprising. Built on the site of a much older town, it has grown up in the last thirty years as the capital of modern Turkey. In company with many other sweeping changes of the last three decades, it owes its renaissance to Kemal Atatürk, who evidently considered that a centrally placed seat of government would be more effective than the 'littoral' and commercially minded Istanbul. It is, like several of the world's recent and federal capitals, rather self-assertive and official in appearance. But the wide, tree-lined boulevards, the flowers, the watered lawns, and the modern railway station with a relatively accurate electric clock are a pleasant surprise to the casual travellers coming down, as we did, from the dry and barren hills around.

However, like Istanbul, it was under martial law, and we intended, therefore, to call briefly for petrol and mail, and then press on. But the chief mechanic of the local Rover agency heard that we were in town, and came cycling down the street to meet us. He insisted that we stayed the night on his family's farm.

"My name Umtaz. I taking much honour you stop my house," he said.

The farm was on the edge of the hills, about four miles from Ankara. On arrival, Umtaz—we never got as far as his second name—hurried off to fetch his friends, while his mother, a huge, triangular-shaped old lady, made us welcome with little cups of tea. Later, in the warm evening, everybody sat out on rugs and cushions in a small arbour under the almond-trees. Umtaz played his *saz* and sang. It was an instrument like an Elizabethan mandolin, and gave a strumming, jangling accompaniment to the folk-songs, which, like all folk-songs everywhere, were concerned with "a man love a wooman."

He was a charming, modest person who was determined to learn all our Christian names and make us his lifelong friends. He told a series of doubtful Turkish jokes, at which we all laughed loudly to please him. Then he talked earnestly to Henry about farming. Both had taken courses in agriculture; the one in Ankara and the other in Cambridge. Umtaz had been taught many of the technical terms in English, and it was an obvious pleasure for him to find some one with whom he could talk his own 'shop.' Then, when we had set up the tape-recorder, he returned to his *saz*, and sang that wistful, smoky song *Uskudar*. Its low and tuneful monotony rolled on and on; even Eartha Kitt, who made it famous outside Turkey, would have agreed that this was the real way to hear it. As the tape played back Umtaz and his friends nodded in time and pleasure. Then they demanded that it be played back again and again.

The lights of Ankara in the basin below were winking out, and the women of the farm had long gone to bed, when Umtaz led us by lantern-light into the farm-house.

It was a dawn start the next day, for we wished to cross the greater width of Turkey and reach the Mediterranean plain, four hundred miles to the south, by nightfall. As soon as it was light enough there was a group photograph of Umtaz, his family, and the Expedition. Then, after repeated farewells, we left. Even after our short acquaintance, we were sorry to go. Already it was a feature of the journey that friends were quickly made and offered us much kindness, then we had to say good-bye and hurry on— adding always that we should call again next year, if we returned that way.

We travelled fast on the easy, rolling surface of a new strategic highway which ran south from Ankara. The sun's hot glare bounced back off the road, a dry wind blew through the dust of the plain around, and far above, wisping in the high blue sky, hung white threads of cloud. The dark shadows on the crinkled hills to the east made every deep, eroded gully seem engraved on copper plate. The tyres hummed, the engine sang to itself, the speed went up to 60 m.p.h., and stayed there for two hours. Now, for the first time, on these vast, uninterrupted plains where one could see for miles, I sensed that we were really moving. Not just down that road but 'overlanding,' starting across a continent. It was an exhilarating, open-shirted feeling.

The good road ended as, unfortunately, all good roads do. It left the wind-swept plateau and, through rougher country, dipped across the basins and ranges of southern Anatolia. Sometimes there were small mud villages, and around the sparsely shaded water-holes flocks of dusty sheep lay blinking in the sun. Groups of donkeys stood motionless except for one ear which twitched against the flies. The road wound out ahead, on and on like a piece of dusty string. The hills were angular and treeless; the only green we saw was through our tinted glasses. The sunlight was like a sabre. We passed a camel, the first that we had seen. But, in the words of my diary, "Did not stop, as there'll soon be plenty more."

By late afternoon the Taurus Mountains were low in the haze of the horizon. Gradually as we drove on they grew clearer and higher. Then the road curled away from the plain and ran under their deep shadow. We climbed up a gradual spur and then, dropping through the gears, started the long, twisting climb to the Cilician Gates.

These thin gorges through the rocky Taurus have been used in trade and conquest for thousands of years. One of the few lines of access between the arid plateau-lands of Anatolia and the fertile Mediterranean seaboard, this series of passes forms a great route of history—and prehistory. The early migrations from the Tigris and Euphrates, the Persians, the Romans, the Crusaders—conquerors and armies before Alexander and long after him—all have passed through the Cilician Gates. On one side of the mountains is an inscription left by the Roman emperor Marcus Aurelius, and on the other side, seventy miles away, is one left by the 92nd Punjab Regiment in 1919.

In ancient times one of the defiles was so narrow that even laden mules had to be unloaded before they could be led safely through. Today modern engineering and explosives have blasted the cliffs well clear. Our cars, dust- and travel-stained by now, wound their way slowly round hairpin bends, up dark ravines, between the pines, and then through the final narrow gap. We paused at the top to watch the last of the sun streak the evening sky. Then we began the descent.

It was dark, and we switched on the head-lights. I stood through the roof-hatch. There is something most refreshing in driving at night among mountains. Except for the twin red lights of the leading car as they moved in and out along the twisting road, we were alone. Unashamedly, I felt as if the whole world was before us. Thousands of miles lay ahead, and yet for us they were still but a mere line across the map.

A tribe of nomads had pitched camp where the mountains met the plain. Their black tents were surrounded by herds of goats and hobbled camels, and the dung-fires glowed in that night as they must have done thousands of years ago when these people pioneered the route. So in one incomparable evening we had swept down from the bleak plateau-lands of Anatolia, through the mountains, and out into the dust and heat of the Middle East.

The Expedition long remembered the next morning, for in preparing breakfast it was found that we had run out of porridge.

"Well," announced B.B., who was the breakfast cook (as opposed to "Luigi" Pat who 'created' the evening meal, and therefore called himself the Chef), "you'll have soup and like it."

"Hell, man," said Nigel, "if you can't look after your porridge supplies you'd better give the job of cook to some one who can!"

"O.K., you've got it!" B.B. retorted. That settled the argument soon enough.

For the next week the Expedition had soup—and liked it. We never ran out of porridge again.

Later that morning we paused in Tarsus. Considering that it was the "no mean city" of St Paul, we were disappointed. I do not know what we expected, but we definitely expected something—which we could not find, not unnaturally. There was nothing to distinguish the town from any other in the Eastern Mediterranean; it was dirty, colourful, and, we judged in our still unhardened gentility, shockingly insanitary. We naïvely observed that the gospels of modern sanitation had yet to reach Tarsus.

After a frustrating afternoon looking for the petrol-station in the near-by and equally unattractive town of Adana we made all speed to the sea. It was shortly after dark when a broken-down jeep-load of three braided Turkish naval officers waved us down and asked for help. Oxford hove alongside their stricken vehicle in order that the repair work might be carried out in the light of her head-lamps, and our mechanics disappeared inside the bonnet to locate the trouble. Meanwhile B.B. busied himself with his camera and flash-gun, for he evidently considered that photos of a Land Rover aiding a jeep (the two vehicles being direct competitors in world markets) would more than justify the whole Expedition in the eyes of the Rover Company back in Birmingham.

The trouble—a broken exhaust pipe—was temporarily fixed, and with much shaking of hands, exchanging of cigarettes, and frequent use of

the only common word we had between us—"N.A.T.O."—we put the
Turkish Navy back on the road and headed on to camp by the sea.

The diary records that "There was the usual nonsense about camping.
Cambridge very choosy." Cambridge usually led the way, as Pat, one of that
car's crew, had the maps. One should not suppose that the six of us were
always in complete accord, either individually or car to car. Haloes
changed to horns quite frequently. This was one such occasion, but it had
happened before. In the second car we (B.B., Nigel, and I) would flash our
head-lights; this was the agreed signal for the car in front to stop. This it
would eventually do, and then there would be a shouted consultation
through the windows.

"Hey, you men! How about making camp?"

"O.K., we'll keep our eyes open."

Clutches were let in. and the convoy moved on. After ten minutes the
occupants of the second car would impatiently start pointing out
reasonable sites along the roadside to each other.

"What's wrong with that place? The others must be blind."

This muttering would go on for some time, and then, concluding that
the leading car was quite incompetent, more light-flashing would begin.
Another shouted exchange.

"You've passed hundreds of places already."

"O.K., old man, keep your wool on. The very next place."

On we would go. By now half an hour since the original suggestion
might have gone by, and the second car would indignantly take the law
into its own hands. Slowing down, one of us would stand through the
roof-hatch and swing the searchlight across the verge. Then, selecting a
good site, the flashing lights would begin a third time. Cambridge might
pretend they had not seen our lights and motor on, tail-lights disappearing
nonchalantly in the darkness. No doubt they hoped that in exasperation
we would surrender our site and meekly catch them up—they always
knew of some superlative site just around the next corner. Now was the
tricky part of the game; which car would give way?

Sometimes, furious, we would motor up the road to find them, ten
minutes later, waiting patiently on some most ill-chosen site with an
innocent comment like, "You had a puncture or something? We've been
here hours." This impertinence merely added fuel to the furnace. On other

occasions Cambridge would eventually come back and try the sweetly reasonable approach.

"Say, chaps, we've found a splendid place along there. A sheltered quarry."

"Well, hell, what's wrong with this? There isn't any wind, anyway, and now you've come back you might as well stay here."

The exact outcome of the problem varied night by night. Usually, however, the car that came back or went forward to meet the other gave way, for, during the ensuing argument, B.B. lit the lamps and stoves, and once they were burning the choice of site was a *fait accompli.*

The approach to camping differed from one person to another. I was inclined to be of the "let's-chuck-the-beds-down-anywhere" school. Pat and Adrian, a formidable bloc, were usually looking for something a little more *sympathique.* B.B. would rather give way completely than come to some "half-baked compromise"—but it took a great deal to make him give way. This 'all or nothing' attitude of B.B.'s extended to other things besides camping! Nigel and Henry were the unknown quantities—get their vote and you had won. But later in the journey, when people attached less importance to these things, the problem seldom arose, and in the desert the solution was easy, for one place was as good or as bad as the next.

On this particular evening camp was eventually made in the middle of a disused coast road. It was obvious that no traffic had been down it for years, but nevertheless the Business Manager was worried lest a fleet of phantom lorries should hurtle through the camp during the night. B.B.'s cryptic comment that there was enough room for a squadron of Centurion tanks to move by without touching us did not help. But, short of going off and making his own individual camp, Adrian had to accept his lot.

That day we had been in Tarsus. The next morning we drove across the plain of Issus, and in the evening took a fill of petrol in Antioch. The centuries are very close in this corner of the Mediterranean, and Time, the fourth dimension, lies very clear across the ground.

Between the mountains and the sea is the narrow plain of Issus. Here, one afternoon nearly 2300 years ago, Alexander the Great, outnumbered ten to one, defeated King Darius of the Persians and the most powerful army of the time that could be set against him. It has been called one of the decisive battles of the world, and, though this is a phrase grown cold with use, it was a great victory, opening the way for Alexander's armies to march as far away as Samarkand and India.

Then Antioch. Once it had a population of over half a million, and, with Rome and Alexandria, had been one of the three great cities of the ancient world. Now, with a population of only 30,000, the crumbling walls stand out a mile beyond the shrunken town.

This was the first of many days when the glare, the heat, and, above all, the dust became really apparent. The Expedition wore its shirt outside its trousers, and put on a floppy hat. On the road to the Syrian frontier the dust that billowed out behind the leading car was like a smoke-screen. It made driving most unpleasant for the one behind, and at times we were forced to widen the gap to nearly a mile.

Over the frontier we turned off the main road to Aleppo on to a side-track. For ten miles we bumped across a desert of bare, eroded limestone until eventually the track ran up a hill, and there on the top stood the silent ruins of Deir Sam'an. Here was the stubby remnant of a pillar whereon, in the fifth century, St Simeon Stylites sat in meditation for forty-two years. Irreverently, but inevitably, some one remarked that he must have been the original and champion pole-squatter of his day. But the old man in perpetual prayer was so harassed by his ever-growing flock of followers that he was forced to have his pillar raised successively higher and higher to escape the earthly distractions below. Even this was not sufficient; the higher he went the farther spread his fame. Pilgrims came from as far away as France and England to seek his blessing. Towards the end of his life he was prevailed upon to preach once a day to the huge throngs below. Then, as he predicted, the crowds grew bigger than ever.

After his death St Simeon's pillar became a Christian shrine, and a large church and monastery were built around it. Then, in time, a Byzantine city grew up too. Today the city lies in ruins, but the church itself still stands, though its roof has stared open to the sky since it was sacked by Arabs thirteen hundred years ago. The workmanship and determination of the builders who raised the carved blocks, the pillars, and the keystones so skilfully into position could not be surpassed by even the most modern mechanical means—they are already perfect.

We camped in the lee of the church, as B.B. wanted to do some filming on the morrow. The afternoon sun had made golden walls and warm shadows of the stones. But now, at night, they cooled in silhouette—black against a clear, starred sky. They were profound and silent, aloof in pride; time was still, and the Crusaders might have passed that way a week ago. In the night the sounds came faint and far from the dark plain below: the crickets, a camel's bell, a nomad's barking dog. The night itself seemed to have its own soft sound; though one could not hear it, only feel. But unless one is a poet these things do not go in words.

It was fortunate that in looking round the ruins the next day we had Rudolf with us. He was an itinerant Austrian architect hitch-hiking to Damascus, and, having seen him standing in the sun at the Syrian frontier, we took pity and gave him a lift. Anyway, with less than a day's instruction, he could do the washing-up. He was even given English lessons, and taught the song about the red-nosed reindeer. This he hummed incessantly, and thought a uniquely English joke. At night he was lent an air-mattress and some blankets, for, though the Expedition did not normally take in guests (there was not room), once accepted they were provided with all 'mod. cons.' Rudolf's main claim to fame, he said, was the design of the finest Espresso bar in all Austria. But, in fact, his knowledge was wider than this might imply, and, besides being a welcome companion, he was able to point out many things of interest in the ruins which we laymen might otherwise have missed.

From Deir Sam'an we returned to the main road, and then through Aleppo towards Tripoli. In the Oxford car we had settled down, during the preceding weeks, to a routine of changing drivers every two hours. Cambridge, on the other hand, were still experimenting, and this as far as Oxford could gather meant that they changed drivers about once every two days. Henry, particularly, would have been quite happy to have gone on driving for a fortnight if the others had let him. Each car had devised what, in the Expedition's growing vocabulary of slang, was called a 'zizz station.' A special stowage of trunks, air-mattresses, and sleeping-bags in the back of the cars made a small nest in which one person could sleep. He lay diagonally across the piled-up kit as if on a reclining-chair and, by the careful arrangement of sleeping-bags, he was wedged securely against the bumping motion of the car. Besides allowing one person to rest while on the move it also meant that the driver and the other passenger (or, in rally parlance, the co-driver) had much more room in front to stretch out and keep cool. As time went on one looked forward to a spell of enforced relaxation in the back, for, traditionally, the person behind took no part in the 'running of the ship'—even if he wanted to.

Some hours south from Aleppo, in desolate country a long way from the road, and overlooking the Orontes valley, was another ruin—the Roman garrison city of Apamea. It was dark when we arrived, so we camped between some tumbled pillars and left our exploration until the morning. In the warm night supper was a leisurely meal, and, as often happened when there was time, we sat by the lamps, talking and arguing about an infinite range of subjects: Grand Prix cars and music, Cambridge friends and Burma, National Service and what our sergeant-majors said. The latter was always a favourite and unlimited topic. That night, for Rudolf's benefit, we included coffee bars and architecture. We were nothing if not varied in our tastes. I once heard Adrian argue about the Chinese Opium Wars while, simultaneously, Pat demonstrated the use of maracas in Latin-American music by shaking a packet of Chicken Noodle soup.

The day's early light revealed the ruins around us. Apamea is relatively little known but is considered, by those few experts who visited it, to be the finest example of urban planning and construction that the Romans built. Running away from where the cars had been parked the previous night were the remains of what was and still is—the longest colonnade in the world. Nothing was spared in this city's construction, but today it lies tumbled by earthquake and pillaged by Arabs as if a giant knife had sliced through at eye-level. For miles around the ground is covered by huge and fallen blocks of masonry. Some of these blocks weigh over six tons, and once formed the upper structure of buildings sixty feet high.

We were welcomed as rare visitors by a white-haired Belgian professor who has lived alone in the city, hermit-like, for over twenty years. He was seventy-one, and yet easily outpaced us all as he led us scrambling, like ants across lump sugar, about the city. The ruins were his life, and, as he enthusiastically told us, he never returned to his hut in the evening without having found something fresh at which to wonder. Besides a fanatical devotion to his ruins, he had one other passionate interest—cranes. But only in as far as they could be the means of uncovering and restoring so much. However, he had no money, his only tools were a few bent crowbars, and so the huge stones remain where they are. Tumbled, heaped, and immovable.

Apamea was the Roman military headquarters for Northern Syria. It had a population of about 100,000 soldiers, officials, and traders. In plan it was as near rectangular perfection as any city ever built. The main streets crossed at right angles to each other at the city's centre; they were both over a mile long, and lined throughout their length by immense fluted pillars set out at precise nine-metre intervals. Thus these streets are the world's longest colonnades, and they must have been among the most extensive structural tasks undertaken by the Romans. The lesser streets divided the whole city into sixty-four perfect squares. No dwelling-house had a portal of less than ten feet high, and those of the public buildings were much higher. Magnificence must have been everywhere. The barracks, the villas, the baths, the temples, the forum, and the amphitheatre can still be clearly seen by following their lower walls. From the four main gates in the ramparts ran roads towards Aleppo, and thence Palmyra; to Asia Minor; to Jerusalem; and to every quarter where the legions marched.

Adrian tritely remarked, "It must have made the Roman camp at Cambridge look a bit of a sentry-box." But that was a thought—ever since leaving Cambridge our tyres had rolled across the dust that once the legions trod.

What was intended to be a brief filming session became a major tour, and, at B.B.'s command each person donned his brightest technicolour clothing and ran hither and thither to stand as a scale against the stones and fallen pillars. When eventually we said good-bye to the professor he showed an envious interest in the winches on our cars. "They could be like the cranes. *Je suis désolé que vous vous en allez.*" But we had to go, to leave him with his city, its heat, and his own contagious enthusiasm. Maybe he will get a crane.

Rudolf and his theme song left us in Homs, where the road for Damascus ran south. We headed on towards Lebanon, and at the border of that country the two cars separated. Cambridge went ahead to Beirut in order to make refuelling arrangements with Mobilgas and the Rover agent, while B.B., Nigel, and I set off on yet a third filming diversion, this time to a Crusader castle. In the sense that the ebb and flow of history has left its mark on Syria and Lebanon, the traces are mixed, the different ages superimposed one closely on another. That evening was separated from the morning by nearly a thousand years; from the Romans to the Crusaders.

For some miles Oxford drove towards the hills. Perched on one summit was a small, low castle. The road was very bad indeed, and in bottom gear we crawled and zigzagged slowly upward. Then, round a spur, the castle appeared high above. It was no longer low and small as it had seemed from the plain—it was huge. Half an hour later we parked beneath the silent walls and looked up to the battlements hundreds of feet above. It was staggering in size, and we had to walk far back to see it in one gaze. This was Krak des Chevaliers. Lawrence of Arabia called it "perhaps the most wholly admirable castle in the world."

Crusader castles are a catalyst to one's imagination. One thinks of the distant march from Europe, and how, for two hundred frenzied years, the Crusaders fought the Infidel to hold the Holy Land. One has read of Richard Cœur-de-Lion and Saladin; the banners and romance of the Crusaders have long become a legend—but never quite a myth. It does not do to search too closely into history, lest one finds that the Knights were not as pure and genuine as one believes. But of Krak des Chevaliers there can be no doubts—it is sheer brute strength and energy in stone.

An old Arab came out, and welcomed us in English, "I work in Michigan for twelve years before Big War." He showed us an enclosed archway in the outer battlements where we might sleep, and then, although a full tour had been deferred until the morning, we impatiently set out for a quick climb through the castle before dark. It took ten minutes to reach the top; through empty halls and passages that smelt of old, damp stone, along the windswept battlements, and, finally, up a tight spiral staircase to the roof of the highest and final keep. The view was magnificent. We could see the plain, two thousand feet below, darkening in the rapid dusk; the sky around was swept the palest blue by the clean wind, and there was a dust-yellow tinge where it curved to meet the land. We held our hats against the wind, and gazed out over a thousand square miles of hill and plain until, in a few moments, the sun was gone and it was dark. We climbed below.

⊛

Loud knocking on our wooden door and a respectful but emphatic "Get up, messieurs," roused us in the morning. The sky was grey with clouds, and it seemed that good colour-filming would not be possible. I asked the Arab guardian if the sun would come. With obvious sympathy for my ignorance, I was told, "Sometime God make cloud, sometime sun. He do what He want." As there was no telling what the Almighty intended, we ate a slow breakfast and waited. However, by eight o'clock a strong wind was rolling away the clouds, and it had been decided that the sun would burn.

Krak des Chevaliers was built at the beginning of the twelfth century by the Knights of St John of Jerusalem. Most of the Knights were French, and they built their fortress to stand, like a steep island, overlooking the hilly gap between the inland plains of the Orontes and the coastal lowlands of Tripoli. Millions of tons of rock were dragged from the surrounding quarries and chipped into blocks as tall as a man, and, inside the outer ramparts, a moat was dug forty feet down and wider than a street. Above, in the huge walls, one sees the slits and covered galleries for the archers, the holes for pouring boiling oil, and the high projecting turrets which over-looked attackers. The castle in its heyday was garrisoned by five thousand Crusaders, and there was enough food inside the walls to last a year's siege. So impregnable were the massive defences that they withstood at least twelve prolonged attacks, and even Saladin withdrew, a wiser man, after he had viewed the indomitable walls. A medieval Arab chronicler wrote of the Krak that for one hundred and fifty years "it stuck like a bone in the throat of the Saracens."

But, after nearly two centuries, the full fire of the Crusades had dimmed. The garrison of the castle had dwindled until there were barely three hundred knights left. At last, in March 1271, the Muslims assembled a large army, calling in contingents from the Assassins and as far away as Egypt. Then, under the Emir of Homs, the siege began. It was not until the fighting was in its sixth week that the attacking hordes of thousands gained final entry. Even then it was by treachery. But, in admiration of their bravery, the Emir gave the remaining knights safe conduct to the coast. The Krak never fell to direct assault.

Today the castle is empty and quite deserted; there are no guides or guide-books. So, in unhurried pleasure, one is forced to work out the plan alone. We walked up the dark entrance passage which runs under the walls for over one hundred yards. For easier defence it had three elbow turns, and could be blocked by a drawbridge, four gates, and a portcullis. We saw the kitchens, where the oven was as big as a small house, the stone chambers, where there were four hundred huge jars for oil, and the stables where once were kept four hundred chargers. The scale of the interior was equal to that of the defences—at times one's mind only worked as a recorder of dimensions. On the roof, above the courtyard, was a round stone table for the meetings of the Master and the senior Knights of the Order. Behind, in the battlements, was the Crusaders' chapel. In there it was dark except for the sunbeams which stabbed through the narrow windows. And, in the sigh of the wind above, one could almost hear the chink of mail and the murmur of a Latin Mass.

We left after lunch and picked our way carefully down towards the plain again. A few hours later we were in Lebanon, and speeding down the tarmac road from Tripoli to Beirut. It was night, and I was driving. Never—before or since—have I driven at such risk; we might have killed or been killed at least eight times in less than two hours. According to our handbook on Lebanon, "it is decreed that the driver should pursue the right-hand side." The word "should" is given the most voluntary of all its possible interpretations. But "pursue" is obeyed to the very letter. With chin on horn, the Lebanese chase some indeterminate object which hurtles along an erratic course at any speed between 50 m.p.h. and 90 m.p.h. The objects are, of course, invisible to all except their own individual pursuers, and, furthermore, there is no liaison between these objects—particularly those travelling in opposite directions. In sixty miles we passed five knotted crowds who were admiring some head-on collision. Those Lebanese who cannot afford the replacement rate on cars have bicycles and hand-carts instead. At night they propel these, unlit, down the white line. Because of this every motor vehicle is equipped with head-lamps of searchlight ferocity, and one's admiration would be complete if these lights had some means of dipping. But that, I suppose, would spoil the system. The results to all parties concerned—dazzled motorists, cyclists, and pedestrians—are spectacular and often fatal.

Cambridge were waiting for us, as planned, in the central square of Beirut, and instead of leading us to a camp on the town's outskirts as we expected, they told us that the Expedition had been lent a dormitory in the British Mission School for Girls. (The girls were, of course, on holiday.) The kind ladies of the mission must have been disturbed by our appearance, for the next morning they hospitably offered us hot baths. Grabbing my towel, I was away like a flash; experience had taught me to move very fast on such occasions. The haste was justified, for, sure enough, just as my month-awaited bath was full, the water, was cut off—during the night a lorry had driven into an unlit waterworks excavation on the Tripoli road and smashed the pipe! Clean and self-satisfied, I earned appropriate comments from the others, who stewed in their dirt for the rest of the day.

The Expedition spent three busy days in Beirut; there was always a good deal to do in towns: letters to write, the cars to check, sights to see, and a small mountain of laundry to wash. On the subject of dirty clothes there existed two schools of thought. One led by Pat and Nigel, believed that the most effective method lay in dumping everything in a bucket, adding water and soap-flakes to taste, and then poking the mixture spasmodically for the next twenty-four hours. The other school, B.B. and I, advocated scraping the dirt off with a maximum of scrubbing-brush. Neither method was particularly successful; the former removed only half the dirt, while the latter removed not only the dirt but half the clothes as well. It was not until later in the journey that we evolved a fully fledged washing-machine: clothes, water, and detergent were put in a pressure-cooker, which was then clamped down and stowed in the back of the car. The bumpy roads produced a marvellous lather, and after two hundred miles of corrugation one had a wash of almost perfect whiteness. This Mobile-Pressure-Cooker-Launderette (patent applied for) saved us a lot of trouble. Of course, it could not cope with the larger items such as trousers, but for one's 'smalls' it was a most admirable arrangement. And what matter if the potatoes did taste of soap?

"Bureaucracy on Wheels" might have been a good name for us. Planning was not finished when we left England—far from it. It seemed to go on interminably. In Beirut (and it was fairly typical of most other places where we called a halt to catch up on the paper-work) the Busyness Box was opened, and with both typewriters in action, with files, carbon, and paper all around, the office work began. Most of our business in England went through the agency of the Home Team. A typical letter to them ran to three or four closely typed pages divided into a series of numbered paragraphs. Thus, from Beirut, the Home Team letter contained the following instructions and information (among sixteen other points):

1. Our future mailing addresses and plans up to Karachi.
2. Please check the insurance on the cine camera.
3. Stir up the Burmese Embassy in London about our entry visas.
4. B.B.'s arrangements for airmailing the exposed film to the B.B.C.
5. Customs clearance details on the above.
6. Possibility of Land Rover demonstration for Persian Army in Teheran—please pass this information to Rovers.
7. Send us a technical report from the B.B.C. on the first batch of film.
8. Statement of Expedition's expenses to date.

Below these headings were further details, but they would only bore the reader, as, on occasions, they must have bored the Home Team. However, if we were to reach Singapore in one piece financially it was all necessary. As Business Manager, this was chiefly Adrian's responsibility.

Other work was dealt with according to each person's particular job. Thus B.B. would turn a lavatory into a dark-room and develop his black-and-white films to the negative stage, caption each photo, and then mail the negatives and captions back to his London agent. The latter dealt with the commercial sales of the pictures. Nigel, as Q.M., would turn a town inside out while he foraged for tinned-food bargains with which to restock the Expedition's larder. My task was to find inspiration for a newspaper article and to keep the Diary up-to-date. Carbon copies of each page in the Diary were sent to the Home Team so that they might follow, in some detail, what we were doing. Pat wrote many of the bread-and-butter letters to those people who had helped us on the road. At the same time he was writing ahead for route information, and to Embassies to check various doubtful points such as camera and Customs regulations. Henry, of course, was concerned with the maintenance of the cars. It did not matter that there was nothing wrong with them—Henry was a perfectionist. In Beirut the cars returned from garage inspection with a thick extra leaf in each rear spring. This, it seems (despite what British manufacturers claim to the contrary), is a necessary and standard local modification to all British cars arriving in the Middle East. If the Expedition thought that it had already seen some rough roads, it learnt that there were some lessons in store.

Although the administrative side of our journey took a good deal of time, we always found opportunities for the lighter side. In Beirut the Club Ski Nautique invited "les étudiants d'Oxford et de Cambridge" to try their skill. For a while we sat in our bathing-suits, shy and hunched in our pristine whiteness, watching bronzed bodies dashing over the water. Adrian, however, saved our honour and surprised everybody by remaining upright on his skis throughout two complete circuits. Then we were invited to meet some Press reporters at *un cocktail*. The newspapers later came out with some amusing comments. The Expedition was, in their opinion, "*très sportif et de grande bonhomie,*" the rivalry between the two cars was exaggerated to wonderful proportions—"A 50,000 kilometre Boat-race on Wheels!" Perhaps the reporters were encouraged by our mention of Henry's past successes with his Austin Seven Special, for he became the ace racing driver "*M. Henri Nott, qui gagne les grandes courses à Silverstone.*" Adrian was called "*M. L'Entrepreneur de L'Expedition.*" But it was Pat who came away with the prize as "*M. Le Navigateur et L'Attaché Diplomatique*"— a title which pleased him no end, and, chameleon-like, he reverted to his French beret, garlic, and a daily copy of *Le Figaro*.

Beirut, sometimes known as the Paris of the Mediterranean, was an expensive and amusing place. Lately it had become the summer Mecca of the oil-rich sheiks from Saudi Arabia. They fly in with more money than they know what to do with, and monopolize the cabaret girls and the motor dealers. From the latter they buy Cadillacs three at a time and, having given two to the former, they throw the remaining one away when the built-in radio fails. Anyway, that is what we were told.

The Lebanese regard themselves as the world's sharpest businessmen. Maybe they are right; certainly the tradition of commerce goes back two thousand years, and today more than ever the economy of their small country is dependent on it. They look at the rest of the world with cheerful cynicism—and not only in matters of commerce. It was in Beirut that we were told the following story.

Three people—two men and a beautiful woman—were wrecked on a desert island. How could this triangular problem be settled? The Lebanese maintain that the solution entirely depends on the nationality of the castaways.

If they were Spaniards, one of the men would shoot the other.
If Italians, the woman would shoot one of the men.
If Americans, the men would merely sit down and talk business
If French, of course, there was no problem.
And if English, no difficulty would arise either, for none of them would have been introduced.

As we left Beirut and climbed inland we realized that we should not touch the sea again until the Indian Ocean at Karachi. As far as we could foresee, there were three apparent 'legs' in the journey. The first was from London to Beirut; that was now behind. The next was to Karachi; and the third ended in Calcutta. After Calcutta it was anybody's guess, but that was still a long way ahead.

THE ROUTE FROM ANKARA TO KARACHI

x = Krak des Chevaliers

5

Middle East

AFTER an hour's twisting climb from the coast the road levelled out across the fertile plain of Bekka. With the rise in altitude there was a fall in temperature. Beirut had been, as Nigel said, "like a whale's inside—hot and sticky," but now the bright air and green fields were clean and fresh. The atmosphere was as crisp as if newly pressed.

In the middle of the plain stood the temples of Baalbek. The Romans and their slaves worked for two hundred years to raise these shrines to Jupiter and Bacchus, but, as elsewhere in the Middle East, the Arab and the earthquake have partially destroyed what the *Encyclopœdia Britannica* calls "one of the grandest architectural achievements of all time." The pillars, the staircases, the platforms, and the gateways are immense, but for all their size, they are most finely proportioned. Near by, lying on its side in a quarry, is the largest piece of masonry ever cut by man—a single block weighing nearly two thousand tons. How the Romans lifted these gigantic stones is still a mystery. We watched a reconstruction gang working with three jacks to raise what, in comparison, was a mere pebble. After an hour of struggling they had hardly moved it.

With all the ruins which we had seen and used as a backdrop for our filming in those few days, it was not their present beauty, their past glory, or their archæological interest which above all amazed us. It was their sheer size. And coupled with this was a consideration of the puny machinery available to those ancient people as set against their staggering products. The unequal scale seems only to have been balanced by their tremendous faith—be that faith in their God, as with the early Christians and Crusaders, or in themselves, as with the Romans. One could not fail to wonder.

The high green hills of Lebanon roll down into Syria, and gradually, eastward through a narrow belt of cultivation, the land coarsens into rocks and sand. On the fringe of the Great Syrian Desert, which stretches for five hundred scorching miles to the Euphrates, is the oldest inhabited city in the world, Damascus. Unfortunately, we were kept occupied in obtaining permission from the Syrian Government for the next stage of the journey, across the Desert. Consequently, I must guiltily admit that, though we visited the bazaar, the most remarkable thing about Damascus of which I can find mention in my Diary of October 1955 was a Chevrolet of 1956— "no gear-lever." Which, I fear, must prove something about us.

Nevertheless, while we were in the city there occurred something which was serious and illuminating in its widest implications. The six of us had been invited to a restaurant in order to meet some newspaper-men. After answering various questions about ourselves, everybody sat down to tea. I found myself opposite an Editor, and, by way of opening the conversation, I remarked that the Middle East was "a very interesting part of the world." It was a trite remark, but one which certainly seemed harmless. I thought that the Editor must have misunderstood me when he replied curtly, "We in this country do not want your interest."

I hastily explained that I was referring to the past associations and history of the area rather than to present politics.

"That is what the British and Americans have always said, but all the time you have ideas."

"What ideas?" But, as I asked, I knew the answer.

"Israel. Why do you British send arms to the Jews when at the same time you complain that Arab countries buy arms from Russia? I will tell you—because you are an imperialist nation and wish to control this part of the world."

It was clear that our views were so wide apart that argument would be pointless, and, under the circumstances, undesirable. Instead, I asked what solution he saw to the problem of Israel.

"There is no problem," he replied, with a calculated smile. "We wait until U.N. support for Israel has faded, and then we attack. The Arab nations will finish the Jews." He made a dramatic gesture with his hands.

This intensity of hatred is a thing of which we in Britain have no comprehension. But, despite their constant talk of "sweeping the Jews into the sea," it seems that the Arab countries are in deadly fear of Israel. They know that her army is more formidable than all of theirs put together. This fear is covered by bluff and propaganda. Thus the Arab leaders are able to maintain the confidence of the masses—but the bluff is not always as cool as was the Editor's. A foreign diplomat whom we later met predicted that the Israelis would "break out within the next three years." If they left it longer, he explained, the Arab nations would have sufficiently caught up in the arms race to compete with the Jews on equal terms. "Then the Jews will be in trouble. The next war will start here." He was quite definite about it.[2]

✇

From Damascus to Baghdad there are three routes across the desert—"round the bottom," "round the top," or "through the middle." The most popular, on account of its reasonable oil-pipe-line road, is the route south to Mafraq, in Jordan, and then seven hundred miles east from there. For the route "round the top" one goes north to Homs and then eastward across the desert by following the other pipe-line, which runs from Tripoli, on the Mediterranean, to the Kirkuk oil-fields, in Iraq. On the last part of the route one swings away from the pipe-line and drives down the Euphrates valley. This northern crossing has been used for thousands of years. It approximates to the Fertile Crescent of Old Testament times, and it passes close by the ancient caravan and trading city of Palmyra, which now lies in drifts of wind-blown sand.

Before leaving England we had heard of the third, the 'slap-through-the-middle,' route, and of the unique vehicles by which it was pioneered. Although the Expedition was advised against following it in the cars, B.B. and I determined to find out more about this route's interesting story. The Expedition split, and the next few days are best explained by a letter written to the Home Team at the time.

Damascus
7th October

DEAR H.T.,

An interim note to tell you about a slight change of plan. Tim and B.B. have become interested in the Nairn Buses which, as you may know, make the journey from here to Baghdad straight through the desert. Consequently, they are staying here for a few days in order to get some dope for an article or two. Meanwhile, the rest of us are taking the cars over by the northern route (Homs, pipe-line station T.4, Palmyra, T.3,

T.2, Abou Kemal, Ramadi, Baghdad). Parts of N.E. Syria are military areas and we are, at present, delayed in getting permission to go through them. However, we hope to leave Damascus P.M. tomorrow and should reach Baghdad in three days. By that time Tim and B.B. will have got the photos and notes for their articles and will then come over to Baghdad in one of the buses. We will all meet up at that end. By the time this gets to you we'll be in Baghdad anyway and will write again. Yours expeditionally,

OXCAM

B.B. and I saw the others off the next evening, then found ourselves a room in a small hotel. The two of us had already met Mr Fraser, the manager of the Nairn Company, who had given us complete freedom of the bus depot and workshops. He even arranged that a company car should collect us from the hotel each morning.

The Nairn Bus is a byword for reliability in the Middle East. Every afternoon its 170 horse-power diesel engine starts with a great cough, and at five o'clock precisely the silver bus emerges into the bright sun. With a wail on its siren it picks up speed through the suburbs of Damascus, and then after a few miles it swings abruptly east into the desert. Fifteen hours and nearly six hundred miles later the bus—now glaring white in desert dust—draws to a halt with a pent-up sigh from its air-brakes. The Overland Desert Mail is in Baghdad after an all-night dash across half of Northern Arabia.

The design for this seventeen-ton machine (and the eleven others owned by the Company) is unique, and so is the service it provides to travellers in the Middle East. This, the biggest bus in the world, is the result of thirty years' experience and experiment on the part of two New Zealanders—the Nairn brothers—first to realize the commercial possibilities of a direct link between Damascus and Baghdad. Back in 1923, when the Nairns were starting their enterprise, these cities were separated by the unmapped rocks and sand of the Great Syrian Desert. Tiny bands of hostile Bedouin attacked those who ventured forth without sufficient guard, and with summer temperatures reaching 140^0F. the desert was as hot as any place on earth. It presented driving conditions—if you could call them that—unparalleled anywhere else in the world. It still does.

In April 1923 a small reconnaissance party led by the Nairns set out from Damascus in three open cars to find a route across this wild region. Navigating by the sun and compasses, carrying petrol and oil for one thousand miles, and ten days' supply of food, the party actually reached Baghdad in four days. Later they made the return journey, and, in the months that followed, repeated the crossing several times to improve their route. Soon they were able to cut the time to three days. Using open limousines, they instituted a weekly service which enabled passengers and mail to reach Baghdad from London—via Beirut—in two weeks. The previous London to Baghdad journey had taken one right out to Bombay, and from there up the Persian Gulf—an overall journey of nearly two months.

The cars in those days were compelled to carry arms, a week's provisions, and to travel in strong convoys. For, despite the annual £2000 in gold paid to the Bedouin for safe passage, attacks on the cars were always to be reckoned with. Stopping in the desert at night, the convoys formed hollow squares, and the men passengers took their turn on watch with the guides and drivers. Such measures made trouble rare, but during the tribal rebellions of the Druse in 1925 the Arabs made several raids on the convoys with their swift fighting camels. Once the convoy leader was killed, several passengers wounded, and a large consignment of gold was taken. Again, in 1928 Iraqi tribesmen ambushed a small file of cars. Mortally wounding the driver of the passenger vehicle and injuring two others, they forced the mail car to stop, turned out the driver, and dragged the machine away. Camel police, arriving later, pursued the attackers, but never found any trace of the car or its contents.

The Nairns, however, learned to evade the marauders by secretly changing their routes, sometimes by hundreds of miles to the north or south of their usual line of travel. The cars always managed to arrive on schedule—they had to, for the company had agreed to forfeit money for every hour that the mails were delayed, except when due to a *force majeure*. In thirty years the company has never yet had to pay such a fine.

There is the story of a Government official in Baghdad who in 1925 ruefully told one of the Nairn brothers that he would never get to Beirut in time to catch his ship for England and his leave. The ship left the next day. Looking at his watch, Nairn bet him a double fare that he could get him to the ship in time. The official accepted the wager, and was strapped into an overland car which Nairn himself drove to Damascus, and then down to Beirut. The 650-mile journey took sixteen hours, and the amazed but delighted passenger was rowed out to his ship as she dropped her moorings. The car was a wreck.

By the early 'thirties the fame of the desert service had spread far beyond the wastes it had conquered. The open touring cars were no longer adequate for the increased traffic. Larger vehicles, specially designed for desert travel, were needed. Three large, six-wheel buses were specially built in America. But, although they cut the journey to twenty-four hours, their long and inflexible chassis were never entirely satisfactory. Accordingly, trailers hooked on to powerful cars were tried. Allowing more flexibility, they seemed better able to withstand the battering of the desert surface. From this 'tractor and trailer' principle has evolved the Nairn fleet of to-day.

In the twelve modern buses the tractor is basically a heavy lorry—but a faster and heavier lorry than one will ever see on the Great North Road. These machines must pull their seventeen-ton load over an appalling surface at speeds of well over 50 m.p.h. for fifteen almost continuous hours.

Since no manufacturer will build a bus to the Nairns' exacting requirements, the company is forced to buy the various parts from different sources. Thus the two chassis in each bus—an outer one braced by an inner—are supplied from the United States. From another manufacturer comes the engine, while the axles are derived from wartime tank-transporters. The gear-box with its eight forward speeds, the half-ton of springs per vehicle, the tyres, which cost £100 apiece and last for 80,000 miles, the air-conditioning unit, which is driven by an engine strong enough to power a family saloon, the air-brakes, the railway head-lamps, and the electrical system—all are supplied by different makers. Only in the Damascus workshops can these components be assembled into the specially built "Nairn cocktail," as the chief engineer described it.

After two most interesting days the time came for B.B. and me to leave for Baghdad. We had the choice of travelling in the Pullman, which seated eighteen passengers and had a bar, a steward, air-conditioning, and a lavatory, or in the Tourist bus, which had none of these facilities. The latter carried more passengers, and—due presumably to the lack of a lavatory—it made one or two extra halts, and took a little longer on the journey. We chose the Tourist. The manager introduced us to Hassan, the driver, who immediately seemed to regard us as his honoured and personal guests. A few minutes before five o'clock we climbed into the dark interior and settled back in our seats. The dust-proof door was slammed shut, the engine cleared its throat, and the journey began.

Our fellow passengers were Iraqis or Syrians. Some wore European clothes and shabby trilbies, while others were clad in the white robes and burnous of the Arab. They regarded us with curiosity—the more sophisticated ones came down the aisle and introduced themselves with offers of cigarettes and chewing-gum. Everybody did their best to make us feel at home.

Damascus was soon behind, and presently the bus turned off the road and eased herself on to the desert. She picked up speed, and it was only then that we fully appreciated the rugged construction of the vehicle, for in the desert there was no road, only an occasional oil-drum set out as a marker. The bus lurched and swayed slightly on corners, but, due to the rubber-mounted coupling between the coach and the tractor, there was little noise from the throbbing motor in front. The rush of the pounding tyres and the sensation of motion was similar to that experienced inside an airliner dashing across a grass runway just before take-off. The dust from the tractor swept past the windows and then began to settle on the glass itself, until in a short time one's view of the desert flashing past outside became dimmer, and then blotted out altogether.

At sundown the bus stopped at the border post, though the frontier itself was still a hundred miles ahead. The door of the coach swung open, and Hassan peered inside and shouted, "You come with me. How you like my bus? Ver', ver' good, eh!" We agreed, and were led inside a solitary mud building, where Hassan sat us down and signalled for coffee. Around the walls were advertisements incongruously telling us what English cigarettes to smoke, and which was Milwaukee's finest beer. A little boy insisted on cleaning our shoes, and then sat back on his haunches extolling his skill until we paid him. The question of customs' formalities was waved aside by Hassan—"you are my vriends," and obviously, therefore, such inconveniences were not for us.

We were invited to travel in the driving-cab for the next stage. It was an experience I would not have missed. In the cab, high off the ground, there is an air of controlled strain. For hour after hour the driver neither speaks nor smokes; silent and expressionless, he leans slightly forward on his wheel, watching the way ahead as the loom of his head-lamps rushes over the rock and sand. Suddenly, for no apparent reason, his hand flies to the gear-lever and the already deafening noise of the engine bursts to a roar, the air-brakes hiss as he dabs with a foot—then one sees what he saw seconds ago. Like lightning, and with wonderful precision, he wrenches the wheel, the bus peels away to one side and goes thundering through a tiny gap in the tangled rocks. The Nairn drivers never err, they never misjudge their speed, and they never crunch a gear-change. With seventeen tons behind them there is no time for a mistake. Sometimes they must move very fast, as the wheels surge into soft sand and begin to slide. They must know every yard of that five hundred miles—the Nairn Track, as their route is universally known. The Nairn Track; no small compliment to the men who drive it.

Rutba, a transport post in the middle of the desert, is reached a little before midnight. Here the east- and west-bound buses meet and refill their seventy-gallon tanks. Then on. After Rutba B.B. and I started to blow up our air-mattresses, on which we intended to sleep in the broad luggage-racks. It was all we could do to prevent the mattresses being burst by the enthusiastic efforts of the other passengers. Cadillacs and Coca-Cola they knew all about, but here was something entirely new—a bed you blew up! Marvellous! Every one blew in turn while the rest applauded, and when eventually we climbed into the rack we got no sleep at all—our helpers prodded the mattresses all night in wonder that they had not deflated.

By dawn we had travelled five hundred miles. The desert sweetened into the palm-fringed margins of the Euphrates, and the bus halted in the little township of Ramadi. Amid more applause, we let down our 'beds' and then pushed, with every one else, into the Iraq Customs House. Here the inquiries were conducted with an informality startling in its simplicity. The official—we decided he must have been the official, because no one in the bus had been wearing pyjamas—courteously asked us, "How many baggages you have?" We replied that we had only one; we were sharing a "baggage." This was clearly not customary among desert travellers, but, nevertheless, he seemed satisfied.

Then over the Euphrates, past the R.A.F. air-base at Habbaniya, and down to the Tigris. I was anxious to catch a glimpse of these famous rivers, and their ancient countryside. But it was not possible, for the dust hung thick upon the windows, allowing only a dim yellow light to filter through. At eight o'clock precisely we pulled into Baghdad. We collected our things and stepped down, blinking in the sunlight. Pat and Henry were there to meet us; Oxford and Cambridge had arrived the previous evening. Hassan came to say good-bye, and when we told him, "Your bus ver', ver' good. You ver', ver' good" we meant it, and he smiled all over.

⊛

Baghdad, like Timbuctu or Casablanca, is a city about which people have highly imaginative and luxurious ideas, but, in fact, it is not the sensual or romantic place that fiction would often have one believe. It is not even a poor substitute for that other Baghdad in Hollywood, and if any dancing girls do exist they would certainly bear no resemblance to that delicious desert rose, Miss Yvonne de Carlo. The Sheiks of Arabee are definitely not around any longer; but one may see their grandchildren, grown rich on oil, ensconced in the latest pink or sky-blue masterpieces from Detroit. What we Westerners call 'civilization' has definitely arrived in the sea of constipated traffic that is Rashid Street, the main thoroughfare. The Faithful are called to prayer by a minaret loudspeaker which plays its 'muezzin' from a gramophone below. Baghdad is a bewildering mixture: mud shanties and ten-story buildings, camels and double-decker buses, women in purdah and Cinemascope. On the proceeds of the country's oil it is a boom town, but not quite sure of the direction in which it is booming. A brand-new railway station had been built, but, as it was built on the wrong side of a rapidly expanding aerodrome, the trains will never reach it. Instead the station is used for Government offices. As the Prophet undoubtedly said, "Time Marches On"—and what if progress does follow with a limp?

However, I should not imply that we disliked Baghdad. It is just one of those places to which one would prefer to return in twenty years' time to see how it had progressed.

Our stay was prolonged by an accident to one of the cars incurred while filming a Nairn bus coming in from the desert. While chasing the bus Cambridge hit a huge and unseen bump. She took off, and remained airborne—as we found from the tyre-marks—for nearly six feet. The damage was not great, but no good had been done to the front axle; it had to be repaired. Repairs were easier talked about than done, for it seemed that there are only two real working days in the Baghdad week. Fridays and Sundays are the Muslim and Christian sabbaths respectively. As it is hardly worth going to work on the one intervening day—Saturday—the week is reduced to the four remaining days. But, even then, it seems that Monday becomes a day of preparation for the forthcoming labours, while likewise Thursday becomes a day of preparation for the forthcoming vacation. Thus on Tuesdays and Wednesdays only can one expect to get things done. However, while waiting for the repairs we caught up on letters, visited Ctesiphon, and in the hot afternoons we observed the dictum that "while there is always plenty to do the best thing to do is to sleep" (Aldershot Traditional).

We were kindly made honorary members of the British Club in Baghdad during our delay. We were to meet its counterpart many more times on our travels, for it seems that wherever our empire-building forebears wandered they formed themselves into standing committees and started clubs. Some have grown large, some have stayed small, but, whatever the size, they extend half-way round the world—from Baghdad to Bangkok, and even beyond. Walk into one anywhere, and, though you might not know what country you were in within five thousand miles, you will recognize immediately the well-stocked bar, the chintz curtains, the immaculate washrooms, and the inevitable copies of the *Overseas Mirror* and the airmail *Times*. It is the British Club—it could not be anything else. But though the surroundings may have the same ingredients, so has the welcome. To us it was always "Right-ho, boys, make yourselves at home. Now, what'll it be?"

Nevertheless, coming out from England, we could not help being appalled at some of the remarks which came from the occasional member. He would talk loudly about "the natives" in the most repulsive terms. This might not have mattered so much had not the barmen and the servants been able to understand—though they pretended not to.

"These people are scum," I was once told. "Do y'know what some of them do with their dead? Well, I'll tell you. They cover them with dung and leave them to rot in the sun. Ugh—and they talk about civilization! Why, they've only just crawled out of the mud." He slid his glass across the bar. "Boy, another Scotch. No, you damn' fool—Johnnie Walker."

Inwardly I curled up; I blushed for my white skin. Had it ever occurred to that person that this method of disposing of the dead was at least practical? No doubt "the natives" are as much horrified at the Western habit of burning the dead. Or might they prefer to do the same if they had the wood? But they have not, and therefore they do what is expedient.

However, I must not imply that these tactless remarks (to say the least) came from more than a very few people. That I must emphasize. Neither were they exclusive to the clubs. But so also must I emphasize that it is just these few who do the damage; in a variety of ways they have caused irreparable harm in the past, and will go on to cause more in the future. Hatred can be spilt by the chance remark of one man, but afterwards the stain cannot be dissolved by the courtesy of ten. Some Britons are not well-mannered (despite the happy tradition). If anything, the women are the worst.

We should not delude ourselves. If I were a foreigner I sometimes should not love the British very much. I should remember that single remark and forget all else. Sometimes I should loathe their guts.

The man at the bar shrugged his shoulders. "It's all very well for you, old boy," he said, "but you don't have to live here."

Does he—and a few others like him?

Eventually the repair was completed, and the following morning the Expedition pulled away from Baghdad towards the mountains of Persia. At first the land was very flat, for this was still the great plain of the Tigris and Euphrates. But outside the narrow irrigated margins of the rivers themselves the country was as parched as the dust that covered it. The tall palms of an occasional oasis shimmered in the dry air, and shielded their water from the jealous sun and the desert around.

Parts of the road were wide enough to allow the cars to drive almost side by side, and thus the following car could keep clear of the dust thrown up by the first. B.B. took this opportunity to do some filming while on the

move, for the sight of the other car racing alongside was particularly
photogenic. When the road was straight the dust rushed out behind, or in
the warm wind drifted across the desert to one side. Sometimes, when the
road was rough, the dust fanned over the wallowing car like the smoke of
a ship in a following sea. With suitable background music, this atmosphere
of travel and distance would have been complete. We turned on the
wireless, and, as if to order, rolled along for the next thirty miles to the
rousing accompaniment of some 'covered-wagon' music. Then later we
found the B.B.C. short-wave, and the News came crackling through—
there were "fog-patches" in the Home Counties.

The Persian frontier runs along the foot of the mountains. We swept
into the walled enclosure of the control post to the unlikely tune of *Land
of Hope and Glory*. At all previous Customs stations the formalities had
been remarkably simple and easy. But not so at this frontier. After the
officials had taken two hours to stamp our passports, we had a suspicion
that they were being over-zealous. This was confirmed when they wanted
to seal our cameras. The British Embassy in Teheran had written earlier, in
answer to Pat's inquiries, that the Persian Government no longer required
cameras to be sealed on entry into the country. We pointed this out to the
officials, and even showed them the letter, but, naturally, they could not
read English. It was apparent that news of the year-old cancellation of the
previous law had not yet penetrated to the one place where it really
applied—the frontier. It was useless to argue, so we compromised by
hiding three of the cameras (after all, the revised law was on our side), and
allowed them to seal another, which was not in use, anyway. Next they
wanted to seal the car radios. We invited them to try their skill, but—well,
how does one 'seal' a radio? They gave up, and turned their attention to
our medical documents. There was further delay, as they had lost their
official doctor, and most of the documents were only translated into
Spanish and French. Until then our conduct had been strictly correct, but
we were provoked when four untidy officials came forward and without a
word officiously started to pull things out of the cars and drop them on
the ground. We stood around dumbfounded.

Then one little man did something which we were always most
careful not to do ourselves. He dumped the sleeping-bags in the dust.
Immediate uproar. The officials were dragged out of the cars, and, amid a

crescendo of protests from both sides, we told them that if they insisted on a formal inspection it would be carried out formally. The cars, we explained, would be driven up the steps of the Customs house, through the double doors, and into the hall itself. There was at least a cement floor in there. This ultimatum, delivered in English and sign language, left no room for doubt in their minds, and it definitely penetrated the linguistic barrier. The officials withdrew. It was bluff on our part, for fully to unpack the cars and then repack again was a two-hour job. But we were convinced that the officials were either naturally stupid or being purposely un-co-operative. They seemed to be saying, "Don't ask us why we are doing this, because we haven't a clue. But officials like us aren't worth our salt unless we show our authority."

We waited. It was now three hours since our arrival, and the Expedition was very close to losing its collective temper. But then the same four men returned. They had the audacity to make another sortie to ransack the cars. This was too much. We removed them by force, and put the ultimatum into effect. The cars, with a great deal of unnecessary but impressive roaring and revving, bounced slowly up the flight of steps. "The Shah will hear of this," threatened Pat.

Suddenly the officials decided that they did not want to inspect the cars after all, and with unprecedented politeness indicated that we could leave. We roared with laughter—to ourselves! The cars reversed down the steps and the exit gates were swung open for our departure with almost formal courtesy. We drove out and away. The sole result of this three-hour delay was that one camera was sealed and each passport now had *five* more pages of stamps and squiggles in it than it had before.

The road climbed steadily into the mountains, and at one point it ran over a pass of 8000 feet. In a few hours the temperature had dropped more than twenty degrees, and yet the heat of the Mesopotamian plains was less than one hundred miles behind. When the sun went down it became even colder, and for the first time on the journey the roof-hatches were closed and the heaters switched on. We motored on through the mountains for an hour or two, and then turned off the road to make camp.

During the past few weeks we had given up rigging the tent at night, for there was no likelihood of rain. Camp no longer went 'up'—rather it was set 'down.' The cars were parked side by side, and the beds laid out between them. Then, by lantern-light, we cooked the supper. This was the big meal of the day; Pat was in charge.

Despite our remarks that there were basically only two kinds of supper (a Boil-up or a Fry-up), Pat was a good cook. He worked on the principle of giving us what he himself wanted, and, considering that the variety of food we could carry was limited, he rang the changes in the evening diet most effectively. The first course was invariably soup. It came out of a packet, as, in fact, do most soups these days. To us the advantages of packet soups were obvious; they were light and compact, and by carrying ten different packets it was possible to have ten different varieties. Naturally, we had our favourites. Egg soup (that is what it said on the packet) was not rated as highly as *potage légumes variés* (we had taken aboard a stock of French-speaking soups in Beirut), while chicken noodle was perhaps the best, providing it was made over-strength. Soup was followed by the main course—usually some kind of tinned meat, such as beefsteak, Irish stew, or corned beef. Accompanying this were boiled potatoes and, if possible, a fresh vegetable—cabbage, carrots, onions, or cauliflower. "Fresh veg. to keep you regular" was Pat's culinary motto.

We tried to avoid the usual trap of constant frying, and often used instead a pressure-cooker. During the first month of the journey there had been much controversy about the length of time that the cooker required, but now it was left to Pat. If he judged correctly he was congratulated, whereas if he left the cooker on too long he quickly threw in a bouillon cube (Pat's French for Oxo), and called the resultant mush a *ragoût*. No one was much the wiser. The Expedition did not normally carry 'pudding' and, if anybody was still hungry, 'afters' was a table d'hôte affair of biscuits, cheese, or jam. There was an unwritten convention that one never complained if the meal was not entirely to one's liking. If one did one was likely to be invited to take over the job of cook and demonstrate one's suggestions. This was adequate deterrent. One either went without (very rare) or proposed a gentle and different amendment, such as "Don't you think it would be a good idea if we kept those Vienna Sausages just for emergencies?"

A final and important evening ritual was B.B.'s issue of anti-malarial pills (Paludrin) and vitamin tablets. We took a double dose of the latter when 'on the road' because then we were eating mainly out of tins or packets, and B.B., as Doc, wished to make up the resultant deficiencies.

It was two days' drive from Baghdad to Teheran, the capital of Persia. I am aware that the correct title of the country is now Iran, but I am prepared to risk the wrath of the diplomats in the British Embassy there—one of whom seemed shocked at my intentional ignorance. I am not reactionary, but Persia is a refreshing, lovely name; Iran is not. Persia means everything from Xerxes and Omar Khayyám to cats and carpets: Iran means nothing.

But I must not imply that the Embassy staff were anything but helpful. In fact, they allowed us to camp inside an empty house in their residential compound on the mountain-slopes above the town.

When we thanked them for the trouble that they had taken in answering our previous letters they replied that they were "so glad that we could smooth your way through the Customs." We said nothing, for there was no point in spoiling their illusion, and our frontier troubles had been no fault of theirs. Nevertheless, B.B. was compelled to shunt from one Government department to another for a whole day in order to get the camera unsealed. When he asked them for a letter pointing out to any authorities we might meet in future that photography was now permitted they replied that this was quite unnecessary. The old law had definitely been cancelled, and therefore, they argued, what was the point in giving us a document to that effect? However, the British Embassy gave us a letter which, though lacking any legal significance, had an impressive rubber stamp at the bottom—which was, after all, the most important thing.

We stayed in Teheran much longer than intended in order to give a demonstration of the Land Rovers to the Persian General Staff. The test took place on the military proving-ground three days after our arrival. Henry and I chose the roughest course that we could find, and practised all morning. The final hill on the two-mile circuit was so steep that, try as we might, we could not get the cars to the top before the wheels started to spin on the loose surface. We tried everything: reduced tyre-pressures, a slow approach, a fast approach, going straight up, going up obliquely; but none of these methods was consistently successful. It was not that there was insufficient power under the bonnet, but that the weight of the empty cars was too light on the back axle and too heavy on the front. This was caused by the $1\frac{1}{2}$-hundredweight winch on the front bumper. Eventually we found the solution—the cars were driven up backward. This solved the problem of weight-distribution, and the cars went sailing up without any apparent effort. If anything, it was better showmanship, for the cars looked far more impressive climbing in reverse than forward.

The staff officers arrived, and we were introduced to the General. The vehicles were thoroughly examined, and through interpreters we answered a host of technical questions. Then came the trials. They were a great success, and afterwards the Expedition was invited back to the Officers' Mess. The General sat us down to a double Pepsi-Cola, and then confirmed an order for one hundred Land Rovers. He also gave us, without hesitation, a most valuable letter of introduction to anyone it might concern throughout Persia, saying that the Expedition were his guests, that we were to be helped without question, and on no account was anyone to interfere with our photography! Altogether it was a most worthwhile day.

It ended with Zawar, the local Rover agent, taking us out to a celebration supper of rice and kebab. Zawar was a young Persian who had spent eight years in England, and knew so much about the English that it was embarrassing. For a while he discussed Tudor history (sic) with Adrian, and then, as every foreigner does, he turned to English cooking, English weather, and English women. Next to the latter, the thing that had most surprised him during his years in England was the way so many men wore leather patches on the elbows of their sports coats.

"Such a good idea," he said. "I have brought home two or three coats like that. All my friends in Teheran think they are very smart, and are following the idea—a new fashion, perhaps?"

He was a genuine admirer of Britain, and said that it was the only foreign country where he always felt at ease, or, as he put it, "comfortable." Many other people we met were to express similar feelings, for, though Britain may not be the most popular country in the world, it is still sometimes respected.

"But," Zawar smiled, "you are becoming so complacent—or is it apathetic?"

"In what ways?" some one asked.

He gave several examples of what he meant. I repeat one, because it was a story we had heard before, and, sadly, were to hear many times again.

Zawar had several businesses in Teheran, and one was concerned with hydraulic machinery. He wanted some water-pumps, and wrote to manufacturers in Germany, Sweden, and Britain to inquire about prices and delivery dates. The Germans instructed their Middle Eastern representative in Baghdad to fly at once to Teheran and discuss the deal; they offered pumps from stock in Germany with a two-months delivery date. The Swedes cabled immediately their estimate for the contract, and sent a detailed letter. The British posted a brochure on which the prices had been over-stamped and higher ones inserted. The manager included his compliments on a printed slip.

"The British pumps," said Zawar, "are the best, but if I order them they will take months, and meanwhile my clients may go to another Teheran dealer."

We heard variations of this story many times. Britain may be able to 'make it,' but she often cannot sell it.

6.

Farther East

WHEN in Britain we hear or read of Persia we may picture a hot and unattractive land. Our impressions may still carry the stagnant traces of Mossadeq and oil and Abadan. Well, it is true that oil is the political theme of the country—it is its wealth. It is also true that Mossadeq is still regarded as a national hero, albeit a misguided one. But our impressions are distorted, for, in fact, Persia is a lovely country. It is a land of unlimited space, of high mountains, broad deserts, and steppe-like plains. It is a land of many colours, not always vivid, but of the rich yet pastel shades of distance and horizons. These colours are in the truly sapphire sky; in the snow-flecked mountains and the dust of the plains; in the poplars, tamarisks, and pines; in the dappled valleys and on the yellow roads. In Persia one often wishes that one could paint—but in water-colours rather than rich oils.

The people are very courteous, and the Expedition's introduction to the country through the Customs was something we found harder to understand as time went on. Afterwards we always met with kindness—not just from Zawar and the General, but from the backstreet barber who, when he heard that I was English, switched his wireless to the B.B.C., or from the lorry-drivers who, when we stopped for lunch, would pull up and ask if they could help—thinking that our cars had broken down. I mention these things briefly because they were the pleasant background through which we drove, and, as Nigel colloquially but sincerely put it, "Persia is a country with a sort of built-in nostalgia."

East of Teheran Persia is like a huge, oval meat-dish (the geographers will slaughter me for this). Around the rim are the mountain ranges; inside is a broad depression. This depression is a salt desert larger in size than Great Britain; it is almost uninhabited, and uncrossed by any motor routes. Both the roads from Teheran to Pakistan skirt along the desert's indefinite fringe, one to the north and the other to the south. The first runs six hundred miles eastward to the holy city of Meshed, and then into Afghanistan. It winds its arduous way through the gaunt mountains of that country for over one thousand miles before at last emerging down the Khyber Pass on to the plains of the Indus.

The other route from Teheran goes south to Isfahan and then east along the mountainous margins of the seemingly endless desert. It runs close by the frontier of Afghanistan and crosses into Pakistan. Thence to Quetta, down the Bolan Gorge, and out to the lower Indus and Karachi. We chose the latter route, for it is, if anything, a little quicker. Afghanistan could wait until our homeward journey. But by either road it is a long way. Persia is a huge country; the distances are immense. One does not realize this by looking at a map, but one knows it soon enough when motoring, when each slow mile is creeping on to the milometer, when a day of desert driving lies between the towns.

We had originally planned that both cars should go down through the mountains of Southern Persia on a photographic diversion to Persepolis, a ruined palace of the ancient Persian kings. But, due to the delays in Baghdad, and now in Teheran, the Expedition was more than two weeks behind schedule. So it was decided that the cars would break company at Isfahan, a day's drive to the south. From there Oxford would go through the mountains to Persepolis while Cambridge expressed east to Pakistan in order to make the final arrangements for the irrigation field-work. Later Oxford, with its photography completed, would drive back through the mountains, turn east, and, if all went well, arrive in Karachi a week after the other car.

It was late October now, and as we left Teheran the poplars were yellowing in the cool autumn sunshine, and the Elburz mountains to the north were crouching under their first mantle of snow. The Expedition was setting out on one of the longest single stages of the journey—over two thousand miles to Karachi, only a little less than the distance from London to the Urals.

By the time we passed through Qum, the other holy city of Persia, it was already dark. There was a religious festival, and we had been warned not to stop, as some of the more fanatical Muslims were occasionally unfriendly to foreigners. That night, on the edge of the desert, was cold, and we put on everything we had before snuggling into our sleeping-bags. Marco Polo wrote when he was on this same road nearly seven hundred years ago that it was "so cold that one could hardly survive by wearing many furs and clothes." That was in 1272, and it had not grown any warmer since.

We were all awake well before dawn—pulling the covering flap of our bags even tighter in an effort to conserve a little warmth. But the cold seeped in, and as the sun burst over the ragged horizon we got up, had breakfast, and were away again as quickly as possible. During the early hours of the day our sweaters came off one by one, until by ten o'clock the sun had climbed high into the sky and we were in our shirt-sleeves. An hour later we rolled into the British Missionary Hospital in Isfahan to deliver some letters to Dr and Mrs Wild from their friends in Teheran. They kindly asked us to stay for lunch, and offered afterwards to show us round the city.

The Persians have a saying, *Isfahán nisf-i-jahán*. It means, "Isfahan is half the world." To the modern and sophisticated traveller this might seem a wishful exaggeration, but five hundred years ago it was probably justified. Then Isfahan was a great merchant city, rich in the trade of silks and furs and spices. It was a staging-post and caravanserai on the long overland trade routes from Turkestan, Mongolia, and beyond, from Cathay and the Indies. But even to-day one can excuse the pride of the people of Isfahan, for theirs is a very attractive city. The streets are broad, and shaded by long avenues of trees down either side, and often down the middle too. In Isfahan they make carpets which are so fine that they are hung on walls like paintings, and their silver-work is far renowned.

But the chief glory of the city is the square, the Maidan-i-Shah, which is reputedly second in size only to the Red Square of Moscow. When laid out in the seventeenth century it was a polo arena. Now, though the stone goal-posts still stand at either end, it is a garden with flowers and trees and an ornamental lake. But the square is above all a setting for the mosques around the edge. Like budding tulips, their high and curving turquoise domes stand clean against the sky. They have the same clear symmetry, and the pale yet glowing colour of that flower. Their domes are flecked with gleaming white, gold, and rose mosaics as delicate as any lace. Inside the quiet courts the faithful are scattered on their prayer carpets, some kneeling and some standing. Islam seems a very personal faith; each person's lips are moving in his prayers, and he takes no notice of his neighbours as he nods his forehead in obeisance to the ground.

During the afternoon we had called several times at the little office of the Isfahan Rover agent. We thought that there might be a few letters waiting for us. But the office was closed—it was the Shah of Persia's birthday, and a national holiday. When eventually a clerk appeared he opened it up, and showed us three letters, but refused to give them to us without instructions from his manager. He took us to the manager's home, but the house was empty. We pointed out to the clerk that the letters belonged to us as surely as his wrist-watch belonged to him.

"Letters—me." Then, pointing at his wrist, "Watch—you; letters—me."

We showed him previous letters with the same English stamps. It was no use. He had his orders. A compromise was reached—we read the letters in his presence, and then handed them back to him. Returning to the hospital, we told Dr Wild of our trouble, and he spent the next hour on the telephone trying to locate the manager. When he found him there was a short conversation in Persian, and then the doctor replaced the receiver and told us that our letters would arrive shortly.

"One must always be so polite when being rude in Persian," said Dr Wild, "but one can be quite rude all the same."

"What did you say?" I asked.

"Well, there's no direct translation, but, more or less, 'Is it not a pity that your servant saw fit to deny my guests the pleasure of their letters?' In Persia that's strong language!"

The letters arrived within five minutes. Dr Wild reckoned that the manager, who was a rich and influential merchant in Isfahan, would feel under an obligation to him for many months to atone for his servant's discourtesy. The hospital itself might benefit—a few bags of cement would be most handy for re-flooring the surgery.

With the letters in our possession, the three of us in Oxford were anxious to be heading on, for there was a good deal of mileage to cover in the following few days. We checked that each car had its own passports and maps, and then said good-bye to Cambridge; they were going east and we were going south.

"See you later, men."

"Yes, much later!" said Henry. "Send us a telegram when you get to Quetta so that we know when to expect you in Karachi."

"O.K. We'll be about a week behind you, so if you get stuck in the burning sands just sit down and wait—we'll be along to pull you out!"

"Huh, that'll be the day."

There was, I should explain, a certain amount of sarcastic rivalry between the cars.

After another extremely chilly night on the roadside some hours out of Isfahan we in Oxford turned through the hills and concentrated on putting the miles behind us as quickly as possible. Contrary to what many people have written or implied, one can travel quite fast on most main roads in Persia. In fact, the faster one drives, the smoother the road seems to become. Above a certain speed the car lifts itself out of the regular corrugations and rides from crest to crest. These corrugations are the predominant feature of these loose and pebbly roads; sometimes they run like little waves for twenty or thirty miles on end. No one knows how they are formed, but B.B., who was inclined to be the Expedition's scientific consultant, suggested that it was "some function of the harmonic frequency of lorry springs" (!) which, over the years, had pounded out the ripples. Below 15 m.p.h. the car rises and falls as if in a lively swell, but at any speed above this the whole car vibrates as if it is thrashing over a series of low brick walls. This tooth-loosening motion gets worse as the speed increases, but then, at just over 40 m.p.h., one pierces a sort of 'shudder barrier,' and the car, like a speed-boat, rises up on its 'step' and rushes along contentedly with the note of the engine purring through, where before it was drowned by the crashing and banging.

Once or twice there was a creeping smudge of dust on the lonely road ahead, and a few minutes later we would slow behind a flock of goats or fat-tailed sheep, then wait until the herders had parted them to give us passage. These men, with their women and children following behind on donkeys and mules, were the stragglers of the nomadic Kashgai tribe travelling from their summer to their winter pastures. The rest of the tribe had probably moved the month before, and these few rearguards that we saw were now hurrying south with their flocks to reach the warmer valleys before the onset of the winter.

By the time we arrived at Persepolis the light was too pale and the shadows too dark for good colour photographs, so we went on down the road for another thirty miles to Shiraz. It is a small city, but one famous

throughout Persia for its beauty, and as the birthplace of Hafiz and
Sa'di—two poets revered above Omar Khayyám by the Persians. We
stopped in the centre of the town and asked the policeman on point duty
the way to the British Missionary Hospital. He demanded to know who
and what we were, so, by way of explanation, the General's letter was
produced. He read it in the light of the head-lamps, and then
immediately climbed into the car, offering to direct us personally. A few
minutes later we found Dr Coleman and gave him a letter which Dr
Wild had given us the previous day in Isfahan. Dr Coleman opened it,
read it, smiled, and asked us to stay the night—"Perhaps you'd like a hot
bath too?" Luxury indeed. But Dr Coleman was almost horrified that we
intended to return to Persepolis and the north the next day. "You must
see Shiraz," he said in indignation. "You stay here two nights or you don't
stay here at all." So we put our camp-beds up in the Colemans' sitting-
room and did as we were told.

The hospitals of the Church Missionary Society in Persia are
interesting—not for their buildings and equipment, which are often old
and inadequate, but for the work being done by the doctors, who often
work singly and with very little assistance. Dr Coleman saw at least sixty
out-patients each day, performed three or four operations, and did the
rounds of fifty beds. Besides this he was responsible for the training of his
nurses, and for all the administrative and office work. After evening surgery
he took us round his hospital. The town's electricity supply was running at
half-pressure, and the lighting in the wards came from paraffin lamps and
dim bulbs hanging by long flexes from the ceiling. The patients we saw
were being treated free, though there were a few private wards where the
wealthier patients might pay up to 10s. per day. There were no visiting
hours, because the Persian prefers to have his friends and relations
continually around him in order that they may cook and look after him.
Thus he recovers quicker. The population of the hospital was therefore
about three times the number of patients. Dr Coleman introduced us to
some of the rather shy Persian nurses whom he had trained, and then led
us through the wards.

We saw a policeman who had been knifed, a man being cured of
opium-smoking, and a wizened old woman who had been there a year—
"She's our senior inhabitant, and as she hasn't got anywhere to go she just

stays here." We saw two old tribesmen from the hills with pneumonia, a ward of maternity cases, and a small boy recovering from an operation with his father curled up asleep on two chairs beside him—"He'll only leave when his son can go too." Then there was the operating-theatre, with its bare walls scrubbed spotless; the main operating lamp was an upturned tin basin with a cluster of four bulbs suspended inside—"Well, it's almost shadow-less!" We saw the doctor's two newest pieces of equipment, which had been sent out to him by an English parish. One was a surgeon's head lamp, and the other was a machine for sucking the discharge from wounds and operations—"Now they are here I can't think how I used to manage without them."

I think that the British public's idea of a missionary as a tall, gaunt man with a white topee, determined ideas about hell-fire, a Bible under his arm, and a portable halo on his head would amuse no one more than Dr Coleman. These mission hospitals may not bring in hordes of converts, for the Muslim is as intractable as the Christian, but just because of this the medical work seems all the more practical and realistic.

No mention of Shiraz would be complete without reference to its other hospital. We spent an interesting but disturbing afternoon being led over it. This new hospital—American in staff and design—had been opened by the Shah only two months earlier. It is huge, and cost millions of dollars. It has four hundred beds and twenty doctors. It has air-conditioning in summer and central heating in winter. It has six opaque-walled operating theatres with batteries of chrome machines and special floors that earth static electricity. It has a telephone system of seventy lines, and beds that reputedly cost £100 apiece. Its kitchens have electric cranes to lift the rice from the hoppers, conveyor belts, sterilizing steamers, and trained dieticians. Its beautiful ten-acre grounds have luxurious nurses' quarters with each room finished in a different colour, a cinema, lawns, trees, and pools. It has a water-supply from the surrounding hills, and its own electricity plant. The incoming patient undergoes a rigorous examination to fit him for the card index, his bed-linen is changed daily, and he is assured of every possible human and mechanical care for his recovery. The governing body sits in New York, and, in the words of our American guide, "There are only two other hospitals in the world like this one—and they're in California."

There are four hundred beds, and when we visited the hospital there were twenty-three patients. But, we were told, "This is a long-term policy. Some one must show these people what a modern hospital is really like, and then the idea will catch on." There are only about two hundred trained nurses in the whole of Persia, and the staff quarters were almost empty. Unfortunate? "Well, we're going to train them." They will bring a courteous but poor people, who take more interest in their poets than in their plumbing, from the point where they wash a hypodermic in a running gutter—because the Koran teaches that flowing water is pure—to the point where they will sterilize their knives and forks in super-heated steam twice daily. From illiteracy to the card index. But then this is "a long-term policy," and what if the bedside tables are provided with angled book-rests when nearly all the local sick are illiterate? "The idea will catch on"; show a man a book-rest and he will want to learn to read.

The Americans probably have a greater store of material knowledge than any other nation, but one suspects that their ideas of what to do with it occasionally lag behind. However, it was not to be foreseen that some of the lavatories would have to be reorientated since the designers in New York had faced them towards Mecca. On the other hand, the governing body might have known that the treatment fees could represent the life-savings of a tribesman—if, in fact, a tribesman saved. Which, apparently, he does not. I admire the Americans, and, as a member of the Expedition, I have had cause to be grateful to them on many, many occasions. But, having seen that hospital, I can only wonder at their impatient, impetuous, and amazing generosity.

Although the original purpose of our diversion to Southern Persia was to visit Persepolis, we much enjoyed our sojourn in Shiraz. It is quieter and smaller than Isfahan, and flanked by wrinkled mountains which, even at that time of year, were already traced with snow. We should have liked to stay much longer, but, having already delayed for an extra day, we took our leave of the Colemans very early on the third morning and drove back along the road which we had travelled three days previously, towards the plain of Fars and Persepolis.

Five hundred years before Christ the palace city of Persepolis was built, to be the spring capital of one of the largest land empires the world has seen, an empire which stretched from Ethiopia to the Danube, from the Nile to Samarkand. Persia dominated the ancient world, and the royal palace was built accordingly. From every quarter of his huge realm King Darius summoned artisans and craftsmen to the plain of Fars, the empire's original homeland, and there on a terrace cut in the hillside the builders— twenty thousand of them—worked on the construction and the carvings for three generations. The great halls and the palaces reserved for the royal court were built of immense stones hewn from the surrounding hills; staircases, pillars, walls, and pavements were enriched with thousands of relief carvings showing members of the many subject nations bringing gifts of homage to the king; stone capitals of double-headed bulls and lions were set atop pillars sixty feet high (as each of these capitals weighed over ten tons, architects are still at a loss to explain the engineering methods used to raise them); statues of the royal family were encrusted with gold and studded with gems; roof beams of cedar-wood were brought across six hundred miles of desert from the Lebanon. Nothing was spared in the raising of this city, which, for two centuries, was the palace of the world.

Then came Alexander the Great. In ten short years the empire crumbled.

To-day dragonflies and lizards flicker about the roofless halls and columns of Persepolis, as they have done ever since Alexander's armies pillaged and burnt the place after smashing the Persian empire to disintegration at the battle of Gaugamela (331 B.C.). The loot and treasure taken from the royal coffers was fabulous, and the story goes that Alexander had to wait several weeks, while his men mustered the four thousand camels necessary to carry it away. Some say he ordered the destruction of Persepolis as an act of victory and vengeance against the city from which the Persian armies had set out to conquer Greece two hundred years before. Others, finding such wantonness inconsistent with his character (for it was one of the few cities he took intact and then sacked), suggest that the arson was really the work of a celebrated courtesan who, presumably in return for her faithful services, asked one of Alexander's generals at the victory feast if she could fire the place.

We spent all day slowly wandering among the rocks and stones. Here, on this sunburnt hillside, had once been a great city, and, despite the two millennia since that time, Darius and Alexander no longer seemed to be mere antique myths and legends; they became men who had really ruled and fought, marched with armies, raised cities, held great empires and even greater ambitions. Of Alexander particularly one wondered. What fierce compulsion was it that could drive a man to march from Greece to India, taking all before him? What kind of man was he who, nearly always outnumbered, could always be triumphant? He died in Babylon of malaria when only thirty-two years old. But what more might he have done if he had lived? Yet what else was there left for him to do? He had already marched eastward the breadth of the known world, and made himself the master of the greater part of it.

But among all the ancient glories of Persepolis we were surprised and interested to find something rather more recent, something of which we can find no mention in the books or learned papers of historians. At the base of a pillar was the carefully carved inscription: "Stanley—New York Herald—1870."

In the evening we paid a fleeting visit to the tomb of Cyrus the Great at Pasargardae. Then, in the darkness, we motored north for an hour or two until we made camp by the roadside.

To join the main road running east to Pakistan there was the choice of going all the way back to Isfahan or trying a short cut through the mountains. We decided on the latter, as, although we had been warned that it would be a rocky and rough hundred and fifty miles, it would cut the journey by at least two days' driving.

Sometimes the track was very rough. The speed dropped right down as the car, in second gear, growled its way into the hills and up through the twisting passes. Then down the other side and on to the bare and level plain again, where we would gather speed and head out for the next far range of hills. Occasionally the way almost disappeared as it ran across broad patches of sand. The surface was a hard and salty crust, but, if this crumbled, the back of the car swayed in the sand, and the driver would have to change gear quickly before the wheels began to spin. It was surprising how, after only a few minutes of this sort of going, one could recognize the firmer patches and pick one's way accordingly.

We did not see another vehicle all day, and in a way the silence and loneliness were rather exciting, for there are not many places in the world where one knows that one is quite alone. It was like being in a yacht far out at sea. There was only the sun, the huge sky, and the torn and jagged mountains which rose like barren islands round the skyline. The car was a mere slow-moving speck in such wide surroundings. Even when we paused to change drivers or have a drink the only sound came from our voices, and the tyres which rushed on in one's ears like the wind.

In the evening, just as the milometer was registering that we should be coming to the main road, we saw its accompanying telegraph-posts dipping across the horizon in front. A few minutes later we turned east. As Nigel remarked, "Next stop, Karachi."

We reckoned that at an average speed of 40 m.p.h. and three hundred miles per day we should reach Karachi in rather less than a week. For mile after mile the car sped across those timeless hills and desert plains. As our tyres drummed along the road, through the mountains, over dried-out river-beds, and across the desert, they threw up a streaming cloud of dust which billowed away behind like the vapour trail of some jet-aircraft creeping high against the sky. Once or even twice a day we might pass a camel caravan or a small convoy of vastly overloaded diesel trucks staggering across the desert like listing tramp-steamers under huge tarpaulined cargoes. Their drivers would give us a wave and a shout as, after what seemed hours of hooting on our horn, we crept slowly through their wake of dust and overtook them.

Occasionally on this drive we noticed long rows of little craters running out from the foot of the mountains on to the plain. We had heard about these earlier; they were holes going down to water tunnels, or *qanats*. This system of transporting water must be unique. In the dry summer temperatures of over 110°F. any water flowing in an open channel would soon be lost in evaporation. So the Persians lead it from the springs in the hills to their arid villages on the plain through tunnels many feet below the surface. The vertical shafts we could see from the roads were the holes down which the tunnellers went during construction, and afterwards to clear the accumulated mud and silt. Some of these subterranean water passages are said to wind their way under the desert rocks for over thirty miles. There seems no limit to the tenacity that men will show for water. But, as we had been often told in the Middle East, water is synonymous with life. In the rare oasis patches there was water, trees, and emerald green. But they met the desert at a razored line.

Ancient oasis and caravan cities like Yezd, Kerman, and Bam were spaced infrequently along the route. Secure in their isolation, they are the homes of ancient cults, of Zoroastrianism and fire-worship. It was a good day's drive between them, and, although we did not really need to travel with our fifty-gallon tankage always full, we usually took the precaution of 'topping-up' on arrival in these towns. More important, we filled our water jerry-cans whenever possible, and always kept one full can for reserve in case of a break-down. Occasionally on the road, miles from anywhere, we passed two or three men laboriously scraping the gravel from the roadside back on to the middle of the track. Usually we stopped to give them a drink of water and a cigarette—for which small courtesy they called upon the Prophet to bless and guide us on our journey.

But in some ways the road could be monotonous. On the plains between the hills the road ahead tapered away to the skyline; there was no other traffic; there was not much more to do than keep the car running straight. Once I committed the unforgivable crime of dozing at the wheel. True, I was only 'off' for a second or two, and, in fact, no damage was done. But this was luck, and no credit of mine. If it had happened in many other places it might have been very serious.

By now our desert routine was well established. At dusk—and it only lasted a few minutes—we would turn on to the desert and stop. Out came camp-beds and sleeping-bags, food and cookers. After supper and the washing-up we went quickly to bed. By now we had learnt how to stuff our mosquito nets (which were carried for later stages) with odd clothes to form a quilt against the cold. Before sleep caught up we would lie peeping through the folds in our sleeping-bags at the clear night sky. We, from the clouded latitudes, could see millions of stars which we had never known existed. The Milky Way stretched across the night like a glorious tiara, and the stars seemed so clear and brilliant that one might have reached and rearranged them if one had wished. But they were perfect, and we did not wonder that people worshipped them.

DIARY FOR 1st NOVEMBER

W. of Kerman to 160 miles E. of Bam (305 miles)

B.B. had us up at 6.30 A.M. Breakfast—porridge and tea—over in ten minutes. Cold until the sun got up. While I packed the car Nigel cleaned the plugs and checked the springs and engine oil. B.B., as always, boiled the water and made Thermos tea to keep us going for the rest of the day. Then we were off. Reached Kerman by mid-morning. Picked up petrol, water, bread. This Persian bread comes in lumpy, unleavened sheets about two feet long. It is gritty, and needs pots of jam. B.B. drips like a tap about it; says we should have taken his advice in Baghdad and got a stock of biscuits—"But no one would listen to me. The only thing this stuff is any good for is as a blanket—or engine gaskets!" The petrol man in Kerman reckoned that Cambridge were through five days back.

A little way outside Kerman we stopped for photography: a small village with a beautiful blue mosque in a garden of flowers, poplars, and dark green pines. Behind were the mountains of Kuh-i-Hazar— snow-capped and rising to 14,000 feet.

For the next hundred miles the road was fast, but there were a few rougher stretches through some wadis; the dust was terrific. Also quite a lot of sand blown across the road near Bam (reached 3.30 P.M.). Didn't stop, as we had plenty of petrol, and the police always hold one up while they look at passports.

An hour's halt for a very late lunch—tea, sardines, and a melon. Cambridge must have gone off with all the spoons and forks, because we haven't got any—but we've got all the cups and knives instead. Nigel thinks that the lack of a tea-spoon entitles him to stir the tea with his dark glasses.

We overtook only one other vehicle today (a big diesel). In its dust it was impossible to get closer than twenty yards, and, after more than ten minutes of futile horn-tooting and light-flashing, the driver still hadn't noticed us. So we took off on to the desert and drove round him. Nigel suggests that a solution to this overtaking problem is to carry thunder-flashes. We would drive as close to the lorry as possible and then throw them out of the window. When they went off the lorry-driver would think he had a puncture, and probably stop to investigate. Then we get past!

This evening the road ran through a flat, sandy area for many miles, and, according to the map, we have been coming downhill all afternoon. To-night is certainly much warmer than it has been for the last week—in fact, I'm writing this in my shirt-sleeves. Another 100 miles or so to the Pakistan frontier. The mountains we could see to the N.E. just before dark must be in Afghanistan. Bed.

I have read of the so-called magic that the desert throws over travellers. Now I could more than understand. To see the dawn breaking high in the sky, touching the clouds from pale gold to silver, and then to glaring white and the day; to see the bony mountains across thirty miles of plain shimmering in the noon heat; to see the rich twilight swiftly streaked in rose and crimson; to see the stars and to hear the silent night—these are the desert. The enchantment of space and loneliness is undeniable, and I admit to nostalgia even as I write about it. I would travel that road across Southern Persia again any time.

The next morning we were in Zahidan, which, though still some way short of the frontier itself, is the recognized border settlement. The arrival of a motor vehicle in any Persian community is something of an event, and Zahidan was no exception. The proceedings followed an accustomed pattern. As soon as one stops in Persia the car is surrounded by a curious crowd. One of them will usually point at a friend and say, "Him English." This is not, as one might think, a reference to the fellow's nationality, but merely that he is reputed to have a certain fundamental grounding in our language; he may have been a seaman down on the Persian Gulf. Anyway, "English" comes forward with a toothy grin and courteously poses his first question (it is always the same), "'Allo, 'ow are yoo?" We, wishing to preserve the formality of the occasion, reply, "Very well," and add, "How are you?" But this question has already overstepped the bounds of English's linguistic knowledge, and he counters with a somewhat inconclusive "Yes." Then, thoughtfully cocking his head on one side, "Where from you come?" To this we answer "Inglistan," and he nods in a knowing fashion as if England were just across the desert, and he has been there often. Realizing that further conversation is not much use, "English" insists on shaking our hands, we give him a cigarette, and he withdraws, proud in his internationalism, to the admiring crowd.

However, in Zahidan there was a slight amendment to the story. When we stopped a second time to ask if we were going the right way to the Pakistan Consulate a young boy pushed forward and said, "I will take you, please." So in he climbed to guide us. He was learning English at school, and could speak it surprisingly well; yet in his twelve years he had never been out of Zahidan.

The Pakistan Consulate was housed in what had once been the British Residency; the whitewashed stones which patterned its dusty grounds in careful squares and circles as if they protected some imaginary suburban lawns clearly betrayed its origins. But that was not all. The Consul made us very welcome, and, leading us inside, he went into a rapturous stroke-by-stroke analysis of the Test Series in which Pakistan had just narrowly beaten the touring New Zealanders. The scenes of this triumph were still some seven hundred miles to the east.

There were several things to do in Zahidan. We had to take on petrol for the next 450 miles to Quetta; obtain frontier clearance from the Persian Army post; and, most important, call on the Indian Consul. There is not much love lost between India and Pakistan, and either of them is likely to take offence if the Englishman appears prejudiced in favour of the other. Therefore, Expedition protocol dictated that our call on the representative of Pakistan should be quickly followed by a call on the representative of India. In fact, as we later learnt, the Indian Consul already knew of our arrival in the town, and would have been seriously offended had we forgotten him.

In touring the small town on these errands we were guided by the small boy who had helped us before. While we had been hearing about the Test matches he had apparently run back to his school for permission to accompany us, and then returned to wait by our car. "Please, sirs, I have come for practice of my English." He looked after us most efficiently and, running into the shops in advance, took great pains to see that we were not cheated in our various purchases of petrol, fruit, and bread. He produced his English text-book and read from it with justifiable pride. But

I wondered what he made of *Jack and the Beanstalk* or the extracts from *Treasure Island*.

He asked if he could join the Expedition, and questioned us about our journey, particularly about 'Inglistan.' When he solemnly said good-bye he would not even take a tip—not once had he mentioned the almost inevitable 'baksheesh.'(For this alone he is worthy of mention.) Instead we gave him a small model Land Rover, with which he was immensely pleased.

We had intended to leave for the frontier that evening, but when we returned to say farewell to the Pakistan consul he was almost hurt by our indecent haste. "You cannot go. Just now my man prepares your room."

So we stayed. The consul said something at supper which I remember very clearly, for it seemed a very neat remark.

"Your country," he said, pointing at the floor in the corner of the room, "always busy blocking up the mices' holes, but lately, I think, too many mices make too many holes!"

Being a devout Muslim, he was up at 4 A.M. to say his prayers, and then, though he did not have any himself, he gave us breakfast and saw us off for Pakistan. The actual frontier is the sandy bed of a dried-up river; it is mentioned in practically all the accounts of people who have journeyed along this road, for they always manage to get stuck in it. We too churned about in the sand for a minute or so, but got clear by using the low-ratio gears and four-wheel drive. On the far side of the wadi the road was different to any other we had been on for some weeks, and on the smooth, uncorrugated surface the car opened its lungs accordingly. Nevertheless, we were rather worried as to which side of the road we should be on. There was a rumour that Pakistan had recently changed to driving on the right, and we had forgotten to ask the consul about it. But the important test did not come for another eighty miles. When eventually a lorry approached we drew off the road to watch it pass. It drove by on the left; the rumour was unfounded.

Shortly afterwards we pulled into Nok Kundi, the first settlement, and the official Pakistan frontier post. We stayed the night in the Dak (Travellers) Bungalow, and made our first acquaintance with the Commode, or "Thunder Mug"—a traditional object of sanitation dating from the days of British India, consisting of a small tin pot set in a lidded wooden box. As B.B. announced after formal inspection, "A marked improvement on anything I have seen for the last four thousand miles, and twice as comfortable."

The next morning we were rolling our camp-beds and preparing to leave this outpost when a Pakistani dressed in baggy cotton trousers wandered past. Then, on seeing our Land Rover he stopped in his tracks and peered closely at the lettering on the door.

"Oxford and Cambridge! By Jove! I thought you were a bunch of foreigners—Krauts or something. Oxford and Cambridge, eh? Well, my word, that's a bloody good show. Just come across that damned desert, have you? Driven all the way? That's bloody marvellous. M'name's Khan. I was in Italy with some of your chaps during the War."

He shook us each warmly by the hand, and welcomed us to Pakistan—though we might have been excused for thinking that Mr Khan, of the Post and Telegraph Department (as his visiting-card told us), was even more English than the English.

"Fine show beating the New Zealanders like that, don't you think? I say, is there anything I can do for you chaps?"

We asked him where we could change our few remaining Persian rials into rupees.

"Certainly; give it to my man and he'll do it for you. Oxford and Cambridge; jolly good."

We gave the money to his servant, and Mr Khan went on talking while we finished packing. When we were ready to leave B.B. asked him if his servant would be coming back soon with our rupees.

"Oh, my word, yes. No bloody hanky-panky here; by Jove, no." Then, by way of emphasis, "This is Pakistan, you know."

I am sure that had Mr Khan known we were coming he would have worn suede shoes and a regimental blazer!

The road onward to Quetta ran across what our route report called "uninhabited desert"; this was the rocky and desolate province of Baluchistan. The Baluchis say that their country was made from the debris which God raked together after he had built the rest of the world. As we drove, the slowly changing desert around was dotted with little twisting whirlwinds of dust, and the glaring sunshine beat down from every quarter of the sky. If anything the land looked even more burnt and arid than parts of Southern Persia. But, though the landscape was monotonous, the road was straight, and had an excellent surface. On one stretch, with the car charging along like an express train, we flicked past a hundred and twelve mile-posts in two hours.

The sunset was glorious, and a little later the road wound through a mountain range and we could see the lights of Quetta below. We stayed the night with a Pakistani whose broken-down car we towed for the last few miles to the town.

This strategic town of the North-West Frontier had been badly damaged in recent earthquakes, and much of it was not yet rebuilt. But the new army of Pakistan seemed to have slipped easily into the boots of the departed British garrison—who might have left only a few months before. Many of the streets have English names, such as Lytton Avenue and Curzon Road; there are notices "To the Q.M. Stores," "Grindlays Bank," "Imprest," and "M.T. Park." Outside the town is a sign-post pointing purposefully to the west: "London 5866 miles."

The next day we shared the narrow road down the Bolan Gorge with countless bands of Kuchis and their camel trains. These Kuchis are one of the few true nomadic tribes left in Southern Asia; for hundreds of years they have wandered with their flocks between the summer pastures high in the cool valleys of Afghanistan and their winter encampments on the Indus plains. The tribe was an impressive sight as it snaked slowly down the ravine. The women, unveiled and superbly handsome, wore silver bangles and ankle rings which twinkled in the sun, and their long, swirling skirts of reds and yellows swished as they swung along beside their camels. Many of the camels had jingling bells and bright trappings. Each carried a mountain of a load; beds, tents, cooking-pots, lambs, chickens, the old people and the children—the whole enormous cargo dipping and swaying with the camel's rolling gait. The Kuchi men were tall and gaunt; they looked fierce as hawks, and carried ancient flintlocks by their sides. This tribe recognizes no frontiers, pays no taxes, and lives by no laws but its own—even the orderly British once held clear and looked the other way.

At the bottom of the Bolan Pass the road emerged from the contorted hills and we drove out across the bare and almost treeless plains, until we reached the irrigated lowlands of the Indus. We were in a land of fields, villages, dogs, and people. Our driving reactions, dulled by the empty desert roads, were tested many times by swerving camels and creeping ox-carts, by lunatic cyclists and blind pedestrians. We had arrived, to use an awkward term, in the 'Indian sub-continent.'

Two days later, as we passed the international airport just outside Karachi, a huge hoarding exhorted us to "Be in London in Sixteen Hours." We had taken just over two months.

Cambridge were waiting for us outside the main post-office, as arranged in our telegram from Quetta. They led us to the billet they had found in the Y.M.C.A., we had a cold shower, sat down to read a pile of letters, and then both cars swapped their versions of the last ten days.

As I have said before, the Expedition exchanged an almost weekly letter with the Home Team in Cambridge. They, more than anyone else, allowed us to proceed along our way in the confident knowledge that a whole multitude of our affairs in England were being surely dealt with. They never let us down. As an inadequate example of the trouble they took on our behalf I now reproduce the exchange of letters at Karachi.

Cambridge
1st November

THE OXFORD AND CAMBRIDGE FAR EASTERN EXPEDITION,
c/o BROOKE BOND (PAKISTAN), LTD,
KARACHI, WEST PAKISTAN.

DEAR EXPED.,

Your Home Team (happy euphemism!) sits hunched in duffle coats around its gas-fire and thanks you for the various letters just received from Teheran. We note with envy your tales of the "wild blue yonder," the sands, the sun, the camels and the dark-glasses. Lucky bastards! But to business.

1. As you suggested from Beirut, Adrian, we are getting a brief news sheet to send to the sponsoring firms and others. It will contain a résumé of your travels so far and also a captioned list of the photo negatives which have arrived back to date. The firms can then order the prints they want from Camera Press. Rovers seem interested in a

series on the cars and Brooke Bond have been in touch about those ones you took of camping in Turkey—keep their tea well to the fore!

2. Having slightly rehashed your articles on the Nairn Bus we have sent one to the *Evening News* and the other to *Everybodys*. Both think they can use them but haven't done so yet. We will keep you posted. Meanwhile send us more.

3 Yes, the carbon copies of the diary are definitely useful—especially for this sponsors' news sheet we're doing. But give us a bit more dope so that we can ginger up the articles.

4. Have been on to the Burmese Embassy in London several times by phone and letter. They now say that permission to enter their country by land is entirely up to the Government in Rangoon. You should get in direct touch with the Brit. Embassy there. We see from your pre-departure files that you have already started this. In short, there is nothing we can do about Burma from this end—over to you. The Foreign Office say they have just written to you in Karachi.

5. B.B., when you send the cine film home, let us have the freight order and flight number by separate letter. This is essential if we are to clear the stuff through Customs quickly—they were a bit sticky about the last lot from Beirut.

6. Went down to the B.B.C. yesterday and saw the first two batches of film—*i.e.*, Europe and Middle East up to Beirut. B.B.'s typed commentary was a great help in explaining what it was all about. B.B.C. seemed quite pleased and their comments are enclosed. Most of the criticisms are technical: they thought you used the wrong lens for some of the Nairn Bus shots and want you to watch the exposure the whole time. (Anyway, all this is enclosed.)

7. No, Adrian. We have looked at the insurance policy and think there is about as much chance of the insurance people paying the ransom if you get captured by Burmese bandits as there is if you get swallowed by Dodos! But, if you do run into trouble, keep the camera grinding.

8. The Rover agents in Singapore want to know where they can get in touch and your approx. schedule. Over to you.

9. Give us all the dope on your movements through Pakistan and India. In your last letter you mention the possibility of the cars splitting

up for a while. Let us have mailing addresses and who is splitting up where.

10. I.T.V. showed a short film of your Persian Army trial the other night—though didn't see it 'selves. Rovers should be pleased. But who took it and where did I.T.V. get it from?

11. Rubber Hammers Ltd and The Glass Nail Company[3] have both written asking how you are finding their products. Perhaps something of the 'unsolicited testimonial' nature might be in order! They expect to hear from you.

12. Your finances are not too bad—but don't go on a 'blind' just because we have said that. We'll keep the £56 you left in the account here to cover the home expenses which crop up—airmail postage is already quite a large item. Make the cash you've got with you pan out as long as possible. We, at home, haven't a clue where you'll get any more. Ideas? Keep the articles and photos coming as they can turn into useful pocket money.

13. When you write can you co-ordinate all your requests into one letter? At the moment the different things in different letters take some sorting out. But personal letters—always welcome.

Cambridge . . . as usual.

Will write again to Lahore as you seem to think you'll be there some time. Meanwhile try to look intrepid—it goes down so well!

Yours,
JOHN AND PETER

⊛

Reply to: c/o Lahore Autos,
The Mall, Lahore

7th November
DEAR JOHN AND PETER,

Thank you for letter No. 6. The Exped. is now in one piece again, Oxford arrived here the night before last and seemed to have had a pretty fair trip. B.B. appears very pleased with the film he took at

Persepolis—though how it comes out remains for you to see. As most of the daily details of the Exped. are contained in Tim's diary carbons which he is posting to you shortly we'll confine this letter to explaining our plans and to business.

1. There was a letter waiting here from the Embassy in Rangoon answering an earlier one of ours. They seem to think that the Burmese might give us permission to enter by land but are uncertain because, as they point out, it will be setting a precedent—the Burmese have not given anyone this permission before. Anyway, the embassy will keep working on our behalf and they suggest we tackle the Burmese Embassy in Delhi when we get there.

2. The letter from the Foreign Office has arrived. The gist of it is that they are prepared to let us have a go at Burma providing "the Expedition understands that it does so at its own risk." In other words, if we come unstuck they won't be around to pick up the bits! Seems reasonable enough.

3. Yesterday afternoon we thrashed out plans for the next couple of months. We have had to change from the original because (a) being behind schedule, we are short of time and (b) there is a strong possibility that a road into Nepal has just been opened. In which case, B.B. wants to drive up to Kathmandu for photography and filming.

We have fixed on January 12th as "D. Day" for Burma. Our two pet geographers reckon that the monsoon will be finished by then and that the unbridged (?) rivers in N. Burma will be fairly low. But, as January 12th is only 9 weeks from now it will not be possible for both cars to complete the Thal fieldwork and get up to Nepal.

Therefore the cars will separate. We will all spend three weeks together in the Thal and then the Oxford car (Tim, B.B., Nigel) will go on in advance to India and try to drive up to Nepal. The other car (Cambridge—Henry, Pat, Adrian) will stay on in the Thal for another two weeks doing the research and then make an express run (1000 miles) to Calcutta. By that time Oxford should have finished in Nepal and will also head for Calcutta. In other words, both cars 'regroup' there just before Christmas. We will probably be there about 10 days 'organizing' for Burma.

4. Pat and Henry have spent the last four days in and out of the Ministry of Agriculture arranging our forthcoming fieldwork in Thal. The authorities seem very helpful and interested, even providing an interpreter if we want. We will probably be leaving here in two days' time for Lahore and the Thal.

The letter then went on for several more pages dealing with many other points. It ended as usual, "Yours expeditionally—Oxcam."

There was always a great deal of paper-work. The journey was far too long to have allowed complete planning before we left England. Consequently, the Expedition moved in bounds—we drove for two or three weeks and then halted in places like Beirut or Karachi to plan ahead and gather our breath for the next few thousand miles. Letters had to be written and inquiries made about practically everything: petrol supplies, collecting food, visas, route information, Customs regulations, currency exchange, and many, many more. Of course, many of these things could have been left to chance, and in fact they sometimes were, but we avoided this whenever possible. In Karachi our typewriters almost ran hot with use, the airmail bill soared, and no longer could the Busyness Box contain the growing stack of files. Some one suggested that the Cambridge car, with the Business Manager and his complete office paraphernalia aboard, constituted "the only self-propelled filing cabinet in the world." Before we left Karachi, after six days, sixty-three 'business' letters (and several personal ones) had been posted. "Bureaucracy on wheels" seemed a very apt description of the Expedition.

We kept putting off the day of our departure from Karachi, for there always seemed more things to do. But eventually we dragged ourselves away and set off for the north, nine hundred miles to Lahore. From there the area of our researches in the Thal Desert lay only a day's drive to the west.

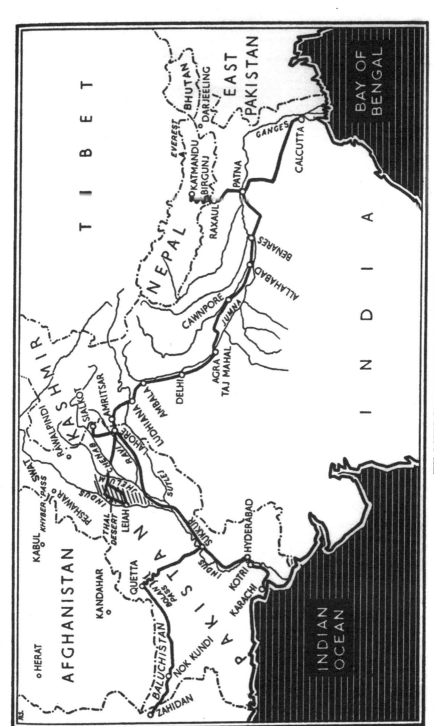

THE ROUTE FROM KARACHI TO CALCUTTA

7.

Pakistan: Water, Sand, and Bagpipes

by Pat Murphy

I SHOULD like to be able to begin my chapter by making some intrepid and evocative remark such as, "Saying farewell to Karachi, the Expedition swung its scientific cloak about its sunburnt shoulders and moved off into the interior." But, despite the fact that such a statement contains more than a grain of truth, Tim has vetoed the idea, and so I will have to be serious.

Besides driving to the other end of Asia the Expedition had the more academic intention of doing three months' research; some of this would be done on the outward journey and some on the way home. Just why we should have had this intention is difficult to say. Certainly none of us regarded it as a mere academic exercise, but neither did we have any grandiose schemes for adding to the world's store of knowledge. Nevertheless, we felt that a serious study of a major irrigation undertaking which was still very much in its infancy could not fail to be useful—to ourselves, if to no one else. I for one am interested in irrigation as other people are interested in ruins or butterflies, and only in moments of rare reflection do I worry myself further for motives. (Though I consider mine to be a more realistic and useful hobby than either ruins or butterflies.) For some reason the other members of the Expedition were almost as keen as I was. So suffice it to say that we were doing research because we wanted to—which is a pretty good reason.

The area of our work lay to the north, and for three days we drove towards it, up the broad plain of the Indus, past carts piled high with raw cotton, hauled by a sneering camel or a pair of doe-eyed bullocks. The drivers of these carts spend most of their time asleep, and it is left to the camels and bullocks to heed the warnings of the klaxon-sounding lorries and buses. They have been doing this ever since the internal combustion engine first made its impact on the Indian countryside, and so dutifully pull in to the left as you approach. Indeed, the quashing of a Bill to change the rule of the road to the right in Pakistan is generally attributed to a group of powerful camel guilds!

This southern part of Pakistan, the Sind, must be very like Egypt: a huge desert with a ribbon of cultivation along a great river which brings life to the land. The river is the Indus; the life is its water. But water alone is not enough; everything depends on its being effectively controlled and directed by man—on irrigation. The canals which fan out from the huge barrages straddling the river at Sukkur and Kotri are the land's arteries, and without them it would die in a month.

The narrow, Nilotic character of the country ends five hundred miles inland from Karachi, where the five rivers of the Punjab all flow into the Indus. To the north the country broadens out into a huge and fertile plain, the core of the richest agricultural province in pre-Partition India—the Punjab, or Land of the Five Rivers. We were back in an almost English park-land, a tree-studded countryside which, as the road wound on, culminated in the shaded avenues of Lahore. Once known as the Paris of India, Lahore is still a most pleasant city, particularly if you have hardly seen a tree since Beirut. The broad avenue known as the Mall is lined with acacias, and the only thing lacking seemed to be the open-air café. One wonders how the face of India might have been changed had Dupleix triumphed over Clive.

Lahore is the cultural centre of Pakistan, and on Partition might well have been the capital had it been further removed from the Indian border, which is only sixteen miles away. The fame of Lahore as a city of stately buildings—its inhabitants say that "Isfahan and Shiraz united would not equal the half of it"—began in the reign of Akbar, the greatest of the Mogul emperors. He built the fort, beneath which now nestles the fantastically crowded and kaleidoscopic bazaar area of Anarkali, named after the beautiful dancing girl who captured the heart of Emperor Jahangir and was walled up in a pillar for her pains. Jahangir's tomb, built by his son Shah Jahan, who also built the more famous Taj Mahal, lies on the other bank of the Ravi, and is certainly one of the most elegant buildings in the East. With these and many other splendours at its disposal, the artistic section of the Expedition had a photographic field-day.

Nevertheless, the part of Lahore we came to know best was the Mall. This was our habitat, from Kim's Gun and the University at one end to Aitchison College (our billet) at the other, with the Brooke Bond offices conveniently situated half-way between the two. Lahore was our base, and, before heading out to the Thal Desert itself, we spent three days gathering the statistical and historical details of the irrigation project we were to study. At any hour of the day it was possible to see members of the Expedition, notebooks in hip-pocket, rushing up and down the Mall from one Government department to another in the process of what was known as 'collecting data.'

Brooke Bond was much more than the source of the Expedition's tea; their offices were our headquarters, mailing addresses, and a lot else besides. The Lahore manager, Mohammed Muzuffar, was one of the greatest characters we met on the trip. He had the loudest laugh in the Punjab, and that's saying something in a land noted for its jocularity. Whenever we called on him (which was almost continuously) all office-work stopped, his minions were sent to bring chairs, cigarettes, iced drinks, and tea. In fact, throughout our time in Lahore his char-wallah never stopped; the kettle was perpetually on the boil. Muzuffar combined a truly English sense of humour (unusual in a foreigner) with his own hearty indigenous variety, and he probably only stopped laughing when asleep. There was a plaque on his desk—"A man should be like his tea; his true strength only comes out when he is in hot water." No one was more amused at the platitude than Muzuffar.

Downstairs from Brooke Bond lived the Rover agent, Zafdar Rashid—ex-Sandhurst, Bengal Lancers, and very much so. Regimental blazer and curly-brimmed hat was the order of the day for Zafdar. He is one of those whom other Pakistanis call a Muslim Englishman, a term which sums it up admirably.

He was an old boy of Aitchison College, a school originally founded by the British to educate the sons of rajahs and nawabs in the English tradition—and still colloquially known as Chiefs' College. Zafdar had obtained permission for us to camp in the grounds, but we certainly never expected the huge blue-and-gold marquee which had been erected next to the school swimming-pool for our accommodation. Neither did we expect the experience of the first morning, when we graduated into the world of 'Sahibism.' We were all asleep, six sleeping-bagged figures curled up on camp-beds, when a moustachioed and turbaned bearer came in, a blanket wrapped about his shoulders. I opened one eye and watched. He was arranging six cups around a steaming tea-pot, and then, having meticulously placed the tea-spoons in position, he turned towards the sleeping Expedition.

"Get up, sahibs," he said, with complete authority.

Not a move.

"Get up, sahibs," and then in encouragement he added, "Bed tea!"

"Fried eggies, sahibs."

True enough, there were three blanket-swathed *chowkidars* (bearers) brewing "bed tea" and frying "eggies" on a little portable charcoal fire outside the tent door. B.B. was out of a job as long as we stayed in Lahore.

The 'sahib' tag seemed quite the normal thing, and after a while we ceased to be amused or embarrassed at this dignified form of address, although, bearded and dishevelled, we were never quite able to equate ourselves with the pukka sahibs of the days of the Raj.

The hospitality that we received from the masters and boys of Aitchison College was overwhelming. In partial return we gave them a talk on life at Cambridge ("it fits one for a life one will never lead"), and another on our journey. We must have rather overdone the latter, for afterwards we were continually accosted by small boys who politely asked for our autographs. We later learnt that a complete set of Expedition signatures was worth the rough equivalent of three bottles of fizz at the school tuck-shop. Such is fame. The College also challenged the "Oxford and Cambridge Touring Hockey Team" to meet their own first team. Only two of us had ever played before; the venue was the best pitch in Pakistan, and our opponents were the crack eleven of the Punjab—a part of the world noted for its hockey-players. It was therefore hardly surprising that Oxford and Cambridge (augmented to a full team by some masters), playing very much on an away ground, were defeated by eleven goals.

But, despite these various diversions, we completed the preliminary teeing-up of our field-work and then took off for the Thal, which lay a few hours' drive away to the west.

Ten years ago the Thal Desert, an area of some eight thousand square miles between the Indus and the Jhelum rivers, was a useless waste of sand and stunted scrub. Summer temperatures reached 120°F. in the shade, and in a year the wholly unpredictable rainfall rarely exceeded eight inches. The story of Thal Development (as opposed to Thal Desert) began in 1947. In that year the British left the Indian sub-continent, and it was divided into Hindu India and Muslim Pakistan; the resultant stream of refugees from one country to the other caused tremendous problems. In the first few weeks after partition Pakistan lost four million Sikhs and Hindus to India, but back across the newly drawn frontier came six million Muslims to replace them. Thus Pakistan had gained two million starving mouths over-night, and her inadequate agricultural economy was strained to breaking-point. Something had to be done to relieve the pressure on land and food, and it had to be done quickly. Accordingly, Pakistan drew up an ambitious plan for intensifying agriculture on land already available, and, more important, for bringing into cultivation desert areas long considered useless. The Thal was such an area.

Lying just beyond the bounds of the Punjab, it is an extension of the largest irrigation network in the world, a network which stretches from the Kashmir foothills of the Himalayas down to the desert of Sind, on the Indian Ocean. This is a land where the "cusec" is king, and where the lack of a basic understanding of the engineers' jargon is liable to make one a social outcast. The cusec, or cubic foot of flowing water per second, is the vital key to Pakistan's economy, and it plays none too small a part in her politics, both internal and external. In fact, the dispute between India and Pakistan over the division of water in the rivers of the Punjab is the most important of all the many disputes between the two countries. The issue of Kashmir, for example, is not so much concerned with mere territorial acquisition (though this is the way it is presented in the world's Press) as one concerned with water. The rivers on which Pakistan so completely depends rise in the mountains of Kashmir; thus India, in control of Kashmir, has control of these waters. India has her thumb on the wind-pipe of Pakistan.

As we drove out to the Thal that morning we crossed over the Ravi, the Chenab, and the Jhelum. Between the rivers were the canals, some of them carrying five times more water than the Thames at Teddington, and the fields of wheat just sprouting above the surface. Along the roads trudged lines of bullock-carts laden with raw cotton for the mills of Lahore, Lyallpur, and Sargodha—the capitals of the canal colonies they serve. This rich land yields two harvests every year, but without irrigation half of it would yield none, and the other half lie victim to the vacillations of the capricious monsoon. Canal water has made the Punjab what it is, and, similarly, it may change the arid wastes of Thal into an oasis of agricultural prosperity.

Thal in its natural state is a desert. But our first introduction to the area was to a completely new and modern town, a forest plantation of young saplings, and a nursery garden whose watered avenues were lined with orange trees and rose bushes. The sand had been pushed back and held by tufts of wiry grasses planted in long rows with military-like precision, emphasizing the purpose of their task. This was the change we had come to see—from desert to development.

The Thal Development Authority (T.D.A.) is the autonomous body responsible for the overall development of this desert. Under its direction the dunes have been levelled and grasses sown to bind them, hundreds of miles of canals have been dug, new towns and villages have been built, experimental farms and breeding-stations laid out, seven hundred miles of tree-lined tarmac roads constructed, agricultural industries started, and finally, most important of all, thirty thousand refugee families settled. All this has been done in a few years. But T.D.A. has still much further to go than it has already come. And there are many problems.

It was with these problems that the Expedition was mainly concerned, for we had come to do much more than merely look and admire. Waterlogging of the desert clays has occurred in some areas, some crops have yielded much less than was expected, and a reappraisal of breeding techniques is necessary. In some respects the scheme is too ambitious for the water available (six thousand cusecs), and there has been inadequate instruction to the new farmers on the techniques especial to an irrigated desert. But these are problems, not failures.

T.D.A. had suggested a programme for us so that we could make the most efficient use of our time, and during the following weeks we motored nearly one thousand five hundred miles all over the project area asking questions, scribbling notes, and taking pictures. The organization was superb. With Henry and me travelled Mr Abassi, the Information Officer, who really was a guide, philosopher, and friend. Not only did he act as interpreter between the settlers and ourselves, but he also had a deep mystical sense which prompted discussion on all kinds of unlikely subjects. He had a macabre turn of phrase, too. Once, seeing a flock of vultures wheeling in the sky, Tim asked him how it was that these birds were so unerring in their knowledge of approaching death. He answered quite seriously. "They develop an instinct like dogs and grave-diggers. In all three cases their food depends on it."

Ahead of us, in their own jeep, travelled a chef and a kind of major-domo. They ensured that lunch was always ready when we arrived at the local rest-house, and then motored on to prepare dinner at the one where we were to spend the night. The meals they turned out were huge—vast, steaming piles of pilao, then a mutton curry, followed by a vegetable curry, a chicken curry, and piles of chapatties. No wonder Punjabis are the size of oxen! Also zig-zagging all over Thal was Mohammed Gill, once Professor at Lyallpur Agricultural College, and now the chief T.D.A. Agricultural Officer. He personally showed us round each of the five experimental farms and gardens we visited. We repaid this keen enthusiasm by bombarding everybody with questions, and Mr Abassi's efforts to get us from one place to another on time failed completely. Sometimes we didn't finish until midnight. The days we devoted to farms, villages, and canals; the nights to cotton, woollen, and sugar-mills. Between times we scribbled in our notebooks.

Since Thal is the most important single development project in Pakistan it is on the itinerary of every diplomat, businessman, journalist, or engineer visiting the country. T.D.A. is thus very competent, and used to handling visitors of all types, but I don't think they had ever experienced anything quite so earnest and inquiring as the Oxcam Far Eastern. All the officials we met really seemed to enjoy being able to remove the conversation from the rather trite plane of "smiling fields and happy peasants" to a more technical discussion of the achievements and problems. Nigel busied himself with detailed inquiries into cost-benefit ratios and other economic mumbo-jumbo. Henry, as our resident agricultural expert, was concerned with the cost of fertilizers and the various strains of wheat. Tim wanted to know all about the composition of the different soils and climatic conditions. I tried to establish an exact relationship between the amount of irrigation water available and the requirements of the crops. B.B. aimed his cameras at everything, from the fertilization of a mango plant to the huge barrage across the Indus which made it all possible. Adrian, however, had committed the heinous crime of admitting that he didn't even know what a cusec was, so the Business Manager was left behind in Lahore to ensure that the Expedition's paper output should not drop while it was in the field.

☿

Apart from the magnificence of the concrete-lined canals threading their way through the desert, and the grandeur of the massive steel and cement edifice of the mile-long Jinnah Barrage, our most vivid impressions were those of Gill's experimental farms and of the villages themselves.

The experimental farms were almost miracles. If it weren't for the sand-dunes only a mile or two away one could imagine oneself in the hot-house at Kew. The sugar-cane stood twelve feet high, the Egyptian clover was greener than the grass in Ireland, and the wheat-yield had more than doubled in three years. Mohammed Gill, the top of his turban waving in the breeze, enthusiastically showed us guavas doing this, mangoes doing that, and four different varieties of orange doing yet something else. The papayas, he regretted, would not be doing anything until next year! Every question we asked was greeted with a torrent of encyclopædic information. Day by day our notebooks filled, and at the end of each visit we always had the cheerful assurance from the genial Gill that we hadn't finished with him yet, but would see him on the morrow at yet another of his garden oases.

☿

Village-visiting, or *chak*-bashing, as we called it, was conducted along somewhat different lines. The five of us, with Mr Abassi, would draw up at the appointed chak, shake hands with the turbaned elders, exchange "*Salaam aleikum*"s, and then take our seats round a table in the headman's courtyard. The normal chak is about a thousand acres, with sixty families each farming a fifteen acre holding. Sometimes two or more chaks are adjacent to each other, and the community is big enough to warrant its own school or dispensary. Soon after our arrival the word would get about that some sahibs had come, and the farmers would start drifting in from the fields until there were about forty or so squatting around us. Questioning would begin, Mr Abassi translating into Punjabi.

"What part of the Punjab did you come from? Were your old lands better? What yields do you get? How much do you have to pay in taxes?"

Sometimes it would be difficult to get a question across, for the previous one had touched off a buzz of discussion on some tricky problem. Once there was so much chatter that I asked Mr Abassi what they were talking about.

"What they are always talking about—water," he replied, with a slow, sympathetic smile. "They want more, and one of them says he missed his turn through being away for a couple of days."

"Are there many disputes over water?"

"No, not in Thal. But elsewhere in the Punjab ninety per cent of the murders are over water-disputes."

"What are the remaining ten per cent about?"

"Women."

"Ask them what they most need besides water."

"What does a farmer always want more of?" Mr Abassi replied.

I was non-committal, but asked him to put the question all the same. With a slow shrug he turned to the peasants seated on the mat, and spoke in Punjabi. There was a one-word answer. Mr Abassi translated, "As always—land."

This question is a vital one in the poor soil of Thal, for the Government has tried to settle as many refugees as possible by giving only fifteen acres to each family. Fifteen acres is just economic to-day, but under the Islamic laws of inheritance the land must be equally divided among all the sons and daughters, and then fragmentation of holdings will make subsistence impossible.

"They will have to divide the income, not the land, and leave the eldest son to work the farm. The other children must go and work in the cotton and sugar mills," was Mr Abassi's answer.

"What about birth-control?" we asked.

Mr Abassi's deep brown eyes smiled as he translated, and all the settlers burst into roars of laughter. There were no women present.

⊛

Still laughing and joking, we were all led off into the sugar-cane fields. The Expedition had obviously made a tremendous hit.

"Here is our local industry," they said, as we watched a blindfolded camel walking round and round, turning a wheel which crushed the cane, so that the juice poured into the empty petrol-cans placed underneath. In one corner of the field was an enormous saucer-like vat full of bubbling sugar juice, with a man feeding cane-tops into the fire underneath. The molten sugar was then poured into trays to harden in the sun into brown lumps like small buns. It is sold in this form to the mills for refining, since the farmers make a better income this way than they would by selling the uncrushed cane.

"How is it that the camel is content to keep walking round and round?" I asked.

"He can't see where he's going, and thinks if he keeps on for long enough he'll reach Mecca in the end."

Roars of laughter, and then a final request before we left to ask Mr Gill to arrange for them to have a fertilizer store in the village, on which they could draw when they had the money, and so get crops as big as on the experimental farms. We promised to convey this request, reflecting that at least the notion of scientific farming was beginning to seep through to at least one section of the huge agrarian population of the sub-continent.

DIARY FOR 21st NOVEMBER

Bhakkar to Leiah (Southern Thal)

Up at six and off by seven. Stacks on the agenda to-day. The usual fried eggies and buffalo butter for breakfast. Mustafa, the driver of the jeep, wants a chit signed to testify to his mechanical ability. Authority delegated to Henry, who writes, "Mustafa is a bloody marvellous mechanic, signed Chief Engineer Oxcam Far Eastern."

First call of morning is at a new afforestation area. Discussed difficulties and effects of growing trees in these arid conditions. Unfortunately—for my own interest—they've kept no microclimatological[4] records. But this is typical of Thal—so little was known that methods are still largely empirical. Plant something; if it doesn't grow it's no good; if it does grow, then plant a few more to confirm and then spread the word. Shisham tree does quite well, and on some of the older plantations (five years or so) climatic change can already be noticed, for the trees conserve moisture and lower the temperature.

Gill, turban aflow, turned up at about ten o'clock and took us off to another of his 'gardens.' Once again we saw and heard everything, and he talked informatively and incessantly. It really seems a delight to him to be able to show us what he and his staff are doing, to have it appreciated, and to have intelligent questions shot at him in his own semi-technical language.

Soon after we arrived a gardener gave us each a rose to wear in our hats, while for 'elevenses' we ate huge radishes and learnt the difference between Mussambi and Jaffa oranges.

T-budding (or Gill's patent grafting process) is the thing here. They did twenty thousand plants on this garden in September. Gill insists that Abassi also watches how it is done. Poor old Abassi, he's seen it hundreds of times.

I'm still trying to get out of Gill exactly how much water all these crops need, particularly oranges, which in Morocco needed vast quantities, and it must be even more in this very sandy soil of Thal. Gill says we'll have a long session in his office at Jauharabad next week. But he wants Henry and me to go to the Water Requirements Farm at Lyallpur first to see what research is being done there; then, armed with Moroccan and Lyallpur experiences, we'll be able to appreciate better the set-up in Thal. Seems fair enough. He's nothing if not thorough.

Collected mass of details on cotton yields, soil alkalinity, increase of crop-value through budding, and economics of these gardens (this one almost pays for itself on sale of produce). All this gen's going to take some sorting out.

Back to Bhakkar Rest House for lunch. Two pilaos and three curries! I don't now how we do it. Stamina is approaching Punjabi standards.

Off to A.M.O. (Agricultural Machinery Organization), whose task it is to level the land prior to parcelling out to settlers. We were met on the banks of Main Line Lower Canal by the engineer in charge of the A.M.O. unit. He's got a strong American accent, having been trained in America with Caterpillars. These Punjabis must have gone down big over there.

He led us off the canal road, and we were suddenly in the desert—solid sand. Next three miles were very difficult going. Cornering is tricky, since if you go too fast the car slides and becomes unmanageable, whereas if you go too slowly you lose momentum and stick. Interesting low-ratio, four-wheel-drive stuff.

All round were sand dunes being cleared and levelled by about half a dozen red and yellow bulldozers; most impressive-looking as they shoved and snorted back and forth. The dust was terrific, and the drivers were swathed in cloth up to their eyebrows. They work right through the year, and, in summer (when shade temperatures are 120°F., and in the sun over 200°—*i.e.*, about boiling-point), they are on the go from four o'clock in the morning until 10 A.M., after which the bulldozers are driven back to the sheds, but remain too hot to touch for maintenance work until four in the afternoon!

After the land is levelled it is harrowed and handed over to the refugee farmers, who make their own water-courses (based on an Irrigation Department plan) from the canals. We were amazed that no more was done, but were told of the urgency of getting the homeless on to the land; no more time than was strictly necessary could be spent helping them, for there were many more waiting. How they get a living for the first few years is incredible, since there can be no worse farming soil in the world. It isn't 'soil' but dry, useless sand, which runs through your fingers like water. There is absolutely no organic matter in it whatsoever. Yet in a year or two it produces crops of gram, wheat, and sugar. This is all Henry's department, and it looks like he's got some interesting work on his hands.

The other incredible thing is how all this machinery stands up to the conditions. We met an American, the Caterpillar Tractor Company's representative, and he was most informative, but a bit too mechanical in his language for all except Henry and Nigel. The biggest hazard any machinery runs in this area is sand. No matter how efficient the air-cleaners are, it gets in everywhere, and then, mixed with the oil, forms a highly effective and destructive grinding paste. Bearings, oil seals, gears, the lot, are affected, and it can raise running costs by as much as half. Hence daily maintenance and the insistence by World Bank, who made the $3\frac{1}{2}$ million dollar loan to purchase all the A.M.O. machinery, that representatives of the companies from America should come to Thal and supervise the care of equipment.

In the evening we drove about eighty miles south to Leiah for the night. We must be amassing a pretty considerable mileage.

There was a retired Pakistan Army major staying in the Rest House, and we had a most interesting discussion during and after dinner about the Punjab Boundary Award and how, on Partition, the award of the Muslim-majority District of Gurdaspur to India made it possible for India to accept the accession of Kashmir. Without Gurdaspur India would have had no link with Kashmir, since of course all the natural routes lead into Pakistan. This is obviously going to be relevant once Henry and I get cracking on the water dispute between India and Pakistan, since the Jhelum and Chenab flow through Indian-held Kashmir.

After a few more days we were beginning to see the wood for the trees, and began to concentrate not so much on the achievements of the project as on some of the problems yet to be overcome. Chief among these was waterlogging and the associated problem of salinity. Neither of these are peculiar to Thal; they are endemic in any irrigated arid zone, but they are particularly serious in Pakistan, where thousands of irrigated acres are being rendered useless by these twin scourges every year. Thal is a new project, but already the disaster of waterlogging has occurred in certain areas.

As you drive through the Punjab you will come across patches of uncultivated land which seem to be covered with a light hoar-frost, or even snow. This land once gave good crops, but now salt has appeared at the surface, and nothing but the most resistant scrub or reed will grow. Continued irrigation has caused this, for the water has percolated through the soil and collected together all the previously diffused salts to form a layer several feet below the surface. As more water percolates downward the salts accumulate, and slowly the layer rises. The plants on the surface aid the ascent of this salt layer by sucking up the moisture from below. With the heat of the sun the process accelerates, until finally the salts choke the plants, which then wither and die.

Where this has occurred in Thal, T.D.A. is trying to reclaim the resultant waste-land by putting it under rice, and applying very heavy irrigations to drive the salts down again. However, the real answer lies not only in heavier irrigations but also in the installation of a drainage system to take the excess water away once it has done its leaching work, and given sustenance to the crops. And here is the vicious circle, for there is no more water available for heavier irrigations, while drainage is a most expensive business.

An American irrigation expert who was surveying the salinity problems in West Pakistan advised the Irrigation Department that they should concentrate all their water resources on to a third of the land being irrigated at present.

"But what about the people living on the other two-thirds?" he was asked.

"That," he replied, "is a social problem, not one of effective irrigation."

It is small wonder, in view of this water-shortage, that Pakistan views with frantic concern India's intentions to use all the water from three of the Punjab rivers entirely within her own territory before it ever reaches Pakistan. It was, in fact, this other aspect of the irrigation difficulties of the Punjab which we intended to study on our way home to England. Meanwhile we had our hands full in Thal.

After a fortnight we all returned to Lahore for a few days' follow-up work in the University Geography Faculty and the Irrigation Department. It was now the beginning of December, and as time was short the Expedition prepared to split into two groups—the scientific, and the artistic, camera-strewn rest. The artistic, or Oxford Group got ready to leave for India in order to jazz up various embassies concerned with our onward passage to Singapore, and also to see if they could get permission to drive up to Nepal. Meanwhile, the Cambridge car (with Tim aboard instead of Adrian, who was going to Delhi to deal with the embassies) would continue the field-work for another two or three weeks. The plan was that we should all meet up again in Calcutta four weeks later, just before Christmas.

There was just one more thing that had to be done before the cars went their different ways. Some weeks before in Karachi, Tim and B.B. had seen something in an airmailed Scottish newspaper which aroused their interest; they had been vaguely talking about doing some journalistic and photographic follow-up work on it ever since. Now they had the chance. Perhaps, then, it would be best if I ended this chapter by quoting the article which Tim subsequently wrote on this intriguing subject. So, with the kind permission of the *Manchester Guardian*, over to Tim.

FROM THE "MANCHESTER GUARDIAN,"
JANUARY 13, 1956

We read in a Scottish newspaper that "grave concern is being expressed in bagpipe circles about the impending import of foreign pipes." It sounded as incredible as tinned haggis from Japan, but on reading that the cause originated from here in Pakistan we decided to investigate. Inquiry led us to the border of Kashmir, to the industrial town of Sialkot. It is not an industrial town in the sense of mills, mass production, and machinery but rather in the sense of tiny workshops open to the sunny street, of turbaned craftsmen who spend their lives fashioning cricket bats and tubas, footballs and bugles, furniture and saddles, drums and lacrosse sticks, shotguns and wooden spoons, anything, in fact, that depends on human skill for its making. Their lathes, their looms, their drills, their forges are worked by hand and patience, and here it is they make bagpipes.

We saw the bagpipe 'factory'—output, four pipes per day—which, because it recently sent a price list to a prominent Edinburgh retailer, is causing the present "grave concern" in Scotland. Everything—including what the firm's pamphlet describes as the "tatans and bony ribbons"—is made by six men squatting on the workshop floor. As one watched them shaping the pipes and chanters with their hands and feet—for they use their toes to hold the rough wood steady while they work—one could not help thinking that these must have been the methods used by the crofters and villagers of Argyll and Aberdeen in days long past. The owner was worried about the reported Scottish reaction to his offer. "After all," he said, "it is their instrument, but they taught us to play and now all Pakistan loves the music, so they should not be angry now that we make our own pipes."

We learned from him the history of the pipes in Pakistan. Rather less than a hundred years ago, after the Indian Mutiny, it became the custom to station a permanent garrison of British troops on the turbulent North-West Frontier. Among the regiments that came to guard the Khyber Pass and to protect the route to the fertile plains of India from the hill tribesmen were many from Scotland—the Black Watch, the Gordons, the Seaforths, and the Cameronians—and with them they brought their pipes. They were surprised and gratified to find that the tribesmen of the Himalayan foothills appreciated the primitive music of the Highland pipes, for, with their own antique wooden flutes, the tribesmen were—and still are—great pipers. What more natural, then, than that some pipe majors should start instructing a few of their eager admirers?

In later years, when the Indian Sepoys were formed into locally raised infantry and cavalry regiments, they adopted the bagpipe and its music for their own. It often happened that a Scottish colonel was appointed to command such a regiment, and he would encourage the Highland tradition still further by dressing the regiment in his own clan tartan. And when, in other cases, an English colonel was appointed, he would look enviously at the cheerful plaids of a neighbouring regiment and would take recourse in devising his own tartan; thus, incidentally, were established the only English tartans on record.

When, in 1947, the British withdrew from India, among the last troops to embark were those of a Scottish infantry regiment. As their troopship cast off and *Auld Lang Syne* was piped from ship to shore there were few who thought that the music of the pipes would last for long in old India. They were wrong. The pipes and plaids have remained, for they had found a place in the new army of Pakistan, and now not even the most ardent nationalist could persuade the pipers to change their tune.

So that we might see the military pipes for ourselves we telephoned the commanding officer of the Pakistan Military School of Music (in Lahore) and arranged to photograph one or two pipers in their ceremonial dress. The next morning we arrived at the parade-ground and there, drawn up in ceremonial order, were not one or two

"Six itinerant British subjects" in Turkey after ten months on the road

Tim   Adrian   Pat   BB   Henry   Nigel

Iran: A rare oasis in the Great Salt Desert is an idyllic setting for the Ma'an mosque
Lebanon: Ba'albek, massive columns of the Temple of Jupiter

Iraq: Breakfast in the desert
Syria: Krak des Chevaliers, the 12th century Crusader castle

Pakistan: Beating the Retreat at the Lahore Military School of Music
"Crossing the Ganges was rather a problem"

India: Shadufs on the Ganges Plain, traditional method of irrigation
"Some indigenous Assamese ceramics"

Nepal: The high-road to Kathmandu, newly built by Indian Army Engineers

Ablutions for all on a festival day in Kathmandu
Having fun on the chains round a Rana's statue

The mountain train to Darjeeling seizes priority on the shared roadway
At the station, the orange seller takes his midday nap

The tea-estate bridge "was only made for ponies"

Stilwell's military highway - ten years on

Stuck in the Chindwin "we did very well till we got to the middle"
Relic of war: a Japanese two-man tank

Panning for gold; it collects in the cells of banana stems
Irrawaddy fisherman

Burma: Lake Inle, where they all row with their legs

Tweedledum and Tweedledee (*top left*)　　　Nepalese ten-year old carries 30kg over the mountain (*top right*)
Magnifying mirror never fails to break the ice

Jungle escort breaks down once again
"They would never have made it without us"

Brooke Bond's Julia tea estate, our Assam base-camp. Our kit for "the assault on Burma" after non-essentials had been shipped home.

Henry   Adrian   Pat   "G⌐suir"   Tim   Nigel   BB

pipers but one hundred and twenty. And with them were twenty drummers, twenty buglers, and seventeen drum majors. The sight of seventeen drum majors all throwing their maces together was unforgettable. Every man wore a different uniform; there were the plaids of every clan in Scotland and turbans from every part of Pakistan. There were men from the Frontier Force, from the Bengal Lancers, from the Khyber Rifles, from the Punjabis and the Pathans, and there were the tartans—Stewart, Mackenzie, Buchanan, McLeod, from every clan north of the Tweed. A Scotsman would have been proud had he seen the perfection of their drilling and the skill with which they played that imperfect and yet altogether wonderful instrument.

For nearly three hours they marched and counter-marched, they beat the Retreat and formed their own national emblem—the Star and Crescent. Their playing and their marching would have made any Guardsman envious. As we left we thanked the senior drum major and told him—and we meant it—that we had not seen such a sight since the Coronation. He did not understand English very well, but he smiled from beneath his six-inch moustache, and told us that he was amongst those who had marched "in the column of the Maharanee Elizabeth" that day.

8

India and the Highroad to Nepal

by B.B.

AFTER a few days in Lahore, during which Tim and I got our story on the bagpipes, the time came for the cars to separate—one east to India and the other west, back to the Thal.

Adrian, Nigel, and I expected some Customs difficulties at the frontier, because Tim, who was down in the *carnet* as the official owner of the Oxford car, was not coming with us, but remaining behind on the Thal field-work. Surprisingly enough, however, the Pakistan officials were not the least perturbed, and readily accepted my signature on the various documents instead of Tim's. But when we came to the Indian barrier it was a different story; it was "quite impossible" for us to proceed. We could not go on unless we went back and fetched Tim. The authorities were also disturbed by the sight of our water jerry-cans on one of which, in red, we had painted "Gin," and on the other "Tonic." India was in the throes of impending prohibition, and for us to enter with what purported to be 4½ gallons of gin was obviously asking too much. They could not understand that it was really only water. "If water, then why you put Gin?" they asked, reasonably enough. We were clearly bootleggers.

However, waiting for us at the frontier was a welcoming committee of Brooke Bonders: Mr Herman, a manager; Mr Jaganath, a local branch manager; and Mr Hariharam, a company photographer. They helped us explain ourselves to the Customs, and after an hour's delay—during which time various officials stuck suspicious noses into our 'Gin'—we were allowed to leave. Once through the barrier we were initiated into a routine which was to sweep us across India. Mr Jaganath suddenly produced three rose-petal garlands, which he hung about our startled necks; Mr Herman conjured up a large tin of tea which he presented to Adrian; and, while they held the pose, Mr Hariharam clicked his shutter. We were surprised and rather flattered; it was some days before we really got the hang of it all.

We set off for Amritsar behind a sky-blue Ford station wagon, with Mr Hariharam filming us out of the window. On the outskirts of the town the cavalcade pulled in to the road-side, where a number of little red vans were gathered, each piled high with packets of tea. We got out. We shook hands. We drank a cup of tea. We were photographed. We shook hands again. We moved on. That was the drill.

Amritsar is the capital city of the Sikhs and the site of their holy of holies: the Darbar Sahib, or Golden Temple. We were led to the temple, where, after removing our shoes and washing our feet, we were received as privileged guests. In the yellow light of evening the temple was a sight of very rare beauty. Set in the middle of a pool a hundred yards square, the golden building shone and glowed against a deep blue sky, its reflection shimmering in the dark waters around it. We were led across the narrow bridge which connects the bank with the temple, and then inside we received pieces of sweet biscuit handed to us by a bearded priest through the rails of an inner sanctum where musicians and singers softly chanted. At the farther end of the hall the chief priest hung garlands around our necks. All this was patiently recorded by Hariharam's camera.

Then we were taken to the temple treasury—which was apparently a considerable honour, for a quorum of hierarchy had to be summoned before we could be admitted. Inside were many golden robes and bejewelled ornaments, some of which had been provided by Ranjit Singh, who had gilded the temple at the beginning of the last century. We were also shown an array of vicious-looking swords which had belonged to famous Sikhs of the past. Finally we saw the great ceremonial doors of gold, which are only used on special religious occasions.

Sikhism is an interesting and relatively young religion founded by Guru Nanak only a little over four hundred years ago as a break from the rigid caste system of the Hindus. He held that all men had an equal right to seek for God, there being only one God underlying all religious forms. In this respect his teachings were more akin to the monotheistic Islam than to the multitudinous gods of the Hindus.

Traditionally despising the Hindu and hating the Muslim, the Sikhs have often desired a state of their own—and still do. Two wars were fought against them in the 1840's; as the result of which the Punjab was annexed by the British in 1849, and one of their treasures, the Koh-i-noor diamond, was ceded to Queen Victoria in the peace treaty. Since the 1947 India-Pakistan boundary passed right through the Punjab, the Sikhs' traditional home, it left many of their shrines and holy places in Pakistan. Consequently, terrible carnage ensued at partition. Muslims escaping to Pakistan were annihilated, while in revenge Sikhs were massacred in Lahore. The death-roll exceeded half a million; the mutual hatred between Muslim and Sikh will take decades to heal.

Ⓢ

Staying the night in Amritsar (after a curry supper hot enough to carbonize our gullets), we pushed on towards Delhi à la Brooke Bond. We stopped several times during the day to have a cup of tea at a wayside stall, to talk to the salesman, and move on—after photographs, of course. At Ambala and Ludhiana there were full-blown receptions with banners, garlands, and speeches. We took it in turn to reply to the addresses with which we were always so flatteringly welcomed.

Arriving in Delhi on the third day, we passed under several banners proclaiming "Delhi welcomes you." One even said, "Hail your august majesty." There seemed no limit to Brooke Bond's enthusiasm, until we noticed a flag saying "Greetings to the Lord of Arabia," and realized that King Saud was in town hard on the heels of Bulge and Khrush.

It came as rather a surprise to discover that Brooke Bond had very enthusiastic ideas on how we should spend our time. A representative of their advertising agents, J. Walter Thompson, Ltd, was making arrangements, and, besides a whole host of appointments while we were in Delhi, it seemed that most of our onward journey through India had been planned in advance as well. We jibbed a little at first, but finally agreed to an amended schedule, and then dossed down wearily in the Y.M.C.A.

There was much to do in Delhi; the first thing was to discover if we could get to Kathmandu, the capital of Nepal. Why did we want to go? The main reason was photographic, but, apart from this, it seemed that very few vehicles had ever driven into Nepal. That was sufficient challenge. Nepal is an independent Himalayan kingdom which, like Tibet, its northern neighbour, has long turned a distrustful shoulder on the rest of the world. In fact, it was not until her hereditary line of Prime Ministers was overthrown in 1951 that she eased her doors and, for example, granted permission for the first British Expedition to enter and approach Mount Everest from the south. Previously it had been simpler to attack the mountain from the north, from Tibet itself. In 1952, with a relaxed suspicion of foreigners, the Nepalese allowed the Indian Army to start building a road into their country. The Indian sappers had been working on this road for over three years, and, in fact, we arrived in Delhi only a fortnight after the through alignment had been completed. Even now it was reported to be little more than a winding track blasted over the mountains; it was not expected to be fully open for another two years at least. Nevertheless, it seemed too good a chance to miss, and, if permission was forthcoming from the Nepalese, we determined to go.

Previously there had only been two ways of entering the country— by air or on foot. By air one flew from the plains of Northern India and, fifty minutes later, landed high up on an air-strip outside Kathmandu. On foot one journeyed via a tiny narrow-gauge railway to the base of the Himalayan foothills, then walked and climbed. After crossing the parallel ranges for several days one descended into the Kathmandu valley, the only sizeable valley in the whole country. When still a few miles from the capital travellers were met by a rickety bus. How did the bus get there? The same way nearly everything else did; it came up over the mountains. It was carried by about a hundred coolies in a journey that took several weeks. In fact, all the vehicles in Kathmandu (and there weren't many) had come the same way—even the municipal steam-roller! They were dismantled into headloads on the Indian frontier so that different groups of porters could carry the engine, the chassis, the wheels, and so on. Then, by slow stages, over the mountains to the far side, where everything was reassembled.

However, all this is rather jumping the gun as far as our own story is concerned—though it accounts for our interest in trying to reach Kathmandu under our own steam. On arriving in Delhi we found a letter from the British Ambassador to Nepal in which he said that a car had just succeeded in making the journey, and permission was now being sought for us also. I applied to the Nepalese Embassy for visas, and filled in the usual multiple forms. "There will be no difficulty," I was told; "come back to-morrow with your passports." I was quite flabbergasted by this, and I immediately sent a telegram to Tim saying, "Essential you arrive Saturday morning," for it had been agreed that only if the Nepal trip was on should he be recalled from the Thal research. The next day, Friday, I returned to the Nepalese Embassy. The forms were scanned, the visas stamped in our passports . . . but just as the Secretary was about to sign he saw the magic words "purpose of visit, filming." Quick as a flash he crossed out the visas with the word "cancelled." "Must wait for permission from Kathmandu," he said. "How long will that take?" "Perhaps one week, perhaps two," he replied inscrutably. I left dejected, and sent a telegram to the British Embassy in Kathmandu asking if they could possibly arrange for permission to be sent to the frontier. To me, as photographer, it seemed futile to go unless we had permission to film.

Brooke Bond had arranged a most comprehensive programme for us in Delhi; something had been laid on nearly every day. There was a tea-party where we met the Press, a broadcast over All India Radio, and a visit to the Indian Industries Fair, where we appeared on television. India has no real TV yet, and one imagines that it will be some time coming. But, no doubt with an eye to a future contract, an enterprising foreign firm had given fifty sets to influential Indians in the capital, and was providing an intermittent service from a studio at the fair. None of us, including the interviewer (the Brooke Bond manager), had ever been on live TV before, so the programme was something of a free-for-all, with each of us trying to out-plug the others in publicizing our various items of kit. Nigel brought the show to a literally smashing conclusion by hurling one of our long-suffering cups at the camera. Quoth he, as the object whizzed past the camera operator, "Magnificent—quite unbreakable, these plastic mugs." It disintegrated thunderously on the concrete floor.

Brooke Bond also arranged meetings with the Vice-President, the Minister of Defence, and the Minister of Planning. Dr Radhakrishnan, the Vice-President, formerly Professor of Eastern Religions at Oxford, and one-time Indian Ambassador in Moscow, gave us a most amusing and informal résumé of Delhi's recent visitors—King Saud, and B. and K., among others. The differences in diplomatic method between East and West were disturbingly brought home to us by his account of India's appeal for wheat during a famine; from the West. "What do you want it for?"; from Moscow, "To which port shall we deliver it?" All these visits were most interesting, and we never should have made them without Brooke Bond's push; in partial return they got a free puff in the papers when "Students call on Minister" appeared as a news item. While we were busy in Delhi Tim was fully occupied in trying to join us in time. Owing to there being no through train from Lahore, he was taken to the Pakistan frontier by Pat and Henry; thence he took a local bus to Amritsar. Being rather a curiosity among the passengers, he was given the place of honour next to the driver. Writing in the diary, he says, "As long as I kept my eyes off the winding course along which the bus wobbled, and disregarded the groans of the obviously fractured chassis, it was quite an amusing drive." Purchasing a second-class ticket at Amritsar railway station, he boarded the Kiplingesque Frontier Mail, and made friends with the guard. The upshot of this was the guard's suggestion that Tim's second-class ticket was obviously a mistake; he promptly installed him in a first-class sleeper instead. After an overnight journey, "only partly disturbed by the snores of a huge Sikh in the next bunk," Tim arrived in Delhi the next day.

It was with considerable doubt that I paid a third visit to the Nepalese Embassy. However, surprisingly enough, the visas were forthcoming—though on the condition of "no filming." It was disappointing that I should not be allowed to use the cine-camera, but we contented ourselves with the hope that we might pick up a filming pass at the actual frontier. In any case, we were fortunate in being allowed to go at all.

We were fortunate in another respect too, because, during a visit to the B.B.C. representative for India in connexion with sending various exposed films back to Britain, I chanced to meet Maung Maung Soe, who turned out to be the First Secretary at the Burmese Embassy in Delhi. At his office the next day I saw him make out cables to his Government in Rangoon designed to get us the hitherto never-granted permission to enter Burma by land. The same evening he invited the four of us to a cocktail party. When we arrived—Tim resplendent in his scarlet Technicolor sweater—we found ourselves the very odd men out in a top-notch diplomatic gathering. During the course of the evening we were introduced to a distinguished gentleman with formidable eyebrows, and had a most interesting conversation with him about Burma. "You seem to know Burma quite well, sir," remarked Adrian. "Well, yes, I suppose I do," he said apologetically. "You see, I'm the British Ambassador there." The perfect squelch! Nevertheless, Sir Paul Gore-Booth gave us valuable advice about our Burma plans, and promised to do what he could to help our case with the Burmese Government.

As usual, there was little time for sightseeing. But, led by Mrs Sen, wife of the All-India Radio chief, we spent a day in Old Delhi being shown round the Jamma Masjid and the equally famous Red Fort. Both the mosque and the fort were the work of the greatest of the Mogul emperors, Shah Jahan, in the seventeenth century. Built of pink sandstone and white marble, each is on the grandest scale, and they face each other across half a mile of parkland. Surely no other man can have so many magnificent buildings to his credit, culminating in his *chef d'œuvre,* the Taj Mahal?

New Delhi, designed by Lutyens on the most grandiose scale, and built shortly after the First World War as the administrative capital of the vast Indian Empire, is a permanent and, in many ways, worthy memorial to the British Raj. The mile-long Kingsway (now euphemistically known as Raj Path) runs from the towering India Gate to the Secretariat, a mammoth group of buildings which would dwarf Buckingham Palace. To one side of this is the circular, colonnaded Parliament building which, accommodating both Upper and Lower Houses, is reputedly the largest covered circular building in the world. The shopping centre is again circular, Connaught Place, from which streets and avenues radiate as the spokes of a wheel. Along these avenues are the embassies and residences of the great, all set in spacious grounds with trees everywhere.

Whatever else the British failed to do in India—and our achievements were infinitely greater than some of our critics would have the world believe—we left three things which the country might never have had without us. We left a common language, English, which, in a country of many different tongues, is still the only language understood throughout, and is therefore the only practical means of government. Secondly, where before there had been a disunited spread of petty states, we left a single nation. In fact, in the very process of unifying India we so nourished the seeds of nationalism that they grew to be the final cause of our own withdrawal. Thirdly, we left a capital worthy of such a vast country.

Nigel, Tim, and I felt rather guilty about leaving Adrian behind in Delhi, to do much tedious business work, while we had the prospect of visiting Nepal on what, by comparison, must have seemed a joy-ride. Nevertheless, our respective claims were clear. Nigel, the Oxford mechanic, had to accompany his car; Tim was the scribe, and for article-writing he had to be included; and since I was the cameraman I had the strongest claim of all—providing, of course, that photographic permission was forthcoming at the frontier. It was reassuring to know at such times that we could discuss priorities dispassionately, and avoid the personal recriminations which so often mar or even split expeditions. Adrian took the disappointment philosophically, and did great work by keeping embassies on the move by his daily visits. He also found time to pen a sardonic masterpiece entitled "Confessions of an Indian tea addict," which he sent to Brooke Bond.

The first part of the journey to Kathmandu—which was eight hundred miles away from Delhi—was south-east across the plains of the Ganges. Agra was to be the first halt, where, in order to fulfil a Brooke Bond engagement, we were due at 4 P.M. However, the road wasn't as fast as we expected, and consequently we arrived in the town nearly an hour late. Then we were somewhat messed up by conflicting directions, and found ourselves crossing the town through the narrow alleys of the bazaar quarter, which was choked by a crowd which made a Cup Final exodus look like a country ramble. After jostling through some of India's teeming millions for a time, our attention was drawn to the fact that we had a flat tyre. Fortunately, we were fairly clued up by this stage of the journey, and it did not take long to change the wheel—though the locals who, in their literal hundreds, gave us the benefit of their advice rather impeded operations. In bending over the jack I was concerned to feel my trousers split right up the seat, but in that company such irregularities of dress excited no comment at all.

When we finally showed up at the Agra Hotel the reception committee had been sitting around for a couple of hours, and Mr Lahiri, the J. Walter Thompson representative who was making the arrangements, was getting worried. However, tea was taken, to the usual popping of Hariharam's flash-bulbs, and the gentlemen of the Agra Press were given their stories. We were intrigued to read in one report the next day that we were carrying "a very strong wench on the front bumber" and that we evidently thought "this wench would prove useful in later stages of the journey."

The main reason for visiting Agra was to see the Taj Mahal. One is so familiar with its shape from photographs that somehow one expects to be disappointed in reality. How wrong one is. It is like a huge jewel, perfect in proportions, superb in setting. But above all else is its colour. Built almost entirely of white marble, it shines and glistens in the sunlight, and from a distance looks as if it had been sculptured from a single block of soft white ivory. White, they say, cannot be pale or dark, rich or light; it can only be white. Well, they are wrong. The Taj Mahal is white, but like no other white that I have ever seen.

As I have already mentioned, the Taj Mahal was built a little over three hundred years ago by Shah Jahan; he built it as a tomb for his wife, Mumtaz Mahal, who died on her fourteenth child-bed. The emperor intended to build a similar tomb for himself near by, thus adding symmetry to the whole vast scheme. But before he could carry out this plan he was imprisoned by his son, Aurangzeb. From a prison in the fort across the river he could see the tomb of his wife, and when he himself died eight years later Aurangzeb, being economically inclined, put him in beside her.

The Taj Mahal may well be the most wholly perfect building ever raised. It is one of the acknowledged Wonders of the World. We might, therefore, have been excused a little self-righteous indignation at the lack of taste shown by some of our fellow-tourists. Let me quote from Tim's diary, written that evening:

Men and women wearing baseball caps had come down from Delhi for the day to "do India." Strung about with expensive cameras and exposure meters (none of which they knew how to use), we saw them taking pictures from the benches, they just couldn't spare the effort to stand up. One of the men was writing the caption on a finished roll of film and, turning to his guide, he said, "Say, boy, whadya call this place?"

"Taj Mahal, Sahib."

"Howdya spell that, for heaven's sakes?"

"T-A-J, one word, Sahib, and M-A-H-A-L another word."

Then there was the woman who, looking at the steps leading up to the building, turned to her husband. "No, honey, I guess you'll just have to go it alone; that looks like too many steps for me."

One sadly suspected that they would go away happy in the thought that they could put yet one more tick against the list of 'musts' on their world itinerary, and yet unaware that they had seen something perhaps even more remarkable than the Empire State building. But perhaps I shouldn't be so superior, for one cannot help admiring them for coming at all. Most English people, if they had the means for a world tour, would probably prefer to go to Bournemouth and spend the money on port-and-lemons.

That evening we put Mr Lahiri and the faithful Hariharam on the train; they were going on ahead to prepare another Brooke Bond reception in Allahabad, where we were due two days later. Meanwhile we were to go to Cawnpore and hold a reception on our own, which caused us some embarrassment. Trying to converse politely for three hours with twenty tea-salesmen whom one has never met before was one of the hardest tasks we faced on the whole trip! But we did get some beautiful rose-petal garlands for our pains. Having done our duty, we thought, by our sponsors, we stayed the night in the hotel and sent them the bill.

After a further day in Allahabad we came to Benaras, the Hindu holy city, seething with pilgrims making for the sacred Ganges in which to bathe. No doubt they left with minds exalted and souls purified, but their bodies can hardly have been cleansed by what, sanitarily speaking, must be the most noxious of waters. Brooke Bond arranged a boat for us, in which we made stately progress past the bathing thousands. The air was filled with smoke from the funeral pyres on the banks—the ashes are later cast upon the river. Back on shore we pushed a way between the emaciated bulls which are released to roam the streets in the names of the dead. Then we were taken down a narrow alley where beggars, piteously crippled and distorted, stretched skeletal hands to us for alms. We visited the Monkey Temple, where scores of monkeys picked each other's fur for fleas, and whose droppings made our bare feet walk more delicately than Agag.

Benaras was, as Tim Somewhat irreverently says in his dairy, "*not our* favourite city." I myself would merely add, see Benaras and leave before you die.

⊛

The Brooke Bond tour necessitated driving to a very tight schedule. Fortunately, however, we were travelling down the concrete of the famous Grand Trunk road, and so, by keeping one hand on the horn to warn the bullock-carts, and with brakes and steering adjusted to perfection, we were able to bat along at full speed, thus keeping our numerous appointments. In five successive days we passed through five great cities—Agra, Cawnpore, Allahabad, Benaras, and Patna. Some of these are among the oldest cities in the world; and though it was a tiring itinerary, we certainly would not have missed it.

We arrived in Patna one evening to find the entire local Brooke Bond staff waiting to greet us with garlands, handshakes, tea displays, and a scarlet banner of welcome. The Indian manager lamented that he had been thwarted in his intended *pièce de résistance*—two trained "elly-fants" had been engaged to come and drop garlands over our necks with their trunks. But, as our arrival date had been advanced by a couple of days, it was now found that these special elly-fants (which had to come from some distance) could not run fast enough to reach Patna in time. "After all," said the manager rather sadly, "the Indian Government had an elly-fant for their Bulganin and Khrushchev, so we of Patna branch wanted to have *two* for our expedition." I think we were even more disappointed than he was.

Patna branch certainly pushed the boat out. Literally, too. For we had come to Patna to cross the Ganges on our way to Kathmandu. The Ganges was rather a problem, for there was no road-bridge over this huge and holy river for hundreds of miles up or down-stream. However, with characteristic efficiency, Brooke Bond had arranged a boat; they took us down to see it the next morning. Surely, we said, looking at a diminutive craft tied up to the bank, there must be some mistake—we wanted to take the car across as well. No, they assured us, there was no mistake; that was definitely our boat.

No matter which way we looked at the vessel, we came to the inescapable conclusion that nothing smaller for the carriage of a fully laden car had ever been launched. Loading operations were delayed while I prepared the photographic set-up—this was obviously going to be quite something. When all was ready Nigel inched the car up the creaking bamboo stage, over the side of the boat, and aboard. The vessel settled, and took on an alarming list. However, she was restored to an even keel by carefully reversing the car two inches. With the car thus stationed precisely amidships, the front and rear bumpers were both over the water. The skipper asked us not to move about, as this, he indicated, would upset the delicate trim. As far as we were concerned his request was quite unnecessary.

The crew hoisted a tattered sail, cast off, and away we drifted on the current. The river is about a mile wide at Patna, but, due to the current, our craft was unable to go straight across. In fact, we expected to drift for at least eight miles in the process of finally working over to a landing-place on the opposite bank; the voyage would take five hours. This seemed like being the lengthiest water crossing of the trip; twenty times longer than the Channel—though, admittedly, that had been by air.

All afternoon the sacred Ganga slid slowly by, until, at sunset, the skipper made his landfall at a village on the far bank. If anything, driving off was even more dicey than going aboard, for there was no jetty, only a couple of planks scarcely wider than the tyre. But, once safely ashore, we paid off the crew, and, considering that it would take them the better part of a day to tow the boat back up-stream, walking along the bank, the charge of 55 Rupees (about £4) was not excessive.

$$\circledA$$

All the next day we drove north, through the dust of the plain, through fields of sugar-cane and rice, through little villages and larger towns. By evening we could see a rim of clouds on the horizon, and then low green hills which grew larger as we sped towards them. We camped the night in a petrol depot at Raxaul, and took our supper at the railway station—as is usually best in India.

Early the next morning we crossed into Nepal, and, as instructed by our Embassy, paused in the frontier town of Birgunj to call on the governor. He was a kindly Mongoloid gentleman who carried a silver-mounted walking-stick, and whose Nepali hat was decorated with little white flowers. With almost ceremonial dignity he handed us a pass which, we were most relieved to hear (for, being in Sanskrit, we could not read it), allowed us to film. We thanked the governor profusely—and blessed the Embassy for their efforts.

In high spirits we set off north again. Now the open country was left behind, and the road became a forest track which led up the gentle slope of the Terai—a wild jungle area where live tigers, leopards, boar, wild elephants, and the rare one horned Indian rhino. Gradually the track became steeper; then up the first sharp hairpin bend, through a long tunnel that led under the first low range, along the gorge of a fast white river, across an ochred girder bridge, round a bend, and suddenly, there ahead, was the solid wall of Nepal and the Mahabharat range rising into the clouds. We were right among the mountains.

All morning we motored on up a deep valley, and every moment the scenery became more beautiful. Overhead the clouds piled up and the sky grew grey and overcast; we rolled down our sleeves and pulled on our sweaters. This was the first really clouded sky we'd seen since Europe; if anything, it added to the exhilarating grandeur of the surroundings. By noon we were quite high up, and could see the tremendous damage done to the road in the last monsoon. Great gashes scarred the mountain-sides, and enormous chunks of road had fallen away into the river below. Bands of Nepalis, at work under Sikh army engineers, stepped aside as we threaded between the boulders they were slowly moving. Lying in the river, just below the village of Bhainse, were the rusty remains of a girder bridge which had been swept away the summer before. A new Bailey bridge replaced it.

Bhainse used to be the old road-head. From here, before the aeroplane came, even his Excellency the British Ambassador had to gird up his loins and spend three days puffing over the mountains, while his Humber limousine followed behind on the shoulders of eighty coolies. It was from Bhainse that the new road was being built. For over three years, with money partly supplied from the Colombo Plan, the Indian sappers have been working on it, but it is a very slow task (I write "is," as the road will not be completed until 1958) because, with heartbreaking regularity, whole sections are washed away each summer monsoon and work must start again.

At the beginning of the new road we were halted at a barrier manned by a khaki-turbaned Sikh. We entered the guard-tent and signed the book, which we studied to find out how unique was our passage; we seemed to be the third civilian vehicle to take the road to Kathmandu. On we went, and, if we thought we had seen wonderful scenery before Bhainse, we now thought again. There can be few mountain roads in the world to compare. With a hairpin bend every hundred yards, it winds up and up, in places doubling back on top of itself a dozen times like a squib, in what the sappers call a giant's staircase. So sharp and frequent are the corners that one's speed very rarely rises above 15 m.p.h. We often stopped to take photos, and to look down at the valleys below, and the mountains high ahead. Sometimes we caught glimpses of a white scar made by the road along the mountainside thousands of feet above; an hour later we would find ourselves looking down from that same scar upon the fantastic contortions of the thin yellow ribbon which had led us there. Winding and twisting, it flung itself along narrow ledges, up spurs, across green valleys, and always it was climbing. Occasionally there were Nepali villages clinging to their ridges, their narrow terraces of crops hanging steeply above and below like hundreds of tiny steps. Once we heard a plane, and, looking down, could see a Dakota flying up a valley on its way to Kathmandu.

We were delayed for two hours by road-building operations, while a dozen Army trucks discharged rubble to make an embankment. The labourers were Nepalis who, in small black flower-pot hats and check-cotton trousers, looked like busy little gnomes. The Sikh sappers who were overseeing the work chatted about their work and gave us each a wet of char; Army tea tastes the same the whole world over—sticky, lukewarm, and delicious. While talking shop with these amusing chaps we noticed that we had driven exactly 12,000 miles from Westminster Bridge. So, during the delay, we borrowed some stones and built a roadside cairn to mark the spot. Then, at last, the road was clear and we could go on.

It had grown cold and dark by the time the road reached into the clouds. Whenever the way levelled out at all we were sure that we had reached the top; but no—on and on, up and up. The trees became knotted and gnarled, with beard-like bunches of moss hanging from their trunks and branches. The road became slippery with the heavy mist, and then, very gently, it began to snow.

Finally, just when jokes about abominable snowmen and oxygen masks were becoming rather repetitive, we came to an Army signpost and stopped to read it in the head-lights. "Simbhanjang Pass, 8162.91 feet" it announced with military precision, and beneath was some sapper poet's amusing effort:

> We are told the plane flies lower,
>> Across the rugged Mahabharat range,
> But to have one's feet on terra firma,
>> This height now gained is not so strange.

We estimated that there were still some forty miles to go, and, rather than spend the night in the snow, we went on. The road had been climbing so long that, now it was over the top, it seemed reluctant to go down; it fell only slowly, and appeared to climb again almost as much. As the car crawled round each successive bend the searchlight beam swung over the edge and flashed out into the night. There was nothing to stop us going over the edge, which might have been thousands of feet below for all we knew. In fact, as we were later told, it was.

Once, on a particularly narrow section, there was a small landslide which we had to clear before going on. But gradually the road made up its mind, and the descent became continuous. Odd lights from sapper camps or Nepali villages swung vaguely in the darkness like uncertain stars; so constantly were we turning, always spinning the wheel hard over one way or the other, that we lost all sense of direction and just followed the never-ending curves as they slowly unwound in the swinging beams of the head-lights. Then, though it was quite dark, we were conscious of being in a deep valley. An hour or two later a barrier appeared ahead and a soldier, shivering in his overcoat, came forward to examine our pass. He swung the gate open and told us that there were only another ten miles to Kathmandu. We were rather excited.

The road levelled out and, almost before we knew it, we were running between low stone walls, temples, and half-timbered houses. The streets were empty, there were no lights, the houses were shuttered and still; we might have come to a deserted city. This was hardly surprising, for, as we later learnt, there has been a curfew in Kathmandu for the past two hundred years. It was mainly by intuition that we eventually found the British Embassy on the farther outskirts; no lights showed, and a dozing sentry told us that His Excellency had already long gone to bed. We were preparing to put our beds down on the office veranda when the Second Secretary, hearing our motor, hove up, rather surprised at our arrival. We had been given up for the night, and, due to the curfew, every one was in the habit of going to sleep early.

A room had been booked for us at the little Snowview Hotel, and, being led to our room, we wondered how the expense would later be justified to the Business Manager; it had always been agreed that hotels should be avoided, but we could hardly cancel the booking and start looking for a camp-site at that late hour.

Next morning we turned up at the Embassy to pay our respects, and to thank every one for the trouble they had taken on our behalf. Colonel Proud, the First Secretary, immediately invited us to stay in his bungalow, and would hear nothing more about camping. We moved in right away, and a magnificent host he was. Sitting round a warm log-fire in the evenings, sipping hot rum toddy, listening to his records, and sleeping under thick eiderdowns—these are among the pleasantest recollections of the trip. The Embassy is a compact little unit, just the Ambassador and his wife, the two Secretaries, the wireless operator, and some bearers. The bearers, known as *chaprassis,* were magnificent men in brown uniform with wide red stripes, little pill-box hats, and enormous buckles on their belts bearing the royal arms.

Apart from the satisfaction of having reached Kathmandu, the main purpose was photographic, and, from this point of view, if no other, our four days there—all too short—were among the highlights of the whole journey. I could cheerfully have stayed there many months. From the many-templed streets of Kathmandu one looks up to the surrounding Himalayan snows, to thirteen peaks of over 18,000 feet. Just outside the town one can climb a rhododendroned hill and, on a clear day, look north to Tibet, only forty miles away, or east, one hundred and eighty miles across the white roof of the world (I can't resist the cliché), to an insignificant speck—Everest.

In four days we did not have time to wander from the valley, but here, in one hour, I could focus my cameras on a whole mass of colour, on the saffron robes of the Buddhist monks, on the patchwork coats of the mountain folk, on the brass earrings and yellow beads of the women, on the small Mongoloid Gurkhas who, when trained, are perhaps the toughest soldiers in the world. We saw Tibetan pilgrims shuffling past in long cloth boots and leggings, but very thinly clad otherwise. Apparently these Tibetan folk find Kathmandu's climate, even in December, unbearably hot after their own 13,000-foot plateau. In the sunny but frosty air we were warmly clad in sweaters, but these Tibetans puffed and panted as if in the last stages of heat-exhaustion.

In Kathmandu there is none of the squalor or grinding poverty of India. The buildings are picturesque, the weather perfect; and the people colourful, cheerful, and almost falling over themselves to be friendly. In the squares traders squat with their trinkets spread about them on the steps of the temples, and children and grown-ups alike take turns on swings made of tall bamboos tied in pyramids. There is no industry, no rush, no neon signs, no cinemas. Time is quite unimportant, and, though Nepal is one of the most backward countries in Asia, one cannot help hoping that it stays that way. Already, however, well-intentioned advisers are flying in by almost every plane with plans for Nepal's economic advancement; one recognizes that there may be much material justification for these plans, but one wonders whether these easy-going people will not lose immeasurably more than they will gain in the sudden acceleration to the nowhere-in-particular which the Western world so fondly calls progress? Why not leave the backward, poor, illiterate, happy people of Nepal alone? A reactionary philosophy, perhaps, but not, I hope, a trite one.

One morning I went down to the river, where there was a bustle of activity. There was an eclipse of the sun later that day, and it was obviously a propitious time for taking a bath. Mothers were washing themselves and their babies, old men were wading about splashing each other, and children scrubbed their water-buffaloes with handfuls of grass. Lengths of cloth billowed from the bridge to bleach, or were spread on the banks to dry after being hand-blocked. Strung about with four cameras and spare lenses, pockets bulging with films, filters, and the other paraphernalia of my trade, this bearded tramp was followed by an enthusiastic crowd of small boys like a Pied Piper. Everybody was most anxious to help, and once, after I tried to photograph a baby who had promptly burst into tears, the baby's older sister later sought me out and anxiously led me back to her charge, whom she had now coaxed into a happier frame of mind. His Excellency invited us to the Embassy several times; what a character he turned out to be. We decided that Mr Boyd Tollinton ("Tollers" to us behind his back) was the very essence of what a British Ambassador to Nepal should be; with an enormous sense of fun, he and his wife provided us with a number of tales which became part of the Expedition's standing jolk-lore. While the three of us "met the Press" (a rather euphemistic description) at a cocktail party, Mrs Tollinton, with practised diplomacy, buttonholed the more staid guests in earnest conversation while Tollers entertained the lighter-hearted with his anecdotes.

The 'Press' were, in fact, three or four Indians; representatives of newspapers and agencies in India, and no different from the other journalists whom we had already met in Delhi and elsewhere. The average Indian (if one may use the rather meaningless phrase) is very self-conscious about his country, and he takes pleasure in hearing its praises sung. He is also very much concerned about Pakistan, a neighbouring and rival country which he views with a hostility amounting almost to a mania at times. Consequently, as we had been in Pakistan, we were always being asked how it compared with India—surely we had not liked it, and surely it was a very second-rate nation? At first we laughed and changed the subject, but this pathological interest of the Indians in what we had thought of Pakistan became very tiring. It was in Kathmandu, then, talking to these journalists, that our mantle of tact fell away and we told our questioners a thing or two. Let me quote from Tim's diary:

. . . same old questions. I had had enough and gave them a few home truths. India, I pointed out, was mad keen to be the world's guiding influence, the uncommitted nation of peace, the moralizer and the country which so often told the West what to do and how to do it. One bright Indian M.P. had even piously advocated that the cessation of H-bomb manufacture should be unilateral as far as the West was concerned; set a sincere example to Russia, he said, and world peace and goodwill would inevitably follow. (This suggestion had been much hailed in India's Press.) Yes, the journalists agreed, that was India's line—to be the great mediating force. Then why, I asked, was India herself spending so much on armaments? To contain a belligerent Pakistan, they said. But wouldn't it be a good idea, I suggested, if India disarmed, and so set Pakistan the very example of trust that she was advocating the West should set in the case of Russia? Oh, yes, they agreed, but in India's case the situation was different, because Pakistan was arming too. Oh, yes, I also agreed, and so was Russia. It is one of the stranger facets of the Indian mind that things are so often 'different' when applied to themselves.

Nigel and I spent a couple of afternoons wandering about the Kathmandu valley outside the town itself, while Tim got down to writing articles and the diary—which already ran to 100,000 words. We visited Bhatgaon, which, though only eight miles from Kathmandu, was once the capital of a separate kingdom. On this particular day most of the population had gone off to Kathmandu on a shopping excursion, leaving behind only the old and infirm. Practically every building was of interest, with intricately carved teak beams under the eaves and windows. Temples were everywhere—very Chinese in appearance, with three or four roofs in tiers, and many fierce statues of wrestlers, elephants, and various mythical creatures guarding the entrances against the evil spirits. As we drove back through the fields we passed the peasants streaming home from the capital in their best clothes, with babies and shopping tied to their backs. We also passed a knot of Tibetan pilgrims who, having only just stepped down from the 15,000-foot passes leading through the Himalayas from their own country, had never seen a car—and ran for their lives when they saw ours.

On the last morning a Nepali with whom we had become friends honoured each of us with garlands of tiny Himalayan daffodils, a Nepali hat, and a kukri—the curved knife of the Gurkha tribes, sharp enough to split open a tin in one swipe. But, despite these happy mementoes, leaving Nepal was sad; how gladly we would go back—even on foot! However, we had work to do in Calcutta, and could spare no longer. The return journey over the mountains was even more eventful than the ascent, for we were delayed by a landslide, a stalled bulldozer, and rain, which made the surface of the road suicidally greasy. Finally, we came round a corner to find an Army truck hanging over an embankment and completely blocking the road. The sappers took three hours to jack it up and haul it clear, by which time it was dark. As we had stopped often to film, there was still another eighty miles to go to Raxaul—which we eventually reached at three o'clock in the morning, very weary indeed.

The next day we were motoring south through the glare and heat of the Indian plain once more until, at sunset, we reached the Ganges and recrossed it back to Patna. One of the boatmen, who could not understand a single syllable of English, amazed us with his word perfect recitations (or so we assumed!) from Shakespeare, Milton, Darwin, and the Bible! He had a repertoire of sermons too, which, together with his other pieces, he had evidently learnt parrotwise from his erstwhile master, an English padre-sahib. He had not a trace of an accent, and one can only assume that the padre must have been very fond of repeating himself.

Thirty-six hours later, after a fast run down the Grand Trunk Road, we rolled across the massive Howrah bridge spanning the Hooghly, and into Calcutta.

Calcutta was our half-way house, and, before continuing on to the east we were to spend ten days there over Christmas. Brooke Bond kindly allowed us to use part of the top floor in their office block as a billet, and, in the three days before Cambridge arrived from Pakistan, we relaxed and enjoyed ourselves in the company of numerous generous hosts. Cambridge arrived on Christmas Eve after a hectic two-day dash from Delhi, where they had picked up Adrian on their way through from the Punjab. The Expedition was now together again, and as usual there was quite a lot to talk about. Before we all started to make serious preparations for Burma we celebrated Christmas. Brooke Bond, whose interest in us had become distinctly avuncular by this time, gave us a magnificent Christmas dinner with all the trimmings, including holly and paper hats.

Then, on Boxing Day, we got down to the business of the next leg—which is where Tim takes over the story once more.

9

For a Variety of Reasons

LONDON to Calcutta is a long way—for us, nearly thirteen thousand miles. But the journey had been made many times before, and it will be made many times again. Provided that one has a car in reasonable repair, and that one plans with common sense, there are no great difficulties. At Calcutta, however, the long road ends and one must take a ship to Singapore, to Australia, or to wherever else may be one's final destination. True, a few people had endeavoured to drive on by land, but, for a variety of reasons, they had given up and turned back. Physical barriers, political difficulties, and sheer lack of information—for a variety of reasons.

Between India and Burma lie the Naga, Lushai, and Arakan Ranges. These jungle-covered offshoots of the Himalayas are drenched in the heaviest rainfall on earth, and, though much lower than their parent chain, they form one of the world's great natural barriers. Their sharp ridges and deep valleys run from the Himalayan borders of China for six hundred miles south to the Bay of Bengal. No permanent road has ever crossed them, nor by land is there any way around. The people and tribes on either side, separated on the map by a mere two hundred miles, have a different religion, a different culture, and a totally different history.

But the last war showed that there are no impassable mountains, and, as Wingate ordered, "no jungles shall be reported impenetrable until they have been penetrated." In the urgency of war, and at fantastic cost, two fighting roads were hacked and blasted through those ranges. The Indian and British Fourteenth Army built one from Imphal to Tamu and thence, across the Chindwin by the longest floating Bailey Bridge of the War, to the plains of Mandalay. The other road was pushed through much farther north, from a village called Ledo in the far corner of Assam. This road, built by the Americans and Chinese under the legendary General "Vinegar Joe" Stilwell, was constructed in one hectic year immediately behind the advance. Its 270 miles cost the United States Treasury 137 million dollars, and it ranked as one of the War's outstanding—though unsung—engineering achievements.

For a few short months in 1944 thousands of trucks rumbled through the hills carrying in troops and supplies against the finally retreating Japanese. But, with eventual victory and the Japanese defeated, the strategic need for these hard-won supply lines was gone. The men who engineered them returned to Britain and America. Their roads returned to the jungle. Since that time—we had been told in letters, in libraries, in London clubs, and now even in Calcutta offices and bars—the roads had been unused.

"Frankly," they said, "we can't help you. We don't know anything about either road."

Prior to arriving in Calcutta most of our collected information was negative. It seemed that under the encroaching jungle the abandoned roads would not have lasted long; their embankments and once graded surfaces would have been washed away by ten years of monsoon rainfall; the latest maps of the region were made in 1944, and told us where there had been bridges—once. Furthermore, the recent earthquakes in Assam might have disrupted what little there was left. But all our informants were speaking from supposition and not from actual facts. We at least should be able to go and see for ourselves.

Besides this major physical problem there were political difficulties too. There were three of these; they were like the vital pieces needed to complete a jigsaw puzzle. Fortunately, by the time we reached Calcutta we already held two of those pieces. First, we had permission from the Burmese Government to enter their country by land on condition that, if successful, we reported to the Army commander on arrival in the first Burmese town. Second, the Foreign Office in Whitehall had approved our plans. This latter was more complicated than one might suppose, for normally, if the F.O. thinks that British subjects are entering an area where their welfare cannot be adequately guaranteed (either by itself or by the Government of the country concerned), it is reasonably inclined to deny permission to proceed. However, we were going to be allowed to enter Burma through an uncontrolled frontier, albeit "at the Expedition's own risk." But the third and last piece in the political jigsaw was unexpectedly difficult. For, while we had permission to enter Burma, we had not as yet permission to leave India.

Our intended route out of India would run for a few miles immediately inside the border, through an area known as the North-East

Frontier Agency. In some ways it is the jungle equivalent of the famous North-West Frontier; it is a tribal area, and one of strategic significance. For a few years past some of the Naga tribesmen have been making an unsophisticated claim for their own independent state—led by a gentleman with the likely name of Mr Fizo. Independence is a world-wide fashion these days, and Mr Nehru, India's premier, is its international champion. Naturally, then, he is anxious that any such claims for independence (no matter how insignificant) as exist within India's own frontiers should not receive undue publicity. It could be awkward for him, while preaching to the rest of the world about 'sovereign rights' and 'self-determination,' if some one should point out that there existed a mote in his own eye. Of course, the Nagas are a very simple people, and could not begin to rule themselves, and neither is the movement widespread through the tribes; it is nothing more than the demands of a few dissatisfied groups. But, nevertheless, the problem could be embarrassing to the Indian Government if misconstrued, and therefore official policy has thrown a blanket over the North-East Frontier.

The British High Commission in Delhi had even pessimistically said that there was no point in even making an application to pass through the area. However, Adrian spent a week camping on the doorsteps of the relevant Government departments in Delhi, and had eventually extracted a promise that our wish would be "given consideration." This was hopeful. But the final word lay in Shillong, the capital of Assam, where lived the Commissioner for the North-East Frontier. Knowing that Bulganin and Khrushchev had not been allowed to visit the area, we could only hope the authorities would realize that we were rather lesser fry, and not the least concerned with the political aspirations of Mr Fizo and his friends. In Calcutta, then, we had to work on the assumption that permission would be granted—though we still had to call at Shillong on our way through Assam to find out. If the all-powerful Commissioner was doubtful we could at least lay our plea before him personally.

As we reviewed the facts in Calcutta, some looked gloomy and others good. Certainly there seemed a much better chance of 'forcing' one of the roads into Burma than we had thought on leaving England. (As I pointed out much earlier, we had always assumed that the difficulties would grow less as we approached them.) We now had odd pieces of information, whereas before we had had none. The Indian Government had told us that both the war-time roads ran through the jungle as far as the Burmese frontier; beyond that they did not know. There was also reassuring news contained in a letter from the British Embassy in Rangoon. "Three years ago," it said, "the Imphal-Tamu road was just motorable in a four-wheel-drive vehicle," but that, once into Burma, it now petered out in an area controlled by rebels. On the other hand, the letter continued, the Stilwell Road which in 1944 ran from Ledo, in Assam, for 270 miles into Burma was "known to be motorable for the last 80 miles of its length from the Burmese end"—from the town of Myitkyina. We referred this information to the map. If at the Indian end the Stilwell Road was 'navigable' for the first 40 miles to the frontier, and if at the other end in Burma it was open for the last 80 miles, then there was an unknown gap of only 150 miles. This doubtful section was through the worst of the steep and sodden Naga Hills. But if we could cross that gap we would eventually reach Myitkyina and there pick up a known road to the south. We decided to try the Stilwell Road in preference to the other one from Imphal—we had no wish to enter the rebel area.

Looking back on it, our planning in Calcutta for Burma was disturbingly reminiscent of that for a small-scale military operation. We were determined to cater for all the foreseeable possibilities; enough would have to be left to chance anyway. The cars were taken away to the Rover garage for a thorough overhaul, and we also set about lightening their load. There was much argument about this. Some one thought tins of vegetable salad were "useless" and another thought sardines were even more useless. Some talked glibly of "travelling light from now on" and "ditching all this rubbish"—pointing at a huge pile of what some one else deemed "essential equipment." There was also the question of leaving a good deal of our personal clothing behind. Various scales of shirts and trousers per man were suggested, but some of the Expedition rebelled against this "regimentation" and "military-kit-schedule-nonsense." After discussion we decided to leave one of the typewriters behind; though it nearly broke Adrian's heart. As B.B. said, when told of this drastic step, "We must be getting really operational." But the biggest struggle was when we tried to persuade Adrian to leave behind his "Busyness Box." After two days' cajoling he compromised by transferring all the most important carbons and papers to a single, though voluminous, cardboard folder. He assured us that it only contained those documents which were absolutely basic to the continuance of the Expedition, and it became known as the "Assault File." B.B. went through our over-complete medical kit and discarded all those items which were unnecessary or duplicated. Despite Pat's protests of "What will I sit on when cooking?" we dumped the two folding chairs, together with various pots and pans, buckets, and washing-up bowls. Each person eventually agreed to cut his own clothing by half.

"One shirt or two?"

"What about a tie? Better take one—never know about these rebels; probably Balliol or Trinity men, and sure to ask us to dinner."

"Well, I don't know about anyone else, but I can't manage on only three pairs of socks. I'm taking the lot."

The cars' tyres were inspected by Dunlop's; they had naturally suffered some wear. But, though the company offered to fit a new set, we wished to try the entire journey to Singapore with the original set on which the cars had left London. Pat, as Navigator, called on Mobilgas to arrange about some town in Assam—as near the Burmese border as possible— where we could take on a final petrol fill-up. The American manager suggested that, in addition to carrying one hundred gallons between the cars, we might also take an old aircraft belly-tank strapped to the roof-rack.

"Yep, you can get 'most anything you want up in Assam—there's everything from spare belly-tanks to Curtis aero engines lying around."

Pat said that he did not think we should really have room for a belly-tank.

"Maybe not a belly-tank, but, brother," said the boss, "where you boys are going you'll need an aero engine all right."

Evidently he did not think much of our chances.

People who called round to view our preparations may not have thought much of our chances, but they wished us well, and all seemed agreed that we were preparing for the worst. In addition to the winch, the fifty-gallon tanks, the heavy-duty springs, the oversize tyres, the searchlights, and the jerry-cans, which were part of our normal equipment, we now took aboard a whole new array of ironmongery. Nigel had scrounged about in Calcutta for these tools to deal with the difficulties of the jungle road and unbridged rivers—sledge-hammers, crowbars, a spare spring, picks and shovels, a block and tackle, a four-ton hydraulic jack, ropes, axes, machetes, two hundred yards of telephone wire, three weeks' supply of food, two crates of beer, and seven pounds of six-inch nails. If necessary, it seemed, we were prepared to build our own road! Certainly no one could suggest to us, as they had before we left England, that we were "going rock climbing in sandals."

Throughout the Expedition there were many arguments. We had no leader, and therefore almost everything had to be thrashed out between the six of us. These round-table soviets could become tiresome, but, while each person was bound to be incompatible with the rest some of the time, trouble only really arose when everybody decided to be incompatible with everybody else simultaneously! People could suddenly become extraordinarily 'bloody-minded' about nothing at all—and least of all was I an exception. But, fortunately, these occasions were rare, and though there were often strong disagreements on small and unimportant things (but how vital they seemed at the time) we invariably managed to discuss matters of 'policy' fairly calmly. In Calcutta, for example, we had to decide if we should carry firearms for Burma.

There were (and still are) in Burma a large number of political rebels and terrorists. They come in all sizes and political hues. Some are conventional Red Communists, and others are the rarer White Communists; some are 'for the workers' and others for themselves; some are motivated by more or less genuine political aspirations; and others are simply armed dacoits. Some are quite gentlemanly in their proceedings, and blow up the occasional railway bridge to provide rebuilding employment during the slack periods for villagers (and themselves). Others murder and ambush civilians as well as waging a series of bitter small-scale wars against the authorities. The arguments in favour of carrying weapons for self-defence were obvious but doubtful. I for one knew from slight experience as a National Serviceman in Malaya that insurgents do not normally attack unless they are fairly certain of winning the encounter. While, then, we might possibly give some account of ourselves if attacked, we were unlikely to come out on top in the end. Secondly, one of the things that insurgents always require is a supply of arms and ammunition. If they know that a small body is carrying weapons, then added temptation and incentive for ambush is merely laid before them. Thirdly, in the eyes of an otherwise genial dacoit a weapon of defence can be very easily mistaken for one of offence, and he may be inclined to shoot rather than follow his original intention of mere peaceful robbery. Therefore, we decided it was much safer to remain unarmed.

Practically everything we did in Calcutta was justified on the grounds that it was being done 'For Burma.' Nigel took the three machete knives and had them sharpened to a murderous edge—"for cutting a way through the jungle." Henry sat for hours poring over a Rover Workshop Manual—"I'm clueing up on the cars in case they go wrong." B.B. had the tape-recorder overhauled—"so we can get some tapes of the rebel chieftain and then play them back to him; he should like that!" Pat made an hour's recording from a friend's radiogram of South Pacific and Swan Lake—"good jungle-camping music." I bought a new 300-page diary—"If everything happens that could happen I'm going to need it." Adrian had a special bush-jacket made to his own unique specifications; it was a cross between a maternity coat and a hacking jacket with a single vent up the back so large that it could only have been designed for riding a camel. Finally, all six of us were given some more injections as 'boosters' to the ones we had had before leaving England. These included one against Bubonic Plague, which, to quote the Expedition, was "an absolute killer"—we referred to the injection rather than to the Plague. For two days afterwards we felt thoroughly ill, and wandered about as if we had been poleaxed.

I have explained the decision to try the Stilwell Road into Burma, starting from Ledo, in the farthest corner of Assam. But we had to get to Ledo first, and it is one thousand miles from Calcutta. It had always been assumed that this part of the journey would present no problems. But normal people do not motor to Assam. As they frequently told us, "We fly." The reason for flying soon became apparent when we tried to work out a route. Beyond Calcutta begin the many-rivered lowlands of Bengal. At least twelve of the rivers have no bridges. Instead they have ancient and irregular ferries. But even the roads between the ferries are uncertain, for, due to frequent monsoon flooding, their dirt surfaces break up and become unusable. Consequently, there are often long detours and diversions. One must know of these in advance, otherwise one can spend days of dismal privation motoring about the bleak rice-lands of Bengal looking for a ferry. The Automobile Association of Bengal, whom we supposed would know the answers, were no help at all.

"Well, you see, one used to go this way, but we had bad floods last year, and now we've had more again this year. So it's all different; everything has been changed."

In Assam too the swollen tributaries of the Brahmaputra are quite likely to swamp a road out of action for months on end. In short, no one seemed to know how we might get north across Bengal and into Assam except by air. But eventually we found help from the unlikely source of the pharmaceutical firm of May & Baker. They had 'a man' up in Assam, and cabled him for information. A detailed reply arrived back the next day; without its recent and accurate data of roads and ferries we might be asking people in Calcutta yet.

The Oxford car was overhauled and ready some days before the Cambridge one. (It was our habit not to allow both cars into a garage simultaneously, as this would have left the Expedition without the convenience of either car for our many errands.) Also, Pat and Henry were still busy writing a preliminary report on the Thal field-work to post to the Royal Geographical Society before leaving for Burma. We in Oxford, therefore, prepared to leave Calcutta a couple of days in advance of the others. Our 'instructions' were to go north to Siliguri, at the foot of the Himalayas, and turn east into Assam. We then had to cross the Brahmaputra and motor up to Shillong, the hill capital of Assam, in order to collect the all-important sanction for the Expedition to make its exit from India through the prohibited North-East Frontier. With this safely obtained (we hoped), we were to go on to a Brooke Bond tea estate, where we had all been invited to stay a few days. The other car would meet us at the estate.

THE ROUTE FROM CALCUTTA TO SINGAPORE

10.

One Thousand ·Miles

THE Oxford crew got up at six o'clock determined, as usual, to be well on the way before the heat of the day. After a busy morning we moved off—also as usual—in the early afternoon. Whenever the Expedition got lost it was invariably in a town, and now for nearly two hours we motored back and forth through the crowded northern suburbs of Calcutta (or 'congested areas' as such built-up regions with a 30 m.p.h. limit are aptly and officially known in India). But at last, by literally taking a rough bearing from the sun, we came out into open country. Calcutta had always been regarded as the end of the trans-Indian-subcontinent part of the journey, and the start of the trans-South-east-Asian stage. After ten days in the city it was almost a relief to be back on the road again. In some ways the Expedition now really began.

The drive that afternoon and evening lay across some of the most featureless country imaginable; mile upon mile of mud-brown, treeless rice-fields which now, in the dry season, were baked and cracking in the sharp sun. We came to the first Ghat (river bank) at dusk. The road ran down to a rough staging. We drove aboard a barge (really an advanced form of raft), drifted for a minute or two across to the opposite bank, rolled down a couple of wooden planks, and drove away once more. In the first two hours of darkness, before we stopped, this same manœuvre was repeated five times.

We were woken from our roadside camp before dawn by the low moaning of the bullock carts as they passed along the road towards the work of the breaking day. If any of the many sounds of India still linger in my mind (besides the altogether unearthly one of a betel-chewing Bengali clearing his throat) it is that of her bullock carts. Theirs is a softly tortured, unreasoned, distracted sound of wood worrying wood, unlubricated. It is melancholia itself, yet fascinating. It winds up from every *kacha* (dirt) road over the whole huge span of the country, and I should know it again if I did not hear it for another thirty years!

Foregoing breakfast in an attempt to catch the first ferry across the Ganges, we were packed and off in a few minutes.

But on arrival at the Ghat the ferry had just gone, and, as the Ganges is a wide river and the opposite landing was some miles upstream, the next scheduled crossing did not leave for four hours. So we waited on the bank, ate a slow breakfast, dozed and talked drowsily about "the whole business"—that was the way the Expedition usually referred to itself, its past, and its future. We reminded each other of the van we had met in Zagreb, and pondered where it might have got to now; of the Persian Army trials; of the field-work; and Mr Khan at the Pakistan frontier. We chatted about Kathmandu, Burma, and where we might be in six months' time ("probably back in Persia"). Then, completely fancy-free, I wondered what time would be best to arrive back in London. But I was cut curtly short. "Let's get to Singapore first," said B.B. Sometimes he could be quite unimaginative! But perhaps not; he was looking thoughtfully at the map, and presently came out with an idea.

"Look, Darjeeling is only forty miles on from Siliguri; we could drive up there for just one quick day. It would be a pity to miss it when we are so close. Probably never get another chance."

We all looked at the map, though, I think, B.B. had already made up our minds. We could reach Siliguri that night if we hurried, and then go up the mountain road to the Himalayan town of Darjeeling the next day. Nigel was completely sold on the diversion. He had done some occasional rock-scrambling in North Wales, and this seemed to entitle him to an almost proprietary interest in the Himalayas.

"Why not to-night?" he asked. "It's only 250 miles, so we can't get there till pretty late, but it's New Year's Eve and there's bound to be a party at the tea-planters' club. We could probably crash it— be the First Strangers over the threshold after midnight!"

Well, we could try.

The ferry, a little landing-craft, arrived back at noon. We drove up her lowered ramp and aboard. Much too slowly, she chugged up-stream, barely able to hold her own against the current. Impatiently I went below to offer the engine-wallah some cigarettes as an inducement to squeeze a little more out of his clattering engine. He took the cigarettes and shrugged, "Already she is go bang-bang. Please, no more faster, sahib." He opened the throttle to the full by way of proof, and I had to agree that if the thumping and bang-banging continued like that for long the engine would probably rock through the bottom of the ship.

"All right, Charlie, you win. Like before."

The journey took over two hours, and when in the end we nosed against the farther bank the crew made such an elaborate fuss of lowering the ramp that they got it stuck half-way. But eventually we drove off, and at full speed left behind the muddy banks of the Holy Ganga.

"If we're to get to Darjeeling to-night we'll have to steam."

The rutted road ran through the hot dust of the rice-plains all afternoon. In our hurry the way seemed diseased with stagnant streams and rivers, each with its own slow barge. Once, half-way across, the barge wallah stopped pushing on his pole and demanded more money for his trouble. We had already paid the fixed charge, together with a handsome tip (apparently, this was the error, for it indicated our affluence), so, without argument, we ourselves picked up the pole and pushed. Our average speed to the north was very slow, we were tired, and none of us was yet really recovered from the effects of the recent injections in Calcutta. Afterwards I was driving and the others were asleep when, long after dark, we stopped at a level-crossing behind a jeep I had been tailing for some miles. Waiting for the train to pass, I switched on the interior light and looked at the map. We could not possibly reach Darjeeling until the early hours of the morning. What was the point? Anyway, no one had the energy to concentrate for two hours' drive up a twisting mountain road. I got out and walked up to the jeep in front. The driver was an Indian dressed in European clothes, and I asked him how far it was to the railway station at Siliguri. He looked at me as if I was drunk.

"It is five miles more, but"—looking at his watch—"there will not now be any trains."

I explained that we wanted to put down our beds in the station restaurant (which we had done before) and then go on to Darjeeling the next day.

"But if you are planters why not stay at the Siliguri Club?"

I told him that we were not, as he thought, planters but—well, I forget exactly how I put it.

"Oh, yes. That Expedition; you are going Singapore-side. I have heard in the paper. Look, why not stop with me at my bungalow? The estate is not far—will you follow?"

I thanked him sincerely. A little later we drove through the gates of the estate, and, on getting out, compared our watches. They all varied, but we reckoned the old year had gone, and celebrated the coming of the new one with a supper of boiled eggs and tea round the table of our hospitable friend. Then he showed us to a room where we slept, undisturbed, until late the next morning.

It was a wonderful drive up to Darjeeling; ahead were the steep green hillls, and away behind, stretching into the horizon, were the yellow plains over which we had so tediously come the day before. Not only was there a contrast in the scenery but in the people too. These looked happy people, much better fed and clothed than the poor, lean peasants of Bengal. Once we had to pull into the side—although up-traffic had priority—to allow a gay convoy of a dozen highly coloured buses to come by. They were decked out in flags and bunting, and in the leading bus was a gramophone and loudspeaker going full blast. Heads were leaning out of every window, and we were given a wave and a cheer as the cavalcade went rattling by. We concluded that this might be some local form of Sunday School treat—it was, in fact, a Sunday.

As it climbed into the Himalayas, the road wriggled along beside the narrow-gauge tracks of the Darjeeling Railway. This is a famous line, for it is one of the steepest in the world. We came upon one of the trains standing in a wayside station; it was a magnificently fairy-tale affair. The little engine—not much bigger than our car—had been made in England fifty years ago, and was embroidered with solid Edwardian brass filigree, all highly polished. On each front buffer sat a woolly-capped and gnome-like gentleman with a box of sand. Theirs (there were two of them) was the duty of pouring fistfuls of sand on to the lines when the way got particularly steep, and the engine's wheels started to slip. Next in the picturesque crew was a man who sat in a box of coal astride the boiler hammering the lumps to a more reasonable size for the engine's consumption. He handed them to the fireman behind, who popped them in the fire-box. The fifth and final person on or around the engine was the driver; this was obviously a position of great prestige, for his name was painted on the side of his engine for all to see. To complete the Emett-like character of the ensemble, the crew wrapped their sandwich lunches in bright bandanas, and kept them inside the capacious brass head-light. The engine did other things beside pulling five miniature coaches up to 7000 feet. It was a mobile—though unofficial—hot-water supply for the villagers along the line. By presenting the driver with a bunch of swedes or carrots they could obtain a bucket of water for the weekly wash, piping hot and straight from the boiler. We saw one woman give the driver a hen, which was, we supposed, a sort of season ticket for this remarkable facility. The Darjeeling Railway is obviously unique in several respects besides its steepness!

On top of the last two coaches were the remaining members of the crew: the brakemen. In long overcoats and fur hats, they sat cross-legged on the roof waiting to wind on the brakes as required. Sometimes, on an especially steep climb, the engine got slower and slower, until finally it ran out of puff altogether. When this happened the brakemen would furiously wind their handles to prevent the whole train running back downhill. Thus secure, the passengers and crew disembarked to have a quick smoke while the exhausted engine regained its breath. The coal-hammerer and fireman, of course, remained aboard. The former bashed coal with a vengeance, and the latter peered at his fire, heaping curses on (one assumed) his swede-and-carrot-hoarding driver. After a few minutes the brass whistle gave a melodious squeak, indicating that the engine was prepared to try again, and everybody climbed aboard. A slowly quickening series of black pants puffed from the funnel, and the train was on its way once more.

But, though it may spoil the tale, I must not imply that such incidents are completely standard or normal procedure. Picturesque it all may be, but at the same time it is surprisingly efficient. The thirty or forty trains snorting up and down the line each day keep to a remarkably accurate schedule, and in the course of the last fifty years they must have hauled many millions of tons to or from Darjeeling.

In order to gain height quickly, the line resorts to several interesting manoeuvres. Sometimes the train rushes obliquely up a slope until it can go no farther. Here it pauses momentarily while some points are switched behind, and then, with the engine pushing, in reverse it starts rolling down towards them. Now, with its downward impetus added to its own power, it gains enough speed to rattle across the points and up the next line to a point a little higher than it reached before. By repeating this zigzag it can climb the hills quite fast. In several other places the line loops round over itself. Here it would be possible for the driver, as he passed above, to spit in the eye of the rear brakeman as the end of the train passed underneath—if he wanted to, and if the train were long enough.

The road and railway run side by side all the way up to Darjeeling. In fact, there are 130 level-crossings in forty miles. Of course, there are no gates, and one must be careful when motoring lest, on rounding a blind corner, one is confronted by a hurtling train and swept off the edge. Unfortunately, this has happened many times, and, as the fall is usually for hundreds of feet, it has been fatal.

After two hours of steady ascent we crossed over the highest point on the road and paused to pull on our sweaters; with the altitude, it was sharply cooler. Then on, down the relatively gentle slope to Darjeeling. A few miles before the town we came round the side of a hill; we slowed to a stop. All eyes—including the driver's—were on the sight ahead. No, not a hurtling train, but sixty miles away, rising in a series of snow-covered peaks and spurs to the clear, unclouded top—Kanchenjunga, the third highest mountain in the world. If we had turned back to the plains there and then, I should probably have said that the diversion had been worth it. Mountains, I have always thought as a non-mountaineer, are rather disappointing. From the valley below the one you want to see is usually obscured by cloud, and when this is not so there are other nearer, lesser peaks in the way. But not Kanchenjunga. From where we stood, high up, we could look out over the dark-blue intervening hills and see even the mountain's massive base rooted in the clouds and smoky mists beneath. And farther to the west were the peaks of the Three Sisters, and, farther still was the tiny summit of Makalu. Behind Makalu, we knew, was Everest.

But Kanchenjunga was supreme. It was so far away and yet so clear that one had no sense of scale. I remember thinking that it did not look all that difficult to climb; surely one went up that spur, along that ridge, down into that hollow, then up that bit, and you were there! It was hard to grasp that it was over sixty miles away, and that 'that spur' was probably quite unclimbable in itself, let alone as a means of reaching the summit. Kanchenjunga has been regarded by some as even more formidable than Everest, and, in fact, it maintained its virgin peak for longer. After many attempts by many nations it was finally climbed in 1954, first by George Band and Tom Brown and then the very next day by N. Hardie and Captain Streather. As we watched, the clouds were slowly drifting up to form a ragged collar round the summit, then that was hidden too. We had been lucky, we were later told, to have seen the mountain so clearly.

It was natural for us to compare Darjeeling with Kathmandu. Both were in the Himalayas, but Darjeeling was much more sophisticated, for it has long been a popular hill-station for the jaded officials and business-men of Calcutta. It is also famous, of course, for its tea, which has a strong flavour of its own, and is therefore much sought for blending. The town has a polyglot population of Indians, Nepalis, Bhutanese, Chinese, and Europeans, though there are fewer of the latter than there were before independence. It was a mixture of old and new: planters' clubs and milk-bars, chromed American cars and Sherpas' head-loads. In the early afternoon, when the clouds had gathered to hide the valleys below, and a faint mist of rain hung in the sloping streets, the upper and more European part of Darjeeling reminded me of an English seaside resort. Perhaps Torquay on a still winter's day? There were grey churches, rock-gardens, statues, and notices "To the Museum," "This way to the Library," and "Let us develop your films." Even Tenzing, who lives in Darjeeling, had, I believe, visiting hours when he would sign your copy of his book.

We walked down to the bazaar. There were a number of Sherpas—it was mountaineering's closed season—leaning against the door-ways and railings. Hands in pockets, nonchalantly wearing blue anoraks, or mountaineering smocks, and climbing-boots, they were obviously the aristocrats of the town. "No, British not give—Japanman," they said, when I asked who had given them their clothing. They had recently returned from the Japanese Expedition to Manasalu, and were, they emphasized (perhaps they thought I was recruiting for the mountains), fully booked for the coming season. With their wrist-watches, cigarettes, and lighters, everything about these cheerful chaps indicated that the local boys were making very good. Apparently they have even formed a Union—I should think a Sherpa shop-steward half-way up a mountain might be very awkward. But they are claimed as the best porters in the world. And for us they posed, laughing, for their photographs, and seemed most likeable and friendly.

We wandered slowly back to the car, and found a young Englishman looking at it closely. He asked us a number of questions, and then introduced himself.

"I'm Tim Mayhew. I wonder if you chaps would care to spend the night with me and my wife? Of course, I'll have to ask her first. Hang on, I'll be back in a minute."

While he was gone we had a hurried conference, for we intended to return to the plains that evening. Already we were on borrowed time, but "Well, hell, Cambridge won't have left Calcutta yet," I reasoned; "they always leave a day later than they say." Then, with more conviction, "Anyway, B.B., you can claim that you had to stay on here to take some photographs."

Tim returned in his Land Rover. Yes, his wife was delighted. And so were we. He explained that his tea-garden was about ten miles away. "Round the other side of the hill. But rather a tricky little road, I'm afraid. Still, you'll manage it; just follow me." We laughingly and rather complacently said that we thought we could manage all right, and followed him out of the town. After all, what was "a tricky little road" to us—we who had already motored thirteen thousand miles?

The first six miles were fine (tricky little road, indeed!). Then the car ahead turned on to a sidetrack which slid down a wooded hill-side. Tim Mayhew stopped and came back to tell us to engage both four-wheel drive and the low-ratio gears. "From here on it gets rather difficult." Partly out of curiosity and partly out of deference to his advice we did as we were told. We started off and eased our way down again. Then came a very steep and acute hairpin bend. We looked at each other. "H'm" was our surprised and only comment. Each person silently admitted that we had never seen anything quite like this before. B.B. was driving, and found that, despite hard lock, the car could not get round without going over the edge. Our car's oversized tyres reduced its turning circle; the Mayhews' Land Rover, with standard tyres, was just able to negotiate the elbow. Nigel and I got out to inspect. By juggling the car backward and forward, and by wrenching the steering-wheel first one way and then the other, B.B. finally crept round. In the next half-hour we drove two miles, and negotiated four more of those corners. It was dark, but in the head-lights we could see on one side the rocky wall in which the road had been cut, and on the other the occasional tree-top which was growing somewhere immediately below. In several places the track was so narrow that the passenger had to lean out of his window and tell the driver how many inches—and it was inches—he had to spare between the tyres and the edge.

"Hey, for Pete's sake, B.B.—keep in. I'm having kittens over here." Finally there was a slender suspension bridge over an eighty-foot drop. Mrs Mayhew came back and told Nigel and me to get out in order to lessen the car's weight, as "the bridge was only made for ponies." Nigel and I obeyed without question, but Oxford was still heavily laden with our kit. As she drove across, the bridge's normal, curving sag sharpened into a definite angle which followed beneath the moving car. We very nearly broke that bridge.

On the far side was the bungalow. We told Mr and Mrs Mayhew of our initial scepticism when they had said that theirs was a "tricky road."

"Yes." he laughed, "I thought you were rather cool when I said that. But I've sent some one back to check the stays on that bridge—you didn't do it any good."

After supper, every one sat in front of the log-fire and talked. They told us of their life on the tea-garden, of the wild game in the valleys below, and we discovered—as is sometimes the case miles from home—that we shared a number of friends in Esher and Eastbourne and all those other places where mutual friends so often live.

B.B. and I still felt our injections, but Nigel was determined to get up very early the next morning and drive back to Darjeeling in order to see the dawn from the near-by Tiger Hill. "Dawn from Tiger Hill is one of the sights of the world," we had read in a magazine months earlier. This seemed a probable exaggeration, but the Mayhews related how groups of people had been known to fly from as far away as the United States to Calcutta, board a local plane to Siliguri, drive up to Darjeeling, rise at 3 A.M., see the sunrise over the Himalayas, and depart back to Illinois or Amsterdam firmly satisfied that it had all been worth while. One couple, having chosen a cloudy time of the year, made the pilgrimage to Tiger Hill every dawn for three weeks until they saw the awe-inspiring sight. They too left satisfied. Long before daylight, while it is still night, the extreme summit of Kanchenjunga grows a brilliant white as her snows catch and reflect the sun's rays, which, to the observer on Tiger Hill, come from below the curve of the earth. Then, as the minutes pass, the tips of the other mountains across the wide skyline flash silver, and gradually the light seeps downward into the night below.

Nigel never made it to Tiger Hill. I heard from under my eiderdown the next morning that after a mile or two he had come to the conclusion that he could not drive along that narrow track without guidance on the corners. In fact, so closely had he hugged the inside edge that he had hit a projecting rock and broken a spring. We were faced with the truly delightful prospect of spending an extra day on the estate while the damage was repaired in the little workshop. "Oh, well," I said, "now we've got a real excuse to give Cambridge. Anyway, they'll probably leave Calcutta two days after they said they would."

The day was spent gently, sitting in the flowered garden looking out over the Teesta Valley (Nigel assured B.B. and me that he did not want any help with the spring). Around the bungalow were the steeply terraced slopes of the stumpy tea-bushes; behind were the green mountains; away below were the jungles in which roamed leopards and Bengal tigers. And to the south, through a saddle in the hills, were glimpses of the plains. It was one of those days when one looks and looks, afraid to miss anything. One takes in sweeping pictures and tries to store them as if on a photographic plate. Clenching one's mind, one thinks, I must remember this. Happily the repairs took long enough to prevent our departure that evening.

But there was no excuse the next day. The empty car was driven across the bridge and loaded up on the other side. We said good-bye to our charming hosts, and regretfully motored slowly up the hillside to the main road.

"That," summed up B.B., "would be the perfect place to spend one's honeymoon." It would be too.

By early afternoon we were back in the heat of the plains and heading east towards Assam. We decided to drive on late that night, as, after the diversion and delay in Darjeeling, there was a lot of time to make up. Some while after dark we came to a fork in the road which was not marked on the map. We were just wondering which way to take when a car drew up alongside. A head leaned out of the window and, nodding towards one of the roads, said casually, "If you're going to Singapore I should think your best bet is that way. How much farther are you going to-night?"

"Oh, another couple of hours, I should think," Nigel answered. "Well, I'm going your way. My place is another forty miles up the road. You'd better stay with me."

Without anything more, he drove off indicating that we should follow. We assumed that he had seen our final destination painted on the back door. This was the third time in succession that we had been unexpectedly invited to stay the night. The hospitality of these tea-planters seemed unending.

Later, over a midnight supper, we asked our host where the other, unmarked road had led to.

"Oh, that one. That goes up to Gantok. It's about as far into the mountains as one can get by road. Only thirty miles or so from the Tibetan border. It's quite an amusing place—cosmopolitan, too."

"Cosmopolitan—why?" I asked in surprise.

"Well, it's probably the only place in the world where you or I could sit down and have a cup of coffee with a Chinese Army officer! I met a couple up there last year—they wanted to buy my watch. Oh, Gantok is quite a party in the summer—Indians, Europeans, Tibetans, Chinese, the lot."

"What on earth are the Chinese officers doing there?"

"They come down from Tibet each spring to pick up supplies for their Army garrisons. The staff comes round by sea from China to Calcutta, then by rail and road up to Gantok. There the Chinese take it over into Tibet on mules and ponies. Sometimes you can see hundreds of ponies. The journey back to Lhasa takes them two months; the trail goes up through several passes of over 14,000 feet. Of course, there isn't any traffic at the moment because it's all blocked by snow. But in the summer they really get quite busy. For a long time Gantok has been the nearest roadhead to Lhasa—about four hundred miles. But, as you may have read, the Chinese have just finished their own motor road from Chungking to Tibet, so they probably won't be coming down to Gantok much more. Before that I suppose it has been cheaper to ship the stuff via Calcutta. Hell of long way round, though!"

It was, to say the least, a most interesting story.

"What time do you want to get up in the morning?" he asked.

"About five? We've got to get to Shillong the day after to-morrow, and, if our directions are correct, there's a ferry across the Brahmaputra late to-morrow afternoon. We don't want to miss it. It's a long way, so we'd better leave plenty of time," one of us replied.

"Yes, the roads from here through Cooch Behar aren't much good, so perhaps you're wise."

His bearer woke us in the morning, and as our host was still asleep we left a note thanking him for his kindness.

That day, for the first time on the journey, we smelt the tropics. Driving towards the Brahmaputra, across its wide alluvial plains, we saw wild banana-trees, bamboos, creepers, uncleared lowland jungle and wild monkeys, and the air too had a damper, heavier flavour. Another thing was the dress of the Assamese women. They were much more *décolletée* than before. In fact, some of them were completely so.

The ferry stage was reached on time; it was at a little bamboo village with the unpronounceable name of Jopigopaghat. Here the Brahmaputra was a mile-wide sheet of calm brown water, and the ferry across to the south bank, with its powerful engine left over from some wartime lorry, was the biggest and best appointed since the Bosporus.

The next day we drove up through the jungle of the Khasi Hills to Shillong, and the Secretariat of the North-East Frontier Agency. The Commissioner had left the day before by air for Delhi, and at first no one seemed to know anything about us. But, fortunately, a clerk presently appeared who said that the Commissioner had considered our plans and, "Wait while I look in the files." We waited with anxious patience. The clerk returned.

"Yes," he said, "the letter approving your exit through the frontier is just now with the Governor. Will you come this afternoon when the Deputy Commissioner will sign it? He would like to meet you."

This was excellent news. In effect, it looked as if the last political barrier was down. While waiting for the afternoon appointment, we drove round Shillong, and then out to the golf-course for a picnic lunch. The little town was most picturesque, as neat and attractive as any we had seen in India. The golf-course, laid out and constructed in the heyday of British India, has the surprising reputation of being one of the four finest courses in the world. It is, in fact, a double course of thirty-six holes, and even to our unprofessional eyes it seemed both beautiful and superbly kept. The large and rambling clubhouse was in the best traditions of Rye or the Royal and Ancient, and I am sure, had we been members, it could have 'done' us an excellent tea of buttered toast and strawberry jam! One other thing about Shillong—I include it for the benefit of any schoolboys who have penetrated this far in my book. The geography books must quickly be amended, for no longer can Cherrapunji (hard by Shillong) claim fame as the wettest place on earth. No, research by the Assam Meteorological Office shows that that honour must now go to the small and neighbouring village of Mawnsynram, which in 1955 topped Cherrapunji's staggering 440 inches of rain by over another 100 inches!

The Deputy Commissioner, to whom we later returned, was a moustachioed major in the Indian Army.

"So you are going down the Stilwell Road. I don't know how you'll find it."

"Do you know the area, sir?" I asked.

"I don't know it well, but I went down the road for about one hundred miles in 1953—I had to meet some Burmese officials about some Naga border raids,"

"Three years ago," I said with surprise. "How was it then?"

"I took three jeeps. I think we took two days on the way. It was hard going, and very muddy. But passable. Of course, if there have been any landslides since then you will find your way completely blocked."

"What about the bridges, sir?"

"Oh, you'll get your feet wet," he laughed. "There were a few left, but you'll have to ford most of the rivers."

The difficulties of landslides and rivers we already knew. But the major's news was very encouraging. In nearly a year of conjecture, he was the first person we had met who was able to give us really first-hand and relatively recent information.

He signed and stamped a small slip of paper, read and checked it, then handed it over to us.

"When do you expect to reach Ledo?" he asked.

"In about a week—we're spending a few days on a tea-estate first."

"Well, when you get to Ledo you must call on the District Officer;

he'll escort you up to the Pangsu Pass on the frontier. He knows you are coming, but I'll send him a telegram to-night confirming the arrangements. Of course, once you cross the Inner Line into the tribal area you won't be able to stop or take any photographs. But," he smiled, "the District Officer will be with you to take care of that. Well, then, the best of luck. If you get to Singapore give it my love—I was there on VJ Day."

We shook hands and thanked him. Not only was the last political barrier well and truly down, but we were to be escorted across it. Landslides were still a major problem, but, we felt, they would have to be veritable mountains to really stop us now. We motored through Shillong, and fairly flew down the winding hill-road back to the plains.

The next day we crossed the Brahmaputra to the north bank again, and motored along the *kacha* roads to where, according to the map, we thought the tea-estate should be. But on stopping in a little village to check the way they told us we had come thirty miles up the wrong road. We cursed, but thanked our stars that Cambridge were not with us, for they could never have forgiven or forgotten such a major navigational boob. On the way back we paused while B.B. took some film of a wayside village potter at work on his wheel. It was almost hypnotic to see the skill with which this man slapped a lump of damp clay on to the wheel, and within a minute had turned a graceful jar. B.B. spent half an hour with his cameras, and suggested that our unintended navigational error was henceforth better described as "a photographic diversion to investigate and record some indigenous Assamese ceramics." And, as he further pointed out, at £10 per minute on T.V., our sixty-mile 'diversion' would probably prove most profitable financially. In any case, when B.B. was happy everybody was happy, and Nigel and I quietly congratulated ourselves on our initial error.

We had lunch on the road and then, going on, stopped every few miles to inquire, "Dekia Juli, Brooke Bond?" It was the same questioning inflexion, raised eyebrows, and vaguely pointing finger which had been naïvely but consistently used when asking the way ever since looking for the Munich Kampingplatz four months before.

We had been talking of the Julia tea-estate for many months. It happened that in Cambridge I had noticed the telegraphic address of the Brooke Bond company; it was "Assambrook." The "Assam" immediately registered, and I wrote to the Company's London office asking if they would be kind enough to give me the address of a tea-planter on one of their Assam estates. Perhaps the planter might have some information on the roads in that corner of the world? The Company not only gave me the address of their manager in Assam but also gave the Expedition enough tea for at least a dozen trips to Singapore. I wrote to Assam, and presently had a reply. Mr Hannay was not able to give us many details of the roads, as, of course, he "always flew," but nevertheless he wrote that "if your Expedition ever gets this far you will all be most welcome to stay with my wife and I for as long as you like." In Cambridge the letter had been put in the Navigator's 'contacts file,' and we had optimistically accepted this far-flung hospitality. And so, in the months that followed, we had glibly referred to the estate which was now only a few miles away as 'our Base Camp'— before 'pushing' into Burma. After all, it was reasoned, "all the best Expeditions have a Base Camp." The title also had the advantage that anything we wrote while at the estate would automatically become a Dispatch. For, of course, from Base Camps the best Expeditions never write mere articles.

"Dekia Juli?" we asked again.

The villager stopped his bicycle. "Wuh Digi," he replied with a matter-of-fact wave of his hand. Undoubtedly, the estate was not far. Nigel let in the clutch and drove on. The Assamese have no measured sense of distance, but rely entirely on intonation to convey rough meaning. When "Wuh Digi" is said in the same tone as an Englishman might say "Oh, it's just round the corner, old man" it means, in fact, just that. If, on the other hand, the reply comes "Wuuh Deegi," in the incredulous tone of "That's the helluva long way—you'll never get there by lunch" it means just that too. The point is, in Assam the same words are often used for almost opposite meanings. One must listen carefully to the tone of voice, for therein lies the answer.

Sure enough, the villager's casual "Wuh Digi" was correct. On the road ahead was a signpost pointing up a side-road. "Julia Estate, J. Hannay, Manager. 3 miles."

We drove up the long estate drive which ran through miles of tea-bushes, and eventually pulled up in a flowered garden. Mr and Mrs Hannay came down the steps of their bungalow and across the lawn to welcome us.

"Well," he said, "it's nice to meet you after all this time. We were beginning to wonder if you'd ever make it!"

Cambridge had not yet arrived, which was not really surprising, as they probably had not left Calcutta until three days after they said they would. We unpacked the car, and, over a long, cool drink, we read our mail. Then Mrs Hannay showed us to a large bedroom with sheets and eiderdowns and bedside lamps.

"Hey, Tim," called Nigel from the adjoining bathroom, "there's hot water coming out of the tap marked 'Hot.'" I ran to inspect this wonder, and, as it was only the second time on the journey that we had seen hot water running from a tap merely for the turning, both of us nearly scalded ourselves.

"Now, you must have a lot of dirty clothes," said Mrs Hannay. "Give them all to me and I'll send for the dhobi-man."

Some Base Camp!

The household had long been asleep when, at three o'clock in the morning, scrunching tyres on the gravel outside announced the arrival of Cambridge. They apologized for the awkward hour, but excused themselves on the grounds that they had "just pioneered an entirely new route along unknown roads," and thus, they claimed, had arrived at least a day (or a night?) earlier than they might have done. Anyway, the Expedition was in one piece again.

The Expedition spent four delightful days at Julia. In spite of our Burma preparations in Calcutta, there were still many things to do. But, in fact, whenever the Expedition stopped anywhere there were always things to do. Now there were the winches to be checked and greased; tins of food to be correctly stowed; photos to take and letters to write. There was congestion at the single typewriter, as each of us, in the traditional style, wrote 'last-minute dispatches from Base Camp,' and, as I find in my diary, "an army may march on its stomach but this Expedition moves on the ends of its ball-point pens." A certain amount of rivalry arose as to who could think up the most hair-raising account of what lay ahead to foist on the unsuspecting British public—or any newspaper that could dream of publishing it. Adrian, our public relations expert, excelled himself. He wrote a blood-chilling dispatch which seemed to include all the inconceivable ingredients of standard 'steaming-jungle' fiction—head-

hunters, crocodiles, giant pythons, mammoth spiders, poisoned arrows, and
carnivorous creepers. We were armed, it seemed, with everything from
cutlasses to light machine-guns. B.B. was prevailed upon to take an
accompanying photograph of us all which was captioned "The last-known
picture of the ill-fated Oxford and Cambridge Expedition. Last heard of .
. ." This photo would naturally, we imagined, have been 'just received by
runner.'

The same evening the week-old airmail copy of *The Times* reported
that the ship carrying members of the Commonwealth Antarctic
Expedition had got stuck in the pack-ice of the Weddell Sea. If they had
heard our laughter I am sure they would have forgiven the irreverence!

While at Julia we took a number of photographs for our equipment
sponsors. For this express purpose Mr Hannay summoned two elephants
to the estate and, donning our coloured anoraks, we climbed aboard the
animals for suitable pictures. Then we turned to our plastic buckets. The
British firm which made these buckets sometimes advertised with a
picture of a London bus running over one—"ten minutes later the
bucket had returned to its normal shape." Not having a bus with us, we
tried to get one of the elephants to stand on our bucket. Mr Hannay
explained to the mahout (elephant man) what was required. The mahout
whispered in the ear of his elephant, and then the animal lifted up a
forefoot, placed it gently on top of the upturned bucket, and held the
pose for B.B.'s cameras. Fine. Now could the elephant put his weight
down and squash the bucket? The mahout looked doubtful, but
whispered some more. The elephant listened, but could not quite
understand. He tried the other foot; he walked round the bucket and
tried the first foot again. Despite repeated whisperings, he just could not
bring himself to squash it. His little beady eyes looked at us plaintively.
"Surely you don't want me to stand on the thing—I'll only squash it, and
then what use will it be to you?" The mahout whispered again and
again—though he himself was lost concerning our ridiculous purpose.
The elephant put his foot gently on the bucket, but absolutely refused to
go any further.

"Now look here," his eyes said, "all my life I have been trained never
to stand on anything fragile, and I'm not going to start now. Not even you,
in your multi-coloured clothing, could be such clots."

Poor elephant, he did not understand, but he tried desperately hard. Actually, I have a suspicion that he understood all along, but just could not believe his own huge ears. After all, what a stupid thing to ask him to do! By way of compromise, he helped Nigel walk up his trunk to offer the mahout some cigarettes, and, with the tip of his trunk, he most delicately accepted the lumps of sugar that we gave him. He was just as attractive as any flop-eared spaniel puppy, and at least a dozen times as intelligent. If only elephants were a little smaller they would make ideal pets—no other animal can be so human or so gentle. The one we met at Julia would look after his mahout's four-months-old son like a benign old baby-sitter. Before the Mr and Mrs Mahout went out they would show the elephant the area in which the baby was allowed to crawl. Then, if the baby wandered outside, the elephant would pick him lightly up and put him back in the middle! Mr Hannay told us many elephant stories, two particularly of which I remember. He had been out shooting from an elephant, and on the way into the jungle he had misplaced his dark glasses. Returning to the road the next day, the elephant suddenly stopped, picked up the glasses from the track, and threw them back to their owner. Then there was the story of the mahout whose wife had died. The old man was naturally upset, but not, apparently, unduly so. A year later his elephant—with whom he had worked for thirty years—died too. The mahout pined away of a broken heart, and a few months after he was also buried.

As our animal left the Hannays' garden he dipped on his front knees and lifted his trunk in a wide salaam. Even in our short acquaintance with elephants we became their life-long admirers.

The Hannays were most kind hosts. They gave us gargantuan meals, as Mrs Hannay thought we all looked thin and needed building up 'For Burma'—she too had caught the habit. Neither of them seemed to mind that we spent so much time checking the cars or writing, and so little time with them. In the evenings they sat listening to their Spanish Linguaphone records; they planned to visit the Costa Brava on their next home leave, and were preparing early.

Pat, of course, was able to give them the dates of all the recognized bull-fight fiestas, and to help in planning their Continental itinerary. Nevertheless, it was strange to hear the Spanish for "No, neither of us take soup, but we should like to see the wine-list" drifting across the verandah in the middle of Assam.

No Expedition can ever have had such an enjoyable or luxurious Base Camp. But we were anxious to be moving on towards the hardest and least predictable part of the journey. We were as ready as we ever should be. So, putting our watches back an hour—for nearly all estates in Assam run an hour ahead of the sun—we wished the Hannays *adios* and dragged ourselves away.

Our next scheduled port of call was Bangkok, the capital of Thailand. I write "scheduled," but, in fact, none of us had any idea of when we might reach there.

11.

The Stilwell Road

TWO days later we arrived in Ledo. This was the extreme end of the Assam Trunk Road, and from here Stilwell had built his supply line southward into Burma. Once this village had been a command post for the Allied armies; it had seen thousands of drab green trucks start off towards the Japanese; it had seen laden transport planes slowly circling to gain height for their flight over The Hump and down into China; it had seen Merrill's Marauders and the Chindits walk away towards their lonely war. Once we listened to the News, and this corner of the world had been important. Once—twelve years ago. To-day you will not find Ledo on any but the largest maps. It is forgotten.

The cars pulled up outside the wooden bungalow of the Indian District Officer. As arranged a week earlier in Shillong, he was to escort us through the jungle to the actual frontier. While he fetched his jeep Pat went over to the Telegraph Office and sent a prearranged cable to the Home Team in Cambridge. "Scrumdown 15," it read. Why the code-word? I hesitate to suggest that all the best Expeditions use code-words. They do not. But, well, "Scrumdown" sounded more fun than an unimaginative "Leaving Ledo on the 15th of January." It was cheaper, too!

The District Officer checked our passports and then, driving off in his jeep, signalled for us to follow close behind. Another jeep brought up the rear. Perhaps they did not trust us. The convoy turned out of Ledo on to the trail that was the Stilwell Road. For the forty miles up to the frontier pass there would be no difficulties, but, with Ledo at last behind, something of an Expedition milestone had been passed. This feeling was furthered when, just before the road climbed off the plain and into the hills, we passed a huge sign-board which had been erected by Stilwell's engineers. It listed the mileages to all sorts of incredible places, culminating in the Chinese town of Kunming, 1079 miles. But the mileage we were really interested in was Myitkyina,[5] 263 miles. That was our goal. It might take three days, it could take three weeks; we hoped for the former, but were prepared for the latter. Once past this sign we officially crossed the

Inner Line, and were now in tribal territory. In the next hour the road became a narrow track as it twisted steeply upward. It became muddier, and the green jungle grew thicker. We crawled up through the damp of the low-lying clouds. Several times little groups of Nagas heard our coming and shyly scuttled off the track into the jungle, there to glance at us rather nervously over their shoulders.

The last part of the drive was up a cloudy valley once known as Hell's Gate. Down it, in the monsoon rains of 1942, had come the survivors of those who had fled before the fire and terror of the Japanese. They had walked for three weeks. Then there had been no road. It was named Hell's Gate by those who received and nursed the tragic few, for to them these people were stumbling out from an unmapped hell. Such was the toll of starvation and disease that, in the 230 miles of jungle between Myitkyina and this valley, four thousand died. Even to-day one does not ask those who 'walked out,' and lived, to tell their story.

Beyond and above the valley was the Pangsu Pass. At the side of the track were two small notices. One merely said "India/Burma"; this was the international frontier. The other, the rusty top of an oil-drum, claimed that it was "228 miles to Myitkyina." The District Officer resolutely refused to let us photograph these signs from his side of the border, so we went a pace or two into Burma and snapped from there. It started raining. We shared a quick 'brew-up' with the escort, and then they said good-bye. Their jeeps disappeared from the clearing, and a few moments later even the sound of their engines was lost as they wound their way down into the valley below. The light rain was the only sound—and it was the first rain since Greece. We removed, as a souvenir, the sign "to Myitkyina." After all, no one would miss it. Then, with exaggerated military nonchalance, Nigel said, "Right-ho, men, you all know what you've got to do." We got into the cars, switched on the windscreen-wipers, and started down the forgotten road into Burma.

Immediately the track left the pass it disappeared. But where once it had been there ran a narrow thinning in the undergrowth. Slowly, and in bottom gear, the cars pushed a way through. The overgrown path—for such it was—wound in short-terraced lengths along the jungle ridges. It seemed that the last of the monsoon was barely past, as the ground was very soft. Many times the engines burst to a higher note as the wheels spun frantically in the mud and the cars sank to a shuddering standstill. But by reversing, by cutting bamboo to lay on the track, by pushing, and by careful driving we got clear and slithered on. The embankments on the steep hillsides had long been washed away, but, with one of us ahead guiding on foot, we eased the cars tenderly over the remaining ledge. In the first hour we covered six miles, which, considering what had been expected, was fast progress indeed. The going became no better, it became no worse. Often we had to bulldoze our way through the undergrowth, but seldom did we bother to cut back the branches, and even then only because they caught in the stubby wireless aerials. In one place a fallen tree lay across the track. The Cambridge winch cable was quickly run out, and then, with the winch whining powerfully, the obstruction was easily dragged clear. It was raining quite hard, and we pulled on our coloured waterproof suits.

"Well, it's not too bad," I suggested optimistically. "At this rate we'll be down the road like a dose of salts."

"Don't count your chickens," was B.B.'s typical reply. "After all the fuss, we're going to look damn' silly if it gets too easy."

"How about a photo, B.B.? We can all look intrepid, anyway!"

He got out his camera and took a suitably 'pioneering' group.

Then, gay in our bright clothing as six of the Seven Dwarfs, we pushed on. The track climbed over ridges and wound down into rain-soaked valleys, the tall jungle always on either side. We splashed through many streams, but one was deeper than the rest. The Expedition dismounted, inspected, and held a conference. A bridge had spanned it once; the crumbled concrete of the buttresses still remained, but of the bridge itself there was no sign. We reckoned that it should be possible to ford. The cars were coaxed down the sharp slope, and then, with engines racing, they surged across. On the far side the muddy track turned through an acute bend before running up a ledge cut in the hillside. Across the ledge lay a large tree-trunk. Nigel was already getting out the axes, but our luck held; there was just room for the cars to squeeze underneath. It was as well—even our winches could hardly have shifted that log.

We went on all afternoon, the wipers droning in the drizzle, and with each slow mile our hopes rose. Gradually, as the track wound down from the higher spurs and ridges, the way grew clearer. At the head of a valley we passed through a clustered Naga village. Still, apparently, prone to the occasional head-hunting raid in settlement of tribal arguments, these Nagas merely scurried off the trail and eyed us curiously—as well they might! Here we noticed the first relics of war. The Nagas had salvaged the jettisoned belly-tanks of aircraft from the surrounding jungle, and were using them as water-butts beside their small bamboo huts. A little farther on the old and rusted chassis of a lorry lay in the encroaching jungle verge where it had been quickly pushed to allow an unhindered flow of supplies to roll in against the Japanese, "Yellow Truck Company, Pontiac, Michigan" read the maker's mildewed name-plate. Our thoughts went back twelve years.

The mud in the valleys was deep. Sometimes the cars would go into slow-motion slides on the slippery surface, and the driver would have to stop and straighten up before continuing. When in the broader patches the cars became momentarily stuck one reversed quickly before they settled—for obstinately to keep the wheels spinning forward when bogged was merely to bog them down farther. Henry was the real expert—his mud-driving had its own calm and coaxing touch. The rest of us soon learnt—if the mud was too much, reverse and reverse quickly; lay down some branches and try again with more speed. But, with the cars in four-wheel drive and the lowest of eight gears, they usually snorted through on the first time of asking. It took a lot to delay them.

The time flew past. It grew dark early, as the trees and clouds shut out the pale sun before its time. In the green twilight we switched on head-lamps and searchlights. Some one stood up through the roof-hatch to swing the searchlight as the driver required. The cars drove farther apart, because the reflected glare from the lights behind dazzled the leading driver in his windscreen. In eight hours the cars had driven nearly fifty miles from the Pangsu Pass. It was much too good to be true, and we discussed our luck distrustingly. Some one made a crack about 'being led up the garden path' towards some barrier beyond. Some garden path! But we wriggled on, and now the trail was wider. In places it seemed that some efforts had been made in relatively recent years to shore up the slumping embankments. This was curious, for, as far as we knew, no one ever used the road. Sometimes our head-lamps' beam picked out thin patches of tarmac which peeped through the mud from the remains of the double-width military highway of the years before. Undoubtedly, sitting behind the engine—now purring steadily, and then roaring under load—with the jungle brushing past the windows, there was romance about that drive along the Stilwell Road.

There were many fords, and, as the trail came down through the hills, they became successively deeper. In the loom of our lights we saw an ancient Bailey Bridge. We inspected by torch; the steel framework of the bridge was still sound, but many of the planks across its floor were decayed and rotten. The river looked too deep to ford, and so, for the next half-hour, we wrenched up the stouter planks and laid them across the bridge in two parallel tracks—appropriate to the line that the tyres would take. Then, with just the driver aboard, the cars were guided across. Several more bridges quickly followed, and each time the stronger planks were rearranged.

We had been driving for twelve hours, and, although it was night, we sensed that the country was more open; it was flatter, and the thick jungle now alternated with broad patches of elephant grass as high as the cars. We were just thinking about making a rough camp when the track led into a silent, sleeping village. Unlike the crude Naga huts, these were little houses built up on stilts. But, being apprehensive of our reception, and of the possibility of dacoits or bandits, we did not delay. However, we could not find where the track continued on the far side of the village. While the cars prowled about seeking the exit a dog began to bark, the doors of the houses swung open, lights appeared, and eyes peered out. Then a man stepped into the weaving headlights and signalled us to stop. We did not want to, but it seemed we must.

He came across to the window of the Oxford car and peered in, astonishment written on his face. He said something which we did not understand. Seeing this, he took off his hat and politely asked, "Where you go?"

"Oh, nowhere. Just down the road, y'know," I replied, with worried nonchalance.

"Road? No, you here stop."

"No, we go."

"You not go. You come Inspection Bungalow—good Bungalow here. Come, I show."

By this time there were several lanterns, and quite a crowd of curious villagers had gathered round. The ones at the back stood on tiptoe to get a closer look at the visitors.

"Englishmans?"

"Yes, that's right."

Their spokesman turned to his friends and gave them this surprising news. They murmured and laughed to each other. Our doubts about their hospitality vanished, for they were only too anxious to be friendly. These were Kachin people, long known for their simple friendship to the British. Not since the War—in which the Kachins played a most loyal part had they seen Europeans drive in from India, and we aroused much interest. They smiled at our mention of bandits—there were none.

They offered us cheroots, and, leading us to the little bungalow, they unloaded the cars and carried our things inside. Nothing was too much trouble; some ran off to fetch water and lamps, others laid and lit a log-fire in the stove; and they all laughed and argued in trying to put up our beds. They considered the Expedition's beards a huge joke. Their spokesman asked us many questions, and translated the answers to his curious friends. They were intrigued to hear how we had crossed the rotten bridges, for, they said, some years previously a lorry trying to drive farther up the road had fallen through into the river below. Anxiously we asked if any lorries ever came up from Myitkyina. Yes, they replied, one or two in each dry season. They were expecting the first for a year in a few days' time. The journey took four or five days, they thought. There were many rivers to ford. This was good news. Provided the rivers were low, we knew that we might now reach Myitkyina. Then, seeing we were trying to cook a meal, the spokesman intimated to his friends that we should be left in peace, and he ushered them out of the door.

"In morning come," he said, and they all nodded in agreement. Everybody shook hands with everybody else, more cheroots were handed round, and then they picked up their lanterns and went down the bungalow steps, chatting about their honoured guests—for, evidently, such we were.

This village was Shingbwiyang, 67 miles from the Indian frontier, known as "Shing" to Stilwell's Americans, and one of his main supply-dumps on the advance. When in 1943 the road had been cut to this point, and fighting flickered in the dense hills around, a colonel of the Combat

Engineers made the exhausted comment, "On this job you don't have to be insane—but it sure helps." For us in 1956, however, it held altogether happier omens. Burma, our fourteenth country, seemed a wonderful place, and we were making good progress.

Supper was a gigantic meal, for suddenly everybody realized that they had had nothing to eat since breakfast. Breakfast—it seemed a week ago. During supper Pat rigged the tape-recorder and, as he had promised for our first night in Burma, played Swan Lake. Then we thumbed through the book which lies on the table of every Inspection Bungalow, and in which under "Burma P.W.D. Circular No. 7 of 14th July, 1908, as amended 8th April, 1927, every traveller using this Bungalow is required to enter his name, rank, and designation." The book ran back ten years, and contained a bare two dozen entries—mainly Forest Officers. Shingbwiyang was well off the beaten track. Each of us signed his name; for 'rank' we concluded that "B.A., Cantab." would do; and under 'designation' wrote "The Oxford and Cambridge Far Eastern Expedition en route London-Singapore." My diary concludes that day, "Left washing-up till the morning—very rare! Exhausted. Bed."

In the morning the villagers gathered again to help us pack up, and then, with yet more cheroots, they waved us on our way. The road was now out of the mountains; the mud, clouds, and water-proofs of the day before gave way to the more familiar dust, sun, and dark glasses. The track was wider, too, and we made faster speed.

A few miles beyond the village was an old air-strip, overgrown and useless. But once—as we found from wreckage on the edge—the landing-ground of Tomahawks and Dakotas. The sound of aircraft revving up for take-off and skimming over the tree-tops beyond seemed far away. Great tufts of grass had sprung up through the tarmac, and there was no sound except our own voices in the hot sun. Throughout the morning we passed the twisted remains of twelve years' rust and rot—burnt-out lorries, jeeps, bulldozers, cranes, tanks, and girders. As we quietly examined these relics we realized the part played by the Americans in the Burma campaign. We in Britain were (and still are) misinformed. Shortly after the War, London furiously demanded the withdrawal of the American film Objective Burma. That was ungenerous. True, the otherwise excellent film made no mention of the Fourteenth Army (more than ungenerous). But that campaign was not an exclusively British affair. Others also fought, some died—Indians, Chinese, Kachins, Gurkhas, West Africans, and Americans. And the latter were not slow in energy or material. In hard cash alone, the very road we travelled on cost them over £50 a yard. Probably the most expensive road ever built. And the maps we carried to guide us down that road were made by the United States Army Air Force in 1944.

Our national pride has ignored the Americans; a legend has grown up which is incomplete.

On looking back, the first hundred miles of the Stilwell Road was much easier than we had ever expected. Anticipating very difficult conditions, we had armed ourselves with everything from three weeks' food-supply to water-sterilizing tablets, from winches to machetes. A part of our success so far was due to luck—the monsoon had been unusually light, and therefore the rivers and hills were not as sodden as they might have been, neither were there any big landslides to block our way. But undoubtedly another part was due to the preparations we had made, and without eight forward gears, four-wheel drive, and winches our overland venture might have come unstuck a dozen times in the first twenty-four hours from Ledo. Nevertheless, it was not all that easy; and, anyway, we were not out of the wood yet.

The broad bowl of the Upper Chindwin is threaded with rivers which ran across our path. Most of the day was spent crossing them. Neither of our cars was in any way waterproofed, but, wisely, the Land Rover carries its vulnerable 'electrics' high under the bonnet.[6] In Birmingham they had told us that the Land Rover's safe 'wading' limit was about 2 ft. 6 ins. Well, we have news for Birmingham—they would be surprised how deep one will go when it must!

The Expedition's fording drill was as follows. On arrival at the bank we reconnoitred for the shallowest way across. This invariably meant that the non-mechanical members were sent in to wade about, awash merely to their waists, until the dry-shod mechanics signalled their approval of the chosen route. Next the fan belt was removed. Even though a fan may be above the water it can, if spinning, blow spray on to the leads and distributor. (This, of course, brings things to a halt very rapidly.) Meanwhile, the floors of the cars were cleared of kit which might be damaged by water. When all was ready each car forded in turn. Thus, if the first car failed to get through, the other car could winch it back. Then we could try again. On the other hand, if the first car succeeded but the second did not, the procedure was reversed—the first pulling forward the second. This was the theory, and, strangely, it worked!

FROM THE DIARY FOR 16th JANUARY

... Cambridge, with Henry at the controls, went in first. The river was about 120 yards wide and by the time he got out to the middle we, in Oxford, were worried. There was an impressive bow-wave creaming around the bonnet and a wake that would have done credit to a cross-Channel steamer. However, Henry kept his foot down hard and pressed on. Eventually, the car emerged on the far bank with water streaming off and out of it like a bedraggled dog after a swim. Our turn next. Away we went, B.B. and I with our nautical ancestry well to the fore and Nigel driving. We did very well until the middle. There the engine died or, as the driver euphemistically put it, 'lost power.' Quite a lot happened in the next few seconds. B.B. and I did an emergency exit through the escape hatch (roof-hatch) and Nigel, with a cry of 'Up Periscope,' followed quickly behind. Then, screwdriver and spanners in hand, he clambered down on to the fo'c'sle (Bonnet) and fiddled inside. B.B., realizing the "unique filmic potential" of the situation, plunged overboard fully dressed towing his cine camera and tripod behind him. I took off my boots and trousers, hitched up my shirt under my arm-pits and waded off to the far bank to fetch the Cambridge winch cable—the crew of that car being so paralytic with laughter at our expense as to be almost useless. With the winch run out and hooked on to Oxford, the long tow began. Eventually we reached "the haven where we would be." All highly humorous—to Cambridge, anyway. It took an hour to dry out the engine.

There were several more like that one, but, with practice, we got better at it. The cardinal rule was to keep your foot firmly on the accelerator. With the engine running powerfully there was enough pressure in the exhaust to keep the water out. But, take your foot off because you thought you were stuck, and—gurgle, gurgle—you had, to quote the Expedition, "had your flaming chips."

The lonely road ran on interminably between the rivers and through the jungle. The dust was such that we resorted to the old habit of driving half a mile apart. It was evening when we came down to the last river of the day. Its name should ring a bell in the ears of those who wear the Burma Star—it was the Chindwin. *Beyond the Chindwin* is more than the name of a wonderful book.[7] It sums up those grim years of defeat and slow return in 1943 and 1944. Above all the Chindwin is the private battle-honour of the Chindits. It was their Rubicon.

Even in the dry season the river was wide and deep, but, fortunately, there was an old raft made of lashed-together Army pontoons, and we crossed by that. On the far side we were greeted by a Kachin policeman. He asked us where we had come from. We pointed behind, over and beyond the clouded hills of the horizon, and, perhaps a little proudly, told him "India." He smiled at us, drew on his cheroot, and asked to see our passports. But he had to believe us, for there was nowhere else that we could have come from in that direction.

He took us to the near-by Inspection Bungalow, and there we stayed the night. These Bungalows, built at the turn of the century, are dotted all over Burma. They are intended for the occasional official touring on duty, but, in fact, it is assumed by the caretaker that anyone travelling must be on official duty, and so we always used them. They are picturesque, stilted houses built of sweet-smelling wood, with two or three small rooms and a little furniture—a table, a chair or two, and a galvanized bath. One is expected to bring one's own bedding, food, and lamps. One 'camps,' in fact, in their shelter.

By noon of the third day we had driven 180 miles from the Pangsu Pass, and the road was improving all the time. There were still rivers to ford, but by this time we had perfected the necessary techniques, and splashed through them as if the cars were amphibians. The expedition was on top of its small world.

The way led straight and clear across the Hukaung Valley, which once, because of its malaria, was the most dreaded region in Upper Burma. Then we passed by the village of Mogaung, and knew that in hills away to the south lay the fabled jungle fortresses of Broadway, White City, and Blackpool. An hour before dusk the road crossed a huge air-field with cracked and warped runways crisscrossing in all directions. A few more miles and on to tarmac. Another mile and we were in Myitkyina. 228 miles in three days.

⊛

That night, under the electric lights of the Myitkyina Inspection Bungalow, the six of us opened up the beer and, with a tin of salted peanuts, held an informal cocktail party in celebration. Nevertheless, our success was something of an anticlimax, and, if the reader is disappointed that we made it so easily, so were we. As Nigel remarked at the time, "All those blasted crowbars and shovels—we've hardly used them. Y'know, this isn't going to look a bit good in the book."

News travels fast in a Burmese town, and within an hour of our arrival the jeep of the commandant of the local garrison drew up outside the bungalow. He had been warned of our plans some weeks before from Rangoon, but seemed most surprised at our actual arrival. We invited him inside for a beer. "Have you brought your rods?" he asked, in perfect English. He had been reading too many Westerns; surely he did not expect us to be wearing six-shooters? "Excellent fishing round here," he added. This in Upper Burma! But the things people expected us to have. (If we ever go on another Expedition we will surely tow a trailer full of rods, tennis rackets, football boots, golf clubs, and a bridge table—all of which we were asked for at some time or other.)

The colonel confirmed that there were no terrorists between Myitkyina and Lashio—our next stop. Beyond there we should ask again. "But," he said, unfolding a map, "this road you must take to Siam—it is very uncertain." On the map he traced his finger along a thin red line which twisted its way over ridge after ridge for four hundred miles eastward from Mandalay.

"You will need escorts; there has been some trouble in those parts. When you get to Lashio go and see the Brigade Commander—I'll send him a signal to tell him you are coming"

This news sobered the Expedition considerably—our self-confidence reverted to more normal proportions. Perhaps after our three-day passage from India, there was not such an anticlimax after all.

12.

Green Hills and Cheroots

THE next morning we topped up with petrol, had our passports checked, and looked at our first Burmese town in daylight. It was evidently bazaar day, for the place was thronged with a gay and chattering crowd of Kachins, Chinese, Shans, and Burmans. Most were dressed in check *lungis* (worn like a sarong), open shirts, and trilbies or brown topees. Wherever the cars stopped they were surrounded by a small crowd who commented to each other what I am sure was the Burmese equivalent of, "Cor', look at this lot." One of them could invariably speak English, and would interpret for the others. The conversation was slow and full of courtesy.

"Excuse me, sahib, may I speak with you?"

"Yes, certainly."

"You have come just now from Indeeya. I think?"

"Yes, that's right."

"Excuse me, may I ask your business?"

"Oh, we're students—travellers."

"Travellers? Where from you are coming?"

"From England. Look, bring your friends round to the back and I'll show you."

Everybody would then move round to the map on the rear window, and I or one of the others would explain.

"From England, then to France, and across to Europe to Turkey." And, tracing a finger along our route, one continued, "Syria, Iraq, Iran, Pakistan, India, Assam, and now Burma—now Myitkyina!" (Murmur of approval from the group.) "Now we go Siam-side to Malaya."

"All the time in your car, sahib?"

"Yes, all the time."

"When you come to Malaya then where you go?"

"Then"—with a sweep of the hand across the map—"back to England."

"I am thinking this is a long travel for you."

"Yes, it is; a very long one."

"You come Myitkyina last night? Excuse me, how you find our country?"

"Well, we've only been here four days, but we like it very much. It is very beautiful—very good."

"Very good. I am happy you find it. How many time you stay in our country?"

"In Burma? Oh, about two or three weeks, I expect. We must go to Lashio, and then to Kengtung."

"You go just now Kengtung-side?" he would comment with eyebrows raised. "There is much trouble, I think. You must careful go."

"Yes, I know. The Colonel was telling us last night."

Then one of the spectators would say something in Burmese to the spokesman, who would listen and turn to me again.

"Please, my friend is ask what your man is doing." He would point at D.D., who might be filming something of interest. "He make cinema?"

"Yes, that's it. He's making a film."

"He will make film of us?" At this there would be a buzz from the crowd, who would start squaring off their *lungis* and straightening their shirts.

"Hey, B.B.; chap here wants you to take a shot of him and his friends."

B.B. would come over and, holding the cine-camera in the normal way, would let a few imaginary feet of film whir through. That pleased everybody no end, and, full of curiosity, they would gather round B.B., wanting to peer through the view-finder. I am afraid that it had to be imaginary film on these occasions, for B.B. was asked to take so many shots of people that, had he complied, the exposed film would have stretched all the way from Hyde Park Corner to Myitkyina.

The conversation usually ended with the 'interpreter' saying, "May I have your introduction, please?" At this I produced one of the Expedition cards, on which were printed our six names together with the Expedition's title. Many Pakistanis, Indians, and Burmese have their own cards (they call them 'introductions'), and unless you can produce one in exchange your stock falls considerably. I handed him one.

"Here you are; this has all our names on it."

He would get out his spectacles. "What is your name, please?"

I would point. "That one; Tim Slessor."

"Teem Salasar? Um. This is much honour for me. Thank you very much. Thank you." Then, looking at his watch with an elaborate gesture, he would say, "I think I go just now."

He would shake hands, and then everybody else would offer their hands, the ones at the back leaning over the shoulders of those in front. Sometimes there might be twenty people to say good-bye. Each person would nod and murmur, "Good morning good-bye"—for this much English they all knew—whether it was morning, noon, or night.

They were pleasant, cheerful people, and everybody in Myitkyina seemed to be strolling about as if they were enjoying a rather private joke. We warmed to them immediately, and our initial impressions of Northern Burma were to be confirmed a hundred times as we drove, in the course of the ensuing weeks, through the Kachin and Shan States. From the Western world, where a premium is set on efficiency and progress, it was delightful to come into this Arcadian land of easy simplicity, wooded hills, sunshine, and cheroots. No one is ever in a hurry in Burma, and though, as we sometimes found, this can be most aggravating, one is forced at the same time to acknowledge that it is probably doing one's soul no end of good.

Among other people we met in Myitkyina was a large Negro. To find a Negro in the far north of Burma was, to say the least, surprising, but— well, we had grown accustomed to the incongruous.

"Ah's in de West African Div. durin' de War, an' ah jus' liked it in Burmah so much that ah jus' stayed. Now ah's got a little garage here— sort o' work-shop, you might say. But ah's still a British subject—yes, suh."

"What part of Africa did you come from?" asked Pat.

"Lagos, yep, ah comed from Lagos."

"Do you think you'll ever go back?"

"M'be, m'be not. Ah dunno—think ah got too much o' Burmah in me now!"

"Well," I laughed, "you're a long way from home."

"Yo' ain't so close yo'self," he laughed, with a belch-like roll. "No, suh, yo' ain't so close yo'self."

He was right at that.

Myitkyina lies in a loop of the Irrawaddy which, eight hundred miles from the sea, was as wide as the Thames at Putney. We crossed on a little pontoon ferry powered by two outboard motors, and on reaching the far bank there was a heaped-up lorry-load of the Kachin Rifles (a battalion in the Burmese Army) waiting to drive aboard as we drove off. As they embarked the soldiers produced bamboo flutes, a gong, an old drum, and a spanner. They struck up their band, and a most melodious sound it was, too. Adrian and I rushed for the tape-recorder, and, having set it up, we delayed the soldiers' departure for the next half-hour. The bamboo flute is a delightful instrument in the hands of a trained musician—and these men were experts. The man on the drum was, as Pat put it, "real groovy," as was also the one with the spanner, who banged away at the side of the truck with a syncopating off-beat. The tunes had a tremendous swing, and then they broke into one which we recognized immediately as *Swanee River*. We later learnt that this and several other American songs have long been absorbed into Kachin folk-music from the gramophones of missionaries. We asked them to play *Swanee* a couple more times, and I am sure that, with their own unique variations, it could have been at the top of the Hit Parade anywhere. When the recordings were played back they slapped each other on the back, and then quietly listened to themselves with a most critical ear. But we could delay them no longer, and they waved and called to us all the way across the river.

> Way down upon the Irrawaddy,
> Far, far away,
> That's where we set up tape-recorder,
> That's where the pipe band play,
> All the world is gay and cheery,
> Everywhere we roam,
> Way down as far as Singapore,
> Then round and all the way home.[8]

This piece of doggerel found a place on the Expedition's song-sheet alongside such other favourites as *Oberlan' Mambo*, *Bumpin' Blues*, *Far Eastern Calypso* ("Far Eastun, Far Eastun; Dat wassa a fine Expedishun"), and the more sentimental *Dust gets in my Eyes*. Had we known anything about the then current popularity of rock 'n' roll we could have worked out something on that too. (In fact, on some of the roads we had been over the title would have been most appropriate.)

The way southward from Myitkyina ran through the hills very close to the Chinese border, and one night we slept only a few hundred yards from the frontier stream. In the morning we went down through the bamboos to the water's edge for a closer inspection. Through the binoculars everything was very peaceful, and we spent a diverting half-hour skipping pebbles across the water into China—well, it's not every day that one can play Ducks and Drakes with that country. Pat and Henry went a stage further. They found a small raft, and poled themselves across the Bamboo Curtain to exchange views with a peasant on the far side. They gave him some cigarettes as a token of goodwill, and then returned to the free world a few minutes later. Pat suggested that he might one day write a book called *Ten Minutes in China,* but, as he reflected, "Probably find some Socialist M.P. has already done it."

Our speed to the south was rather slow, but this was not due so much to the indifferent gravel surface as to our frequent halts for filming. The picturesque scenery of hill forest (rather than jungle) was a perfect backdrop, and whenever B.B. saw a particularly attractive section of twisting road he would stop the cars and set up his cine camera. The rest of us would reverse back down the road, and then, when he had adjusted the focusing and tested for camera angles, he would wave his straw hat. This was the signal for "Action, Camera," and, after a confirming toot on the horns, we would accelerate hard and come tearing past in a most impressive manner. Sometimes our cameraman was not satisfied, and we would have to go back and try again. On a particularly complicated bit he would even insist on a complete rehearsal so that everything would be perfect for the actual 'live' performance. I was the second cameraman, and, apart from loading the cameras, I often took the still pictures while B.B. was dealing with the movies. Sometimes, if I had behaved myself especially well, I was allowed to handle the cine camera. This was an honour indeed, and no apprentice was ever more conscious of his master.

By this time on our journey B.B. had us all thoroughly trained in his Camera Code (a part of Expedition Standing Orders). It was hard, but we had learnt by painful experience.

1. If you hear the camera whir don't look up, just continue what you are doing.
2. Never fiddle with a loaded camera—it may go off.
3. Don't make stupid faces; they aren't funny.
4. Don't ask silly questions—just do it.
5. Ignorance is no excuse.

When the camera was on the tripod B.B. was on his throne, and heaven help anybody who, for an instant, forgot it.

But by no means all the Expedition's photography was egotistical. We often paused in a wayside village to spend half an hour taking photos, walking about, and enjoying our surroundings. This was hill country, and, though warm in the bright sun, it was never hot. The air had the calm sparkle of a clear spring day. In fact, in the Shan Hills it seems to have been spring always—it is that sort of country.

Both Bhamo[9] and Namkham were very attractive. The latter, set in its quiet hills, was the cleanest and most cheerful village we had been in for several months. Shortly before arriving, the shackle pin in one of Oxford's springs broke, and so we pulled up in the village to try to find some old bolt as a substitute. Within minutes the greater part of the mechanically minded population were hunting about in the wartime scrap-heaps for a bolt that might do. From a vast choice which they presently brought us we selected an almost perfect replacement, and then, while the mechanics were carrying out the repair, the rest of us wandered about the village. Many of the little wooden houses had the curved gables and overhanging eaves that one associates with Chinese paintings; around them were fluttering prayer-flags. We passed a group of priests and novices in long yellow garments (worn like togas) who were going round with their wooden bowls collecting rice and other food which had been put out for them on various doorsteps.

But above all, it was the children who attracted our attention. Some of the babies, strapped to their mother's backs with wide bands of cloth, had the most glorious chubby faces—like little cherubs. One woman we saw was carrying her twins like this. It seems a most sensible arrangement, for both the mother's hands are free, the baby is kept warm, and she always has it with her out of harm's way. The slightly older children who had outgrown this way of getting about were running around the streets playing the traditional games of hide-and-seek, cops-and-robbers, and a sort of hopscotch. All were very clean, and boys and girls alike were dressed in bright-coloured rompers, and often woolly hats. They were the complete answer to a photographer's prayer. At first they were shy, but, after gradual coaxing with sweets, they were soon giggling and stretching out their hands for more.[10] Sometimes they would run off to fetch their brothers and sisters to join the fun. Our chief party piece was a small distorting-mirror which we usually gave to one of the bolder children; he would peer at himself with wonderful disbelief, and slowly his face would burble into a smile, and then into a coy bubble of embarrassment. Then they would all gather round the mirror, laughing, and generally being most charming. I seemed to have the task of being Uncle on these occasions, for, being the only person without a beard, they accepted me a little more readily than the others. With all the children jumping up and down for sweets and the mirror, it was rather like feeding a flock of fluttering pigeons.

In a little shop where Pat and I had gone to buy some cabbages we found that we could swap one English cigarette for three cheroots, and on this fabulous rate of exchange we quickly slid a tin of cigarettes across the counter. Soon the whole Expedition were champing away on cheroots nearly four inches long. With five beards, check shirts, battered hats, and now cigars, the Expedition looked very flamboyant. It seemed that we carried our own mobile aura of local colour!

The road ran on through the hills, and every now and again we caught a glimpse of China's mountains away to the north. Although much of the countryside was wooded, it was not jungle. Rather, in this almost temperate climate, it was thick forest, which in the higher parts gave way to pines and gorse. Sometimes it was very pleasant to stop on the road for a few minutes and listen to the drowsy silence and the birds.

On the afternoon of the third day south from Myitkyina we came out of the hills and down to the famous Burma Road. We stopped on the junction, for this was, we supposed, rather a notable moment. The Burma Road had been built before the War through the back door of China. At that time the Japanese were masters of the China coast, and it was only by building this road from Lashio (the railhead of the Burma Railways) to Kunming, in Yunnan, that Chiang Kai-shek's beleaguered garrisons could be supplied. But later, when the Japanese took Rangoon and the lower part of Burma, they cut this life-line at its seaward end, and the Chinese became completely isolated. It was to re-establish a land link with China that Stilwell fought his way eastward from Assam. His armies slogged their way down the alignment of the Stilwell Road (which was built immediately behind them) until nearly a year later he was halted at Myitkyina by the fanatical resistance of the Japanese garrisons. The hand-to-hand siege of Myitkyina lasted seventy-eight days and was one of the most frantic struggles of the War. On one occasion a train of eight trucks was lying blown across the line in Myitkyina station; the Japanese held four of the trucks and the besiegers held the other four. That situation lasted for thirty six hours. But eventually the town fell and the troops pushed on across the Irrawaddy.

When, some weeks later, the advance columns of that army reached the point where now our cars were stopped they saw, across their front, the Burma Road twisting away north to China. The Japanese, who still held Lower Burma, had been short-circuited, and the link had been re-established. Mountbatten, the Supreme Commander, briefly signalled to Churchill and the President, "The land route to China is open."

The land route to China"—for two thousand miles it stretched across three countries, from the docks of Calcutta to the remote mountain province of Yunnan. It was probably one of the longest supply roads of the War, and certainly one of the hardest.

That evening, driving down the once vital Burma Road, we passed only the occasional ox-cart. But the road itself belied the years remarkably well; the asphalt surface and the bridges were still in good condition, and for almost the first time since the Grand Trunk Road in India we were out of the dust and could cruise at over 40 m.p.h. Parts of the surrounding countryside were completely treeless, so thoroughly had the shifting cultivators cleared it. Had we not known, it would have been difficult to tell where in the world we were. It might almost have been Dartmoor or the Berkshire Downs. The milestones went steadily by, each successive one announcing the decreasing distance to Lashio, and then, a couple of hours after dark, we came down a long hill and into the town. We motored around until we found the Inspection Bungalow, and there installed ourselves for the night.

The next day we called on the Brigade Commander of the army garrison. He said that the road farther south to Maymyo was reasonably clear of insurgents, but he warned us not to stop except in villages, nor to travel after dark, as there had recently been a number of minor ambushes in the immediate vicinity of Maymyo itself. We should also call on the C.O. of the battalion stationed at Kyaukme—midway between Lashio and Maymyo—in order that our safe passage might be checked. We decided not to move on until the following morning, as the mechanics were anxious to have a clear day in which to do various maintenance jobs on the cars. So we sent a telegram to the British Consul at Maymyo telling him that we hoped to arrive the next evening. (He had written to us in Calcutta asking us to call on him in order to discuss the further plans of our journey to Thailand.)

The brief prosperity that Lashio enjoyed when it was the starting-point of the Burma Road has long ago gone, and to-day it is a small and sleepy town which has quite forgotten its past fame and importance. Once or twice a week a little train pulls itself through the hills from the plains of Mandalay (180 miles to the south-west), but often the line has been blown up by insurgents and the train must go back to wait until repairs are made. The town was very like something out of a Western film; many of the inhabitants wore tight jeans, check shirts, and cowboy hats; instead of horses they rode in battered jeeps, and these they parked down the main street as if at a hitching-rail.

There was a horse-buggy touring the town with a gramophone on the seat which was grinding out a selection of popular jazz. On the sides of the buggy were fluttering posters advertising the evening's film at the Lashio 'film-house'—*The Prisoner of Zenda*. B.B. and I decided to dip into the Expedition's entertainment allowance on the grounds that we wanted to study audience reaction and absorb some local colour.

The cinema was crammed; it reminded us very much of the Rex in Cambridge on a Saturday night during full-term. The evening started with the Burmese national anthem, at which every one shot to their feet with a good deal more alacrity and feeling than one usually sees in Britain. Then there was nearly an hour of the trailers of forthcoming attractions. These included *Son of Sinbad, Salome, Operation Gobi, Them,* and *Zombie*—Hollywood's most lurid products, and, judging by the audience's reaction to the trailers, the films themselves would go down with a bang.

Then came *The Prisoner of Zenda*; a synopsis of the story was flashed on the screen in Burmese script for the benefit of those who would not be able to follow the English dialogue. After this the film started, and away we went, the audience lapping it up, and getting all the funny situations. They were as sharp as needles; every time Deborah Kerr or Stewart Granger appeared there were enthusiastic cheers, and every time James Mason appeared (as Rupert of Hentzau) he was heartily booed. At half-time the lights went up for an interval, and, while some of the audience went outside to buy soft drinks and pork cracklings from the near-by stalls, the rest of us were entertained by theatre-organ records of *April in Portugal* and *Cherrypink Mambo*. The manager came down to ask B.B. and me how we were enjoying the film, and he offered to find us better seats without extra charge—"At back, more better for you, I think." But we declined his kindness.

Then the lights went out and the film continued. Towards the end the film became really exciting, with Mason and Granger having a ding-dong sabre duel in front of a distraught Deborah Kerr. The whole audience moved forward on its seat and was right in there with its hero. B.B. and I joined in the shouts of encouragement, and altogether, as a united audience, despite several anxious moments, we won our hero's day. The lovers leapt into each other's arms and the villain dived into the moat and away.

As the two of us filed out it was quite surprising to realize that this was Lashio; without overmuch imagination we could have hopped on our bicycles, pedalled down Castle Hill, along King's Parade, and back to College.

During our short stay in Lashio we had a string of visitors at the Inspection Bungalow. The Immigration Office and the police both sent representatives, who sat down and copied out the facts from our passports. Then there were other callers—students, ex-civil servants of British days, and school-teachers—who, hearing we were in Lashio, came to 'exchange views' with us. In this respect Burma was like India or Pakistan, where it is assumed that anyone who has been to Oxford or Cambridge is automatically endowed with wisdom, understanding, and a complete philosophy of life. Where they get this idea from it is difficult to say, but our guests expected us to sit by the hour and talk with them about war, peace, politics, religion, economics, education, the supernatural, the world hereafter—the lot. It was tiring work trying to live up to this reputation, and, I confess, the Expedition ran a rota system whereby each of us took it in turns to put the world aright with our visitors. Often the conversation came round to the fact that they wanted to go to Britain for further education or, in the case of the older people, they wanted to send their sons. How should they set about this? Could we help? How much did it all cost? Could we write them a letter of introduction? It was all very difficult, for one did not want to hurt their feelings. One knew that their chances of going to a British university were almost nil, but they were so sincere and earnest that it was cruel to be unsympathetic. Should one be realistic and pour cold water on their impractical aspirations or should one encourage them with false hope? Rightly or wrongly, we usually did the latter, for it seemed kinder at the time. But these questions troubled us.

We moved off to Maymyo the next day, and were soon rolling south through a sunny countryside of hills and forest. We often drove with the wireless on, and we had a happy knack of tuning in to the most appropriate or the most incongruous accompaniments—depending on which way you looked at them. Sometimes the car ahead would slow down and a head pop up through the roof-hatch with some shouted information for the car following.

"Hey, try the 31-metre band—Radio Ceylon is coming through clear as a bell."

"O.K., we've got some bird in Moscow giving off with the usual co-existence bilge. Whereabouts did you say?"

"Thirty-one-metre—up at the left-hand end."

Radio Ceylon was our frequent companion; in fact, it is the most powerful commercial station in the world, for it took over the wartime S.E.A.C. transmitters. On this occasion it was playing a Latin-American selection, and for the next thirty miles or so we tangoed and rumba'd merrily on our way.

We stopped at Kyaukme to report our safe arrival to the military commander, and to get his permission to proceed on to Maymyo. He confirmed that there had been no bandit activity on the road ahead for several weeks, but warned us to reach Maymyo before dark, as the guards around the town's perimeter were liable to be a little trigger-happy at night. There was not much time to waste, so we got into the cars again and drove out of Kyaukme at full speed.

The cars travelled like things possessed. If there had been any bandits around, Oxford and Cambridge would have been the most fleeting and impossible of targets! In seventy miles we only slowed once, and that was to take a few quick photos of the Goteik Gorge, where suddenly, in a succession of tarmac loops, the road fell headlong down the wall of the ravine for over one thousand feet. Then across a small bridge at the bottom and up the other side on to the forest plateau again.

The evening sky was growing dim and the head-lights had just been switched on when the forest ended and the road ran out across some open fields. Then our lights lit up the barbed-wire gate ahead, and as we slowed the soldiers came running out with their Sten guns at the ready. They surrounded the cars, but, having inspected our Government pass by torch, they opened the barrier and we drove through. On the far side was Mr Onslow, the Consul. "Well, I'd just about given you up for to-night. In fact, I was wondering what had happened," he said.

We stayed a couple of days in Maymyo—four of us with the Onslows, and B.B. and I with the Cassies (the Consulate wireless operator and his wife). They were easy days, for, apart from a letter home or so, even Adrian decided to relax and let all the 'admin' go to the winds. Maymyo had the sort of climate one dreams about—open shirts in the day and log-fires at night—for, although it is only forty miles from the heat of Mandalay, it is some thousands of feet higher, and was before the War the recognized hill station for a large part of the British administration. It is even claimed that strawberries will grow as big as apples and tomatoes will ripen all the year round in Maymyo.

The hospitality of our hosts was boundless; it ranged from golf and tennis to open cocktail-cabinets and sewing on buttons. Once, when Mrs Cassie overheard B.B. telling me about the wonders of his mother's sticky cakes, she slipped away and concocted a deliciously sticky trifle to console him. On another occasion we spent a most amusing morning with Cranley Onslow whacking (I claim no more) our way round the golf-course. Though the course was rather overgrown, it was still a clear relic of the days gone by, and I remember wondering if in two thousand years' time some dome-headed historian from Mars will trace the once mighty spread of the British Empire by plotting its golf courses. (For they are found wherever the British have been.) The Martian may well be perplexed about the rites attached to those hillocks we call bunkers—perhaps he will mark them on his map as "burial mounds" in much the same way as we mark tumuli of ancient Britain.

The British Consulate was guarded by a small detachment of Burmese soldiers. We asked the reason for this.

"Well," explained Cranley ("Cranners" when he was out of earshot), "they're here to look after me. You see, I had some 'visitors' a few weeks back. In fact, they arrived one night when I was in my bath, which was rather awkward. My wife came upstairs and told me that they wanted to see me, so I put on my dressing-gown and came down. There they were, about eight or nine of them, with their rifles propped up against the wall, and making themselves comfortable in the sitting-room. We were all very polite to each other, and they explained that they wanted my money, my typewriters, and my shotgun. There wasn't much point in arguing, so I handed the stuff over and the leader wrote out a receipt saying that the British Government would be fully compensated when their particular gang took over Burma. They were really quite pleasant about it all. But I must say I drew the line when they wanted me to go off to the forest with them for ransom!"

"What did you do?" some one asked.

"I gave them each a stiff whisky and told them I didn't want to go. Of course, if they'd insisted I'd have had to go, but fortunately they were a reasonable bunch, and liked my whisky; so we all shook hands on the doorstep, and off they went. The Army were out the next day, but never found them—in a way I'm rather glad."

He went on to tell us that this was not an isolated incident. Two months before, in broad daylight, a couple of W.H.O.[11] doctors had been kidnapped from their homes just near by. They had been hustled off into the forest and then taken for several days' march along tracks to the bandits' camp in the hills. There they were held for a fortnight until a ransom of several thousand pounds was paid. Apparently the bandits had treated them very well, and had even lent them their blankets at night—though the bandits themselves went without. One of the doctors was an Italian, and had so entertained his captors around the camp-fire with songs and operatic arias that, when the ransom finally arrived, the bandits were genuinely sorry to see him go.

On hearing these tales I am almost certain that Adrian was dreaming up some way to get himself kidnapped. It would have made just the gripping story he was always looking for!

We discussed our plans in some detail with Cranley, and he gave us much useful advice, for it seemed that not all the bandits in the areas through which we should have to pass were quite such Robin Hoods as those around Maymyo. Our immediate intent was for one car to go to the ruby-mining town of Mogok for a couple of days (I'll explain why later), while the other car stayed on in Maymyo. The cars would then meet again and drive south to Taunggyi, the capital of the Shan States.

FROM THE DIARY

Henry, B.B., and I are travelling up to Mogok (about 130 miles). The main reason for this is that B.B.'s grandfather, in 1886, was one of the first Europeans to visit the town. At that time the India Office were considering the annexation of Upper Burma and had been approached by a trading concern who, hearing of ruby deposits at Mogok, were anxious to obtain a concession to work them. Accordingly, B.B.'s grandfather was dispatched up the Irrawaddy from Rangoon and after a long journey by boat and mule he eventually reached his destination. He wrote a report on the gem workings and brought out a large ruby which was later put in his daughter-in-law's engagement ring (B.B.'s mother). B.B. is naturally anxious to visit the place.

The three of us in Oxford drove out of Maymyo in the cool crispness of the early morning, and started back up the road which we had come down two days previously. In just over two hours of flat-out driving we had wound down and up the sides of the Goteik Gorge and were back in

Kyaukme. There, as before, we reported to the Army; then turned on to a bumpy track which led out of the back of the town and into the hills. We had been warned by several people that the seventy miles to Mogok would take us at least five hours, so rough was the surface. Others had told us that dacoits were not uncommon in these hills.

The road climbed a little and then twisted in and out along the hillsides. It was every bit as bad as people had said, but, not having a single operatic aria between us, we drove Oxford like an express train—over the most complicated series of points in the world. Driving was hard work and demanded the utmost concentration, for one was always wrenching the wheel hard left or right, a hand was almost continuously on the gear-lever, and one's feet might have been jigging on an organ, so frequently were they dabbing at the brakes, the clutch, or accelerator. In fact, there were many occasions when one wished for three feet—how else could one brake hard, double de-clutch, and twist round a steep corner all simultaneously? (No, you can't 'heel and toe' in a Land Rover—not unless you wear size 16 surgical boots and have a ball-and-socket joint in your ankle.) There was no part of the road which was straight for more than twenty-five yards, and most of the corners were blind. At the end of an hour the driver was exhausted. But there 'wus bandits in them thar hills,' so we did not waste much time when changing round. All afternoon we thundered and crashed along at every bit of 15 m.p.h.

In fact, we reached the low pass overlooking Mogok more than an hour ahead of schedule, and, as far as we were concerned, we had set up an all-time record and broken two shock-absorbers.

We drove into the single street and stopped at an open-fronted shop to ask for Mr Pain. He was our host, and had been sent a telegram by the Consul in Maymyo two days previously asking him to expect us. The shopkeeper came out into the street and pointed at a bungalow and a large yellow umbrella up on the hillside. He gave us to understand that Mr Pain was underneath the 'brella.' We went up the hill, and our host came down to meet us; through his binoculars he had seen the car winding its way down the far side of the valley some minutes before.

Mr Pain was the typical Englishman's colourful idea of the typical Englishman. A Mogok ruby-dealer for over twenty years, he was one of the only three Europeans left in the town. He was coach, critic, and arch-instigator of the local football team, and was almost the unofficial squire of Mogok, due to his intense interest in local affairs. He knew everybody and everybody knew him. He also had other interests which were farther afield—much farther. While we were having tea and listening to his Gilbert and Sullivan records a telegram arrived. It was from the Secretary of the Clare College Boat Club in Cambridge, giving Mr Pain the dates and details of that year's regattas at Henley and Marlow. This ruby merchant came down from Clare thirty years ago, yet he flies home every other year to coach the College eight for Henley and Marlow. A round trip of twenty thousand miles every second summer to give his old boat club the benefit of his support and experience—how English can one get? He seemed almost hurt at our amazement.

"But you've no idea how much I look forward to it," he said. "I take over the crew at the end of the May Races and look after them until Marlow, and then on to Henley." He looked at the telegram. "Marlow seems rather late this year—still, that'll give me more time with the crew than I usually have. But I'll have to nip back here pretty smartly afterwards to get my junior soccer team up to scratch for the Mogok Challenge Cup. I presented the cup a few years ago, so it's rather important that my team should win it."

As I had had the doubtful distinction of stroking my College fourth eight (a crew of redundant old sweats and freshmen) for five successive terms, Mr Pain and I swung into rowing shop as if we had been cycling down the towpath of the Cam. I do not suppose that even the most humble of oarsmen came to Mogok more than once in a year of Sundays, and, hearing that I at least knew the difference between a slide and a rigger, he led me round the photos of his past crews that hung on the bungalow walls. I listened attentively while he gave me an analysis of the individuals in each group.

"Rogers, an Australian—good solid blade-work, but, oh, dear me, awfully slow on his beginnings." "Ah, now, that chap was one of the best oars I've ever had—a bit temperamental on the bank, but as cool as a cucumber once he was in the boat. Killed in the War, poor fellow." "This crew here came on as fast as any I've ever coached, but they lost to Pennsylvania University on the last day when 'five' caught a crab just short of the finish—they were leading by over a length, too. Rather bad luck."

Yes, I agreed, it *was* rather bad luck after going all that way to coach them. Most of the rubies in the world have come from the small hillside shafts around Mogok. It is said that the Black Prince's ruby in the Crown Jewels came from here, and, though no one knows how old the workings are, it seems fairly certain that they go back more than a thousand years. Due to the fragmentary nature of the gem-bearing seams, ruby-mining is very much of a hit-or-miss business, and does not lend itself to modern or large-scale methods. The only company which tried mechanical means of extraction found they did not pay, and it went bankrupt in the thirties. For one thing, it was much too easy for a worker to spot a ruby in the sludge, pop it in his mouth, and sell it later as his own. Thus, of course, the company lost much of its rightful profits. The little shafts and adits are worked as they have been for centuries past, by five or six men and women—usually of the same family, so that each person can trust the others. Most of the mining is done by hand (the shafts are usually only twenty or thirty feet deep), but a few have small diesel engines to pump the sludge up to the surface. The sludge, brought up by bucket or pump, is then sluiced down wooden spillways until the mud and lighter material have run off. The rubies, sapphires, moonstones, sphenes, and many other gems are found among the remaining coarse gravel—if one is lucky, which usually one is not.

Around Mogok—in fact, all over Burma—there are innumerable spirits, or 'nats'; they seem to be rather like hobgoblins and have the most unusual likes and dislikes, which must be carefully catered for if one is to keep on the right side of these 'little people.' In the picnic lunch which Mr Pain's cook had prepared for us to take to the mine there were some egg sandwiches. Now, it happens that those nats whose self-appointed task it is to look after rubies cannot abide eggs, and so, Mr Pain explained to us, we should have to eat the sandwiches before we got to the mine. We also learnt that one must not mention anything about elephants, monkeys, or horses within earshot of a ruby mine. Neither may a pregnant woman cross over water which is flowing towards it. If any of these things happen the nats become very annoyed, and, out of pique, drive the rubies farther into the ground, where they are much more difficult to find. This does not please anybody, tempers get frayed, and work must often stop until the nats have cooled off. It is incumbent on any visitors to co-operate with the miners by being careful about these things, and so naturally we did our best.

We spent an interesting time down the mine, and then hopefully busied ourselves at the gravel heap to see what we could find. We found several very small rubies, and rather more spinel and other semi-precious stones. The three of us became quite excited, but after nearly an hour we still had not got any gems big enough to be worth anything. B.B. took a few photos of these Expeditional mining operations, and then we motored back towards Mogok.

On the way back we stopped in a small village; it was bazaar day, and B.B. wanted to take photos of this gay occasion. A curious thing about these bazaars is their timing; they are held every fifth day all over Upper Burma, despite the fact that in most other respects the country follows the conventional seven-day week. If this week market day is on a Thursday in a particular village, then next week it will be on a Tuesday, and the week after on a Sunday. This means that the travelling traders move round five different villages, stopping in each for one day until they have arrived back at the first. How the timing of these 'five-day bazaars' (as they are known) has grown up no one seems to know, but it would surely make an interesting study to find out.

B.B. had a busy time with his cameras, for it was a very colourful scene. There were Gurkha women squatting beside their vegetables, laid out on green banana-leaves; Madrasi traders in open stalls selling cloth, shirts, shoes, and cheap Japanese knick-knacks; monks in their yellow robes carrying bunches of flowers; Lishaw women in long black gowns and elaborate red and black headdresses dragging little woolly ponies behind them; Sikhs selling knives, lamps, and crowbars; Shan and Shan-Burman jewel-traders, who stood about examining each other's stones—dressed in snap-brim trilbies, and with rows of gold-topped pens peeping from their breast-pockets. There were miners of every variety—Burmans, Shans, Chinese, and Gurkhas—who had come in from the diggings with the rubies they had found in the last few days. It was strange to see these gems changing hands next to stalls of cabbages and swedes, and then to realize that many of them would eventually find their way to Hatton Garden—having increased their price many times on the way.

It was a wonderful jostle of men and women, ponies, dogs, children, jeeps, and old lorries. The noise was terrific. Everybody took a great interest in us (which rather hindered B.B.'s candid camera work), and those few that could speak English asked us questions and politely laughed at all our answers. We met one old man who slyly told us of the fortune he had made by passing off bits of red glass from the tail-lights of lorries as enormous rubies to British and American troops at the end of the War

⊕

We left Mogok the next day and returned down the track to the south. On reaching Kyaukme in the late afternoon we picked up petrol, and were presently joined by Cambridge as previously arranged. They had spent the day before in Mandalay, and Pat was of the opinion that, whatever else Kipling may have been, he was certainly not a geographer. "'On the road to Mandalay, where the flyin' fishes play,' my foot!" he said. "About as much chance of seeing a ruddy kipper!"

The Expedition stayed the night with an Anglo-Burman we had met some days previously in Maymyo who had offered to lay on some Shan folk-dances by some near-by villagers for our benefit. While he was giving us supper the villagers gathered on the lawn outside and peered through the bungalow windows at their prospective audience. Then, after we had set up the tape-recorder, the evening's entertainment began. I cannot honestly say that I thought the music was melodious. A long drum was beaten at regular intervals with the flat of the hand and a facial expression that implied a lifetime's practice; a small brass gong was struck at the same intervals, and with a similar expression; a pair of cymbals was clashed with considerable aplomb between times. This was the 'band,' and for sheer monotony it took some beating. But the dancers were much more interesting. First there was a man dressed up as a peacock—or, rather, a mythical bird which features frequently in Shan legend—with huge cloth and bamboo wings and a white mask. The dance was a twisting affair with arms and legs moving slowly from one angle to another and then back again. In these dances much of the meaning is conveyed by the hands, but, of course, we were quite unable to interpret the gestures. This was followed by the village headman, who, stripped to the waist, did a lugubrious sword dance. He waved his sword into all sorts of improbable positions, but, as he was the headman, we supposed he knew what he was about. Next on the bill was the 'funny man.' Actually, our host told us, this chap was really an idiot, but the village audience thought he was very funny. As is often the case in primitive and, for that matter, sophisticated humour, the onlookers think it is a huge joke if some one is a little insane. Whenever this poor chap faltered or forgot his ditties they roared, but in the end they got tired of his one-track slapstick, and booed him away. (Dare I say it—he reminded me of several better-known British comics.)

We made recordings of all this, and when they were played back everybody crowded round to get a better look at the 'spirit box'—as the recorder must have been to them. They wanted to know how it worked. We explained—through our host—that inside lived a 'nat' who had a prodigious memory, and who, when we turned the switch, could instantly recall exactly what he had just heard. Well, how else could we explain it?

As we travelled on to the south the next day I remember lying in the back and thinking—not of anything particular, but just thinking. Lying there, with my hat over my eyes and my feet propped up on the food-box, there was always plenty of time to wander about, to talk to myself. All of us used to do it, for it was a drowsy, relaxing business. . .

. . . I must write home fairly soon. Taunggyi would be a good place for that—be there a few days. Wonder what I'll be doing this time in a year? Waiting for a bus? No, of course, it's eleven o'clock, so I'd already be at the office. What office? Who cares—there's plenty of time to sort that one out when we get back. Anyway, it's still night in England, so I'd be in bed. Helluva noise on the roof—must be that shovel got loose. Remind me to fix it when we stop. Remind who? Me—remind me; who on earth am I talking to? Oh, yes, offices . . . won't like that much. Well, they probably won't like me either. But one's got to do something. Well, I suppose so. Yes, I suppose one must. But there might be some chap who wants a crew to sail round the world. Could be . . . When'll we get to Singapore? Let me see, three weeks to Bangkok? Yes, about that—probably spend a week there. Then two or three weeks down the peninsula. About two months to Singapore? Something like that. Then we've got to drive home—hell, that's a thought. Oh, shut up and get some sleep. Um, a couple of months . . . but what about that bit where there isn't a road? Hasn't Pat had some letters about that? Oh, not to worry, that's way south of Bangkok. We'll think about it when we get there. There's that damn shovel again—perhaps if I packed it on top of the beds? But didn't I do that this morning? Couldn't have; must remember next time. Beds — what did I say about beds? Can't remember; something about the shovel. . .

And so one meandered on until they woke you and said it was your turn to drive.

Sometimes one had to walk round the car to wake up—then into the driver's seat, make yourself comfortable, adjust your dark glasses, and sit with a foot stroking the accelerator until everybody was aboard and the chap in the back had slammed shut his door. Then up into first, off brake, out clutch, lift your foot slowly and away; hold the speed up, through into second, through into third, and then top.

"What was the last milestone, B.B.?" (He had been driving last.)

"Should be the ninety-third coming up. By the way, watch the corners in the hill sections. Some are a lot sharper than they look."

"O.K. Ninety-third—another forty or fifty miles to go. Should be in Loilem in a couple of hours. What's the form then?"

"Either push on to Taunggyi or stay the night in the I.B.[12] at Loilem—there's one marked on the map. Here comes the milestone. Sorry, ninety-first."

Loilem was only a small place, and had it not been the administrative centre of one of the districts of the Shan States and on a road junction it might hardly have been on the map. We were most courteously welcomed by the C.O. of the army camp, who had been sent a signal about our movements earlier in the week from Lashio. Although it was only mid-afternoon when we arrived, he asked us to wait until the next day before going on the further sixty miles to Taunggyi. This was because the next stretch of road ran through a mountainous section on which there had recently been a certain amount of terrorist activity. He therefore suggested that we should travel with the regular morning convoy, for which his unit provided an escort. Meanwhile he invited us to make ourselves completely at home in the Officers' Mess.

The Mess was very similar to that of any small unit of the British Army in the tropics. The same books were in the bookshelves; the same dog-eared copies of *Picture Post* and the *Overseas Mirror* were strewn about the chairs; the regimental trophies were on the tables; Daily Orders were on the board; the Visitors' Book lay open just inside the entrance; and hardly had we stepped through the door when the Mess Sergeant appeared with beer and cigarettes. In fact, it was almost better than a British Mess.

Other officers came in to meet their visitors, and, as the Mess Sergeant padded backward and forward with the bottles, there was soon quite a party. They could all speak English, and we found we had quite a lot in common; they gave us the impression that they really enjoyed having us. During dinner (in the Mess) they wound up the gramophone and played a series of scratchy and almost antique Victor Silvester records interspersed with others of Burmese songs. Then eventually, when we drove out of the camp to go across to the near-by I.B. for the night, the sentry at the gate gave us a smart present arms.

It was an early start the next morning. Before the sun was really up we had taken our place in the small convoy drawn up outside the army camp. The C.O. came to see us off; he introduced us to the sergeant in charge of the escort, and soothed our somewhat anxious minds with the cheerful news that there had been no ambushes for several weeks past. Anyway, he pointed out, the bandits usually shot up the escort for first choice, as they regarded their war as one against the Government forces rather than civilians. For this reason he was glad to see that our cars were painted clearly in blue, and that therefore they could not easily be confused as a target with the normal drab-green Land Rovers of which the Burmese Army had quite a number. We inwardly thanked the British Embassy in Rangoon for warning us of this very point eight months before. In fact, it had been one of the reasons why we had chosen to be "unnecessarily flamboyant" (as some of our critics claimed at the time) in having the cars painted in Oxford and Cambridge colours.

The road ran level across open grassland for some miles, and then twisted sharply through the ranges. In these—the hill sections—almost every corner seemed a made-to-measure ambush-site; the bends were so acute that one had to slow right down to get round them. There was always a steep cutting on one side—where the road followed a narrow ledge cut into the slope—and a steep drop to the valley on the other side. Every now and again on the verge there was a white disc (about the size of a soup-plate) on top of a small pole. Apparently these marked places where there had been past attacks, though it was difficult to see what really useful purpose they served—unless as mute rejoinders to hurry on. But the soldiers did not seem the least perturbed. They all lit up cheroots, and, though they sat low in the truck with their rifles and Bren guns poking out over the side, it was all mere routine to them. Neither were they in any hurry. The convoy pulled up in several villages along the way for what seemed to be a Burmese NAAFI break of green tea and rice-cakes. Their vehicle too was unwilling to forgo these periodic respites. Built for the War, she was old and tired. These stops were when the driver demanded wire and pliers to make the running repairs.

We reached Taunggyi in the early afternoon, and as we came down the hill towards it the tin roofs glinted in the sun, and then the wide main street opened out before us. Nearly all these towns of the Shan hills are rambling, spacious settlements with little wooden cottages planted in gardens of trees and shade. There are also a number of churches, for some of the Shans are Christians, as a result of missionary work during the last fifty years. All this and the rolling scenery around gives one the impression, as I have remarked before, that if one could put the inhabitants in Stetsons and spurs one might well be in cowboy country.

Perhaps I should explain why we went to Taunggyi, for, in fact, it was fifty miles off our direct route to Thailand. There was one main reason: to make a reconnaissance for the possible return of the Oxford car three months later to do some fieldwork in Burma (a brief survey of the country's mineral industries). Before leaving England we had discussed the possibility of doing this work, but at that stage it had seemed so far ahead that we had temporarily shelved the plan. Now, however, providing we reached Singapore, we could see the way for one car to come back to Burma by sea,[13] and with this in mind we now visited Taunggyi (the capital of the Shan States) to lay our plans before the authorities, and to make preliminary inquiries.

We spent an amusing five days seeing a variety of different officials—the Secretary of the Shan States Government, the Resident, the Assistant Resident, the Chief Forest Officer, the Manager of the Government

Experimental Farm, the Registrar of Shan Co-operatives, the Veterinary
Officer, the Secretary of the State Mining Corporation, the Chief Chemist
in the Government Laboratory, the Education Officer, Uncle U Tet
Maung-Maung, and all. But, without boring the reader further, suffice it
to say that all this 'visiting' was necessary in the interests of our intended
return.

There were other diversions as well. The Expedition was invited to be
the guests of the Taunggyi Rotary, where each of us was expected to make
a five-minutes speech "on any subject." It is one of my chief regrets that I
did not make recordings of those speeches; I have never heard six
supposedly semi-educated people talk such inane piffle! On another
occasion we went to the near-by lake of Inle, where the villagers around
the shores live a uniquely amphibian life. Practically everything is done on
water—including the growing of rice on islands of floating sedge. Even the
smallest children have their own little dug-outs, in which they paddle to
school.

Throughout our stay in Taunggyi there were numerous invitations for
us to have meals with different families, and on more than one occasion
we had to split up—three of us going to one home, and three of us going
to another. These Shans were most kind and friendly; simple, unaffected
people, but cultured and witty too. A few of them had been to England,
all of them had been subjects of the Crown, and, though now zealous for
their independence, they did not look at us as foreigners but almost as old
friends. I do not wish to be sentimental, but I would say that we liked the
Shans immensely.

13.

Kengtung-side and Beyond

Taunggyi to Takaw (172 *miles*)

UP at 5.00. Breakfast, packed, and filled up all tanks by 6.30. Then out to the edge of the town to pick up our escort for the drive back to Loilem. We took considerably more interest in this escort than we had in the one which brought us into the town a few days ago. This interest was due to the tales we had heard from the Colonel of the Union Military Police, who had told us of an insurgent attack on one of his outposts only seven miles from Taunggyi—two nights ago. Apparently it was quite a battle; his troops used three-inch and two-inch mortar bombs, four hundred rounds of rifle ammunition, and even more of Sten, but, even so, the rebels had only withdrawn at dawn. A few weeks ago there was another attack on an Army convoy travelling a mountain road some seventy miles away to the south. The rebels had somehow got wind of the convoy's coming, and they had laid a trap with four Bren guns. Six men were killed.

Our escort consisted of half a platoon of men armed with Bren guns, rifles, and Stens. They travelled in a Dodge 3-ton truck, which was in considerably better repair than the one which had accompanied us previously. We impressed on them our wish to get to Loilem as quickly as possible. It was, in fact, quite unnecessary, for they fairly hurtled through the hills, and at times we had quite a job to keep up. We pulled into Loilem three hours out from Taunggyi, which was excellent progress.

The C.O. (of the Army camp) whom we met a few days ago was away but he had left a message. All his troops were out on operations, so he had instructed the local police to provide our escort for the next stage. We went down to the police station; drawn up outside was an incredibly ancient civvy truck. (The Army and police often have to commandeer civilian lorries, as they have not enough vehicles of their own. Naturally, the owners only lend their most decrepit lorries.) As we knew that this next bit of road was absolutely safe—there had been no incidents on it for over six months—we tried to persuade the superintendent to let us travel without a guard. We could see at a glance that the escort truck was on its last legs, and, with constant breakdowns, it would delay us all day. Without an escort, we estimated that we could reach the Salween river that night, but if we had to travel with this antique truck the journey might well take two days. The superintendent appreciated our point of view, and also agreed that an escort was hardly necessary, but, he said, the C.O. had given him his orders. Nevertheless, he suggested a typically Burmese solution—we should drive on ahead, and the escort would follow behind at its own speed. Thus he could carry out his instructions, and yet at the same time we should not be delayed. We praised the superintendent for this excellent compromise, and said good-bye. As we left Loilem the policemen of the escort began pushing their lorry about the police compound in an effort to get it started. We judged that that was the last we would see of them.

Soon we were driving fast along a narrow track to the east. The country around was undulating, much of it was badly deafforested, and the dry grassland and scrub stretched on as far as one could see. This deafforestation is the result of the shifting agriculture practised by the hill tribes. The slight fertility of their jungle plots is quickly exhausted, and then they move on. The bare land left behind is unprotected from the sun's direct heat or the monsoon rains, and the result is that the ferrous compounds of the soil soon oxidize into a hard red surface known as laterite. This is extremely infertile—even to the encroaching jungle—and the resultant areas of sterile waste become a serious problem. A subsidiary effect (but one much more disastrous in its consequences) is that, on the bare surface, the 'run-off' of the monsoon rains is vastly increased, to cause choked and swollen rivers which flood their lower courses. In S.E. Asia the river deltas are invariably crowded rice-lands, and so there is often considerable loss of life in these floods—the direct result of deafforestation in the hills often hundreds of miles away. It is an interesting example of man upsetting a natural balance. A solution is difficult, for farmers everywhere are a conservative breed, but illiterate hill-farmers are more so than most.

When we had covered fifty miles from Loilem we stopped for a 'brew-up' and lunch. We took our time, and were just finished when we heard a clattering and a spluttering coming through the trees. Lo and behold—the escort truck! We gave an amused cheer as it went wheezing past, and the police stood up in the back and gave an equally jovial shout in return. Presently we motored on after them. Half an hour later we came round a sharp corner, and suddenly had to jump on the brakes and ram our cars into the verge. We had nearly collided with the escort truck, which was stationary in the middle of the track; it was deserted except for the driver, who was poking the engine with an old table knife. During this breakdown the escort had evidently taken the chance to go off into the forest and bag some duck and wood pigeon for its dinner. The driver refused our offer of help, so we went on.

During the afternoon the track became much rougher as it wound its way over a series of high mountain ridges. Another three hours and, as the sky grew pale with wonderful colours, changing as we watched, we hairpinned slowly down nearly three thousand feet of forest hillside into the Salween Gorge. Then quite suddenly we saw the Salween itself. It was about a hundred yards wide, and came roaring down that deep jungle valley like a tide rip. The Shans call it the Mad River, and seeing it rush sleek and solid down that gorge, already a thousand miles from its source, we could understand why. The scene in the dusk was magnificent. The dark hills on either side rose up in a great leap for thousands of feet into the evening clouds, and, in the twilight, the river looked like molten silver. If we had been ancient explorers we might well have written in our journals "and so we come to the mighty Salween." Even to us such a phrase seemed worth while.

We decided to cross the next day, for already it was dark. There was, of course, no bridge, and the current was much too strong for any ordinary ferry. Instead a pulley rode along a steel cable which stretched above the river to the far bank. Attached to the pulley by a rope was a small raft, and when the raft's broad rudder was put hard over to one side the current pushed the "flying ferry" (as this arrangement is known) sideways across the river as fast as a speedboat.

We found the little bungalow which overlooked the river from a narrow ledge cut into the valley wall. Around it were earth bunkers which had been dug two or three years before, when Chinese Kuomintang guerrillas had penetrated to this part, and when the Salween crossing had assumed considerable strategic importance.

Collecting some wood, we started the old stove in the bungalow and made supper. It was a warm and merry meal, for while peeling the potatoes the subject of birthdays came up, and it transpired that Henry's twenty-second anniversary had occurred a few days before. In fact, he had forgotten all about it. Quick to find an excuse for a party, the Expedition got out the brandy ('medicinal') and had what might be called a 'birthday thrash.'

About midnight, just as we were turning in, we heard a grinding and a screech of brakes outside. The escort had arrived. We had forgotten all about them. They had evidently had a successful day's shooting, for, after unloading their cooking-pots, they borrowed our lanterns and sat on the veranda, plucking a whole selection of weird-looking birds. Then, lighting a series of little fires, they threw the birds on the embers, put on some rice, and waited. They were still going strong when we finally fell asleep.

"We left Hyde Park Corner five months ago to-day."

We crossed over on the raft, one car at a time, early the next morning. Some days previously, while in Taunggyi, it had been arranged by wireless that an escort would drive out from Kengtung to meet us at the Salween. And now, landing on the far bank, we were greeted by a detachment of the Kengtung State Police commanded by a little Karen who had a face as weatherbeaten as a walnut. He bounced about in a pair of gym shoes with a pistol at his belt and a carbine over his shoulder, smiling, welcoming us, puffing an enormous cheroot, and repeatedly saying he was a "Catholic Christian-man." Automatically we dubbed him Cheerful Charlie ("Charlie" was the Expedition's generic term for practically anybody whose real name we did not know). But, in his case, this was considered rather too familiar, and so we amended it to the slightly more formal Charles. He, his fourteen men, and their two almost palæolithic jeeps (*circa* 1942) were to lead us over the next one hundred and twenty miles—and three 6000-foot ridges—to Kengtung. Charles told us that, due to breakdowns, the journey out from Kengtung had taken the escort two days; he confidently expected the return journey to take a good deal longer.

He introduced us to his men, and we offered our cigarettes around All carried rifles and bandoliers, and wore the sheriff-like Star of Kentung on their floppy hats. All followed their leader's example in carrying a plentiful supply of cheroots and rice-flour 'goodies' in their ammunition pouches. That they were a picturesque posse there was no doubt, but we hoped (and they must have too) that there would be no undue test of their military efficiency. We shook hands all round, and, after these cheerful preliminaries, Charles briefly explained that we were now entering country where ambushes by refugee Chinese Nationalist guerrillas (the Kuomintang) were not uncommon—"So, gentlemens, please to be careful." He then lit up another cheroot, turned to his merry men, and waved his carbine; they gave their jeeps a push-start, and the convoy moved off. We climbed up a steep ravine away from the Salween.

Twenty minutes later Charles' jeep suddenly stopped. Ambush ahead? No, trouble with a non-existent exhaust system. Four of the soldiers crawled underneath, and after chatting down there for ten minutes emerged with apparent satisfaction and the exhaust pipe. With this stowed in the back, with cheroots relit, and with the appropriate push-start the convoy resumed progress.

The road, in common with several others we had been on in recent weeks, was most spectacular. Now it ran along a high ledge cut in the rock; now into a craggy limestone gorge, and then out along the jungle mountain-side. It may have been spectacular, but it was not made for gentle motoring; in the first hour we covered less than ten miles. How many things can a road do? Turn, twist, wriggle, wind, kink, climb, fall, slide, and descend? Anyway, this road, east and above the Salween, did all these and more, as it slowly thrust its way to the top of the first 6000-foot ridge. When at last we reached the crest we looked out over range after range of dark-green jungle hills; we must have been able to see for

nearly a hundred miles, almost to China. Far below we could look down
to the tiny cluster of a village nestling in a clearing of paddy fields on the
valley floor. Our road, hours ahead, ran through the village like a wisp of
thread.

The descent took over three hours, for Charles' jeep crawled down at
almost a walking pace. Sometimes his men hopped off to ease the load
down a particularly sharp slope. Also we had to stop twice; once to allow
the rearguard jeep to catch up after a puncture (hardly surprising,
considering that the inner tubes peeped through the walls of the tyres in
about a dozen places) and another time to remove a rock which had fallen
on to the path. When eventually we reached the village Charles decided to
call a halt for lunch, and everybody disembarked into the chop-house for
green tea. We ventured to ask Charles, "Why so slow?"

"Jeep," he shrugged, "no brakings." And then added laconically, "I
think to-day not to Kengtung coming."

This, in the opinion of Henry (mechanic and ex-Hon. Sec. of the
Cambridge University Auto Club), was "just not good enough."

He spent the lunch break calling for wire, pliers, and brake fluid while
he rehabilitated the reluctant 'brakings.' Then he turned his horrified
attention to the 'electrics' and the steering. Having dismantled and piled
the redundant components in the back, he sat himself in the driver's seat,
and ill-temperedly ordered one of Charles' men to fit the starting-handle
"and wind your guts out till it starts." The man did as he was told, and
eventually the jeep staggered to life. Then, after taking it off for a trial run
round the village, our mechanic informed Charles that he, Henry, was
driving the escort jeep for the remainder of the journey, and that the
convoy would be leaving in five minutes. Charles and his cheroot
demurred gently, and said something about Henry not knowing the way—
apparently there were several six-lane super-highways branching off!
Henry said he thought he could manage.

It seemed to me that as an added precaution one of the Expedition
should be armed. Accordingly, before we set off again, I asked Charles if he
had any spare weapons. He said he had not. I pointed out that he had a
carbine and a pistol; he could not use both, and I should be grateful for the
loan of one or the other. After some hesitation on his part I took the
carbine.

The convoy set off again towards the next ridge. With the ex-Sec, at the wheel of the leading jeep, our progress was phenomenal. He threw that jeep round the corners and up and down the spurs to such effect that, for the first time in the day, Charles and his men extinguished their cheroots in order to devote their whole attention to remaining aboard their jeeps. We, in Oxford and Cambridge, had quite a job to keep up as Henry streaked along the track as if back at Silverstone. But with the convoy thus reorganized, with one of our own members setting the pace, and myself with a carbine over my knees, the Expedition found the arrangements much more to its liking—and, we were sure, twice as efficient.

We were still many miles from Kengtung by the time we had climbed over the second ridge, and, as it was almost dark, we decided to stop the night in a small village in the valley below. In any case, it would have been dangerous to drive on at night, for neither jeep had head-lamps that worked, and Henry hardly fancied finding his way along the forest track by the glow of a row of cheroots—the only other possible means of illumination. Accordingly, on arrival at the village we moved into the little bamboo hut that served as inn and cooked our supper to an audience of interested locals. They were intrigued by practically everything about us, for they rarely saw visitors, let alone Europeans. Above all, of course, they were fascinated by our distorting mirror, and if I had to give one piece of advice to other expeditions it would be to take one of these mirrors. It is a passport to almost anywhere, and the laughter it causes is mutual and understandable, quite regardless of language.

We discussed the strategic situation, and, inviting Charles to take supper with us, told him that the convoy would be leaving for Kengtung at nine o'clock the next morning. Then we put up our beds on the earthen floor and went to sleep.

⊛

Our decision the previous evening that the convoy would move on at nine o'clock had been made with unfounded optimism, for we had not reckoned with the jeeps. Charles must have known better, which probably accounted for his amused expression. First, there were two punctures to mend, so the Expedition donated tyre-patches; then there was a damaged tyre valve, so the Expedition donated a new one; air had to be put in the tyres, so the Expedition lent a foot pump; lastly, the jeeps were almost out of petrol, so the Expedition had to siphon six gallons out of its own tanks. Throughout these proceedings the escort got the full blast of our copious and cogent advice. Charles was quite unperturbed—he and his cheroot retired to the shade of a banana-tree.

At last we were ready to move, and, as on the day before, Henry led the way and I took Charles' carbine. The file of cars climbed continuously—except for another puncture and an electrical hitch in one of the jeeps—most of the morning. The country at the top of the pass was most beautiful, and at that height the forest merged into pines and flowering rhododendron-like bushes. Then, down the other side, the country opened out, and the hillsides were dappled with little fields of white opium-poppies. At one of the convoy's customary halts for jeep-maintenance some of the police demonstrated the method of opium-extraction to us, and at a village where we stopped to refuel the jeeps (they had run out again) we examined some black pellets of the drug.

Going on, Charles pointed out a favourite Kuomintang ambush position, with the nonchalant comment, "To-day no trouble I pray God" (he was a Catholic Christian-man). Three hours and four breakdowns later we shepherded the escort down into the Kengtung valley, and as we pulled up outside the town's police station Charles lowered himself from his vehicle and remarked with a happy expression, "Well, Kengtung now!" In the course of those two days and 114 miles we had grown fond of Charles, and, in case he should ever have this read to him, we thank him—and his merry posse!

Kengtung is a small town far out in the eastern corner of the Shan States, near where the uncertain frontiers of four countries meet—China, Laos, Thailand, and Burma. It would not be true to say that Kengtung is completely isolated, but it would be no exaggeration to suggest that it is lonely and remote. By road it is nearly seven hundred miles from Rangoon, and in the whole of Kengtung State, an area larger in size than Belgium, it is the only town. A Dakota flies in from Rangoon once a week, but other than this, communications with the rest of Burma are entirely dependent on the narrow road which we had just travelled. And, apart from the risk of insurgent attack, that road is not one to be travelled lightly; in the last two hundred miles it straddles four mountain ranges and three deep valleys, and for the greater part it is only wide enough for a single vehicle. But, having eventually reached Kengtung, the traveller is well rewarded. Here, set far in among its wild green hills, is a place more like a Shangri-La than any other that we had come to. However, it was a Shangri-La with a difference.

The Expedition had been in the town but a few hours, and had just installed itself in the Inspection Bungalow, when it received a summons to meet the Sawbwa of Kengtung. Now, I should explain that throughout the hill country of Burma the system of rule is part modern and part feudal. The people owe an allegiance to the central Government in Rangoon, but to many of them, living in distant valleys only entered by mule or on foot, this allegiance is theoretical, and no more real than it must have been in the days when they were ruled from Westminster; for their direct and personal leadership they look much closer, to their Sawbwa. The word means 'earthly lord,' and, in fact, this best explains the Sawbwa's rôle. He is the hereditary lord of his people. There are over thirty such chieftains in the Shan Hills, and it is interesting to note that in the days of British rule they were entitled to a nine-gun salute. Of them all, the Sawbwa of Kengtung rules the largest area, and is perhaps the most powerful. His domain stretches from the borders of China in the north to Thailand in the south, from Laos in the east to the Salween River in the west. It is an area of some forty thousand square miles, and almost entirely mountainous. Some of the tribes, dwelling in the farthest valleys, still live their lives quite untouched by the rest of the world. Across parts of the map is written the word 'unexplored'—surely one of the most evocative single words in the English language.

We had already heard something of Sao Sai Long (the Sawbwa), and therefore our surprise at meeting this feudal lord was not as great as it might have been. We found him on the state tennis-court, and when he saw us he pulled on his sweater, zipped up his rackets, and came across to greet us. He was a small young man, and as he had been educated in Australia this possibly accounted for his nickname and informal manner.

"Just call me Shorty—all my friends do," he said. Shorty was very interested in the Expedition's cars, for he was a keen motorist and had recently taken delivery (by air from Rangoon) of a smart new Fiat which he drove about his town like a rally driver.

"Well," he said, "you're going to be here for a few days, so you must come along one evening and see the slides that I took last year at Le Mans."

Presently we were joined by Sao Kun Suik, the Sawbwa's uncle. Together we all went along to his house for a drink. One of us asked him what his name meant; he replied that he was the "Lord Chief Bottle Washer of Kengtung," and he continued to refer to himself thus whenever, thereafter, he was with us. (We later learnt that his official name was Prince War Lord—due, apparently, to the fact that he was born on the day that the Great War began in 1914.) Being the Sawbwa's uncle and chief adviser, he was one of the real powers behind the Kengtung scene. But he referred to Shorty, who, though his nephew, was his liege lord, as The Boss.

He was a most pleasant host, and over a series of monumental rums he asked us about cricket—a game which he had personally introduced to Kengtung. He thought that the Expedition might join his newly formed K.C.C. in a game the next afternoon. We demurred, but Lord C.B.W. was a forceful man, and it seemed that we had no real choice in the matter. Kengtung has reached the unusual stage of what one might call 'enlightened feudalism'—feudalism in the modern idiom.

Later in the evening we met two more of the Kengtung 'royal' family, the Sawbwa's aunts. During the ensuing few days they almost became aunts to the Expedition as well, for they took us under their wings, entertaining and looking after us almost continuously. They were charming ladies, and had the equally charming names (when translated into English) of Princess Lily of the Heavens and Princess Moonlit Waves.

It was Princess Lily of the Heavens who suggested that in commemoration of our visit we should form the Kengtung Auto Club. This was promptly agreed, and Shorty willingly became our patron. This was—and still is—an altogether unique society: world membership is exclusively confined to the Expedition's two cars, which, in the months that followed, flew the dragon crest of Kengtung—hand-embroidered by Princess Lily of the Heavens—fluttering from their wireless aerials.

Sao Kun Suik (*alias* Lord C.B.W.) was quite adamant that we should take part in Kengtung's annual cricket fixture. It was an unusual game, for here—with the borders of Red China, Indo-China, and Thailand all within a mere one hundred miles—we took the field as nonchalantly as if on a village green. Instead of bowling from the customary gasworks or railway-station ends, we played between the palace and the pagoda. The rules were a little unusual, too. Among other variations, each batsman was credited with two runs before he had even reached the crease—this precluded the possible embarrassment of being bowled for a duck. To us the score was unimportant, but among the Expedition's members the most distinguished were Henry (17 runs) and Nigel (11 runs). Both were the highest scorers for their different sides. Following the tea interval Henry was put on to bowl from the pagoda end, and after five successive wides he settled down very well, and took Lord C.B.W.'s wicket for two runs (otherwise known as a duck). As this batsman walked off the field a bugler came out of the police-station on the near-by hill and sounded what we could only assume was the Kengtung version of the Last Post. There were numerous spectators, mostly tribesmen in from the surrounding hills for the local five-day bazaar, and now, on their way home with their head-baskets full, they squatted round the edge of the pitch and discussed the incredible goings-on they saw before them. They were obviously amused to see the fielders scampering about after the ball, and on several occasions they themselves entered into the spirit of the game by running on to the field and chasing the ball too. I cannot remember which side won this memorable match, but nevertheless it was one of the most amusing games I have ever played—and certainly the most unusual.

Our delay in Kengtung was due to the necessity of waiting for the weekly convoy which ran a hundred miles southward to the Thailand frontier. But, despite the various entertainments provided by our hosts, there were several other things to keep us busy. Henry and Nigel, for example, had to change the bearing in one of Oxford's rear wheels. This had been getting ripe for some time, and now made a grinding noise almost as disturbing as a sore tooth. The mechanical process involved in fitting a new bearing is not simple at the best of times, for first, in order to remove the metal collar which holds the offending bearing in place, one requires a machine exerting a pressure of twenty tons. As we could hardly have included such a massive piece of ironmongery in our equipment, and were armed only with hand tools, we had to improvise. Our methods were necessarily a little unorthodox. Under Henry's directions, the collar was cut with hacksaws and then chipped with a cold chisel, until eventually it cracked and came off. Then, having fitted a fresh bearing in place, the next problem was to put on the new retaining collar—this officially requires a 2½-ton press. Our method was to heat the collar in a pressure cooker until it had expanded a little; it was then slipped down the axle, and finally assisted into position by a few hefty whacks with a hammer. Of course, all this is enough to make the Rover designers shrivel up under their drawing-boards. But, under the circumstances, it was difficult to know what else we could do.

While on the subject of repairs, it would be foolish of me to pretend that the cars ran like birds the whole time. Even the best designs have faults, and I do not think the Rover Company would persuade one otherwise. But, although we tested several components of our cars to destruction, we are agreed that if ever we repeated the journey we should not hesitate to take Land Rovers again. There are, it is true, a few other vehicles which would have had adequate performance, but they would have been either too small (*e.g.,* jeeps) to carry ourselves and all our kit, or too large (*e.g.,* a Dodge Power Wagon) to have negotiated some of the jungle tracks. The Land Rover, with one or two modifications, fitted the bill almost exactly. It is a first-class vehicle, and, above all, it has a most excellent engine.

In the hills of Kengtung state they illicitly but somewhat proudly grow some of the best opium poppies in the world. Much of the raw opium finds its way out by little-known paths to Thailand or Indo-China, and thence by air or sea to Hong Kong, Singapore, and everywhere else that there is a demand. On the road to Kengtung we had already seen many fields of poppies, and it was strange to think that here, in this beautiful countryside, from the harvest of these pale white flowers, began a clandestine trail that might end in almost any of the world's great cities.

✺

To prevent the growing of the poppies would be an almost impossible task, for many of the patches are far away in the hills, and could only effectively be surveyed from the air. Even then, it would take more than an army to follow up into the inaccessible valleys. Nor can the Government of Burma prevent the traffic in raw opium across the frontiers, for smuggling can go on at any of a thousand places. The United Nations has sent its experts, and has repeatedly requested that the growing of the poppies should be prohibited, but, as in other cases, that organization makes no practical suggestions as to how its requests might be executed. Opium is the cash crop; a patch of poppies can provide enough money for the cultivator to buy the food that he and his family need. But if that same patch were planted with hill rice it could not produce anything like enough. Opium is, then, the livelihood of many of these people, and it is not only impractical to talk about its prohibition by force but it is also impractical to talk about it until some acceptable alternative of like value can be suggested. This is just another way of stating the obvious—that opium is more profitable than any other crop which could be grown in this difficult country. It is no good considering the raising of opium poppies as a moral question of right or wrong; it is a question of simple economics.

I have already mentioned that we were waiting in Kengtung for the weekly convoy to Thailand. For the last hundred miles of our journey through Burma we were heading into an area much troubled by roaming bands of Kuomintang guerrillas (the K.M.T.). However, there was no other route which we could take. It is true that on many maps there are several other roads which appear to lead from Burma to Thailand, but, in fact, they are either wishful thinking or sheer fantasy on the part of the map-makers—it is strange how disconcertingly fey these people seem to become when their pens move over South-East Asia. On occasions the Expedition could almost see two or three cartographers sitting round their work in London or Washington or wherever else they 'make' maps (the inverted commas are not entirely irrelevant).

"I say, old chap," says the first map-maker, "don't seem to be many roads in this part of the world."

"Oh, let's have a look," says his colleague. "Yes, you're right. But surely there must be some? I know what—let's put a few in."

"O.K., how about one from here to there for a start?"

"Fine; that ought to do the job nicely."

Having thus briefly levelled my sights on these obliging fellows, I will return to the narrative—to the K.M.T. Let me relate something of their story; for, apart from the Expedition's personal concern at the time, it is an interesting tale.

It is everyday knowledge that most of Chiang Kai-shek's Nationalist (K.M.T.) troops took refuge on the island of Formosa following their defeat on the Chinese mainland by Mao Tse-tung's Communist armies. But it is not so well known that some elements of the K.M.T. were cut off before they could reach the Chinese coast and Formosa. They were abandoned by Chiang Kai-shek, and forced to fend for themselves. In time they were pushed farther and farther down into Southern China by the Communists, until eventually, defeated and harried on all sides, they fled into Eastern Burma. Here they were relatively safe, for only at Burma's request could Mao Tse-tung's armies cross the frontier in pursuit.

Originally there were some twenty thousand of these K.M.T. refugees, and for some time they had things very much their own way, marauding at will across the greater part of the Shan States. But eventually, after a series of fierce campaigns, the Burmese Army managed to drive them back beyond the Salween river into the inaccessible country of Kengtung State. Nevertheless, Burma was in an awkward position; her army was not really strong enough to contain these well-armed guerrillas permanently, and yet, at the same time, the Chinese Communists were itching to cross the frontier in order to come to final grips with their enemy. But Burma realized that, should she accept the Communists' pressing offer of help against the K.M.T., it was unlikely that the Communist army, having once entered Burma, would ever leave. In other words, if Burma accepted the offer she would merely have been jumping out of the K.M.T. frying-pan into the Communist fire.

The problem was taken to the Security Council, and was temporarily solved when Chiang Kai-shek said that he would accept any of the K.M.T. who came forward to be repatriated to Formosa. Under U.N. surveillance a large number took advantage of this offer and came down from the hills,

to be flown out from Kengtung and various air-fields in Northern
Thailand. Before the last of these evacuations, in April 1954, Chiang Kai-
shek publicly disclaimed all those who chose to remain behind.

In fact, some five thousand K.M.T. decided to stay, and these people
are still in Burma to-day. Officially they are not recognized by Formosa,
but Chiang Kai-shek can hardly be disappointed that some of his ex-
followers have chosen to maintain a Nationalist base on the Asian
mainland. This suggestion (which is constantly denied in Formosa) is
given added weight by recent events. For example, it is hard to equate
Chiang Kai-shek's disownment of the K.M.T. who remained in Burma
with the fact that they have recently been re-equipped by air with
modern arms and ammunition, and that certain Nationalist generals have
been seen in Formosa one week and reported in Burma the next.
Modern arms (including 75 mm. artillery) are used in the now annual
skirmishes with the Burmese Army. Some of these weapons have been
captured by the Burmese. Many of them come from the flotsam and
jetsam of the war in Indo-China, but others—and this is more than an
intriguing side-light—are of contemporary United States Army pattern,
and have undoubtedly been flown in via Formosa. The United States has
long accepted the sponsorship of the Chinese Nationalist cause, and the
Pentagon must surely know that some of the arms currently supplied to
Formosa are, in fact, finding their way to Burma. The United States
Government may not be taking any direct part in supporting the
K.M.T., but it has certainly not shown any undue anxiety to check this
illicit traffic. The Burmese have made no secret of their indignation, and
a few years ago, to add point to their case, they terminated the U.S.
economic aid programme to their country. As a Burmese Cabinet
Minister is reported to have said at the time, "We were beginning to feel
like brothel-keepers. With one hand we were accepting aid, while with
the other we had to fight bandits armed by the same people who gave
us the money."

The United States has always regarded Chiang Kai-shek and his cause
in a somewhat idealistic light (to British eyes, at least). It is reasonable to
assume, therefore, that the State Department's connivance at this redirected
flow of part of the supplies is due to some plan for containing Chinese
Communism, rather than of causing inconvenience to Burma. But this is

small comfort to the Burmese—especially when they are the people against whom the weapons are usually used.

The way these arms are flown in to the K.M.T. would make an interesting story in itself if more was known about it. From Intelligence reports it seems that the supplies are brought in by light aircraft which land on remote air-strips along the Mekong valley; the planes are probably piloted by that colourful and almost legendary internationale of 'operators' who, for a price, have long flown the unscheduled routes of opium and gun-running in South-East Asia. One of the air-strips is known to be in Burmese territory only fifteen miles from the Chinese frontier, but in such a difficult and remote position as to preclude any successful attack by the Burmese Army. Another lies just across the Mekong in Laos. The limited range of the light aircraft must mean that they operate from some base nearer at hand than Formosa. There are good grounds to suggest that this base is somewhere in a remote part of Thailand.

The K.M.T. encamped along the Mekong have an almost complete monopoly of the opium trade in the valley, and, in return for their airborne supplies, they fly out about a ton of raw opium each month. The cargo finds it way into the hands of three or four Chinese magnates in Bangkok who control the trade, by which time the opium has increased in value several-fold, and fetches £45,000 per ton.

The control wielded over the hill villagers in the Mekong river area is complete. The K.M.T. issue travel permits and have set up check-points around the fringe of their domain to ensure strict security and to levy regular tolls on opium, food, and silver coin. This is the hard-core area of the K.M.T., and one may ask why the Burmese Army has never attacked it. There are several reasons. First, there are a lot of K.M.T.; they are well equipped and experienced—some of them have been fighting on and off for twenty years. Second, theirs is mountain country, and a guerrilla's dream; it could only be entered after a long march on mule or foot; any but the largest-scale attack would be dissipated long before it reached the objective. But perhaps the main reason is that there is evidently a tacit agreement by which neither side provokes the other too far. Both realize that they have too much to lose by disturbing this truce, although it is an uneasy one. However, elsewhere in Kengtung State there seems to be some distinction between the hard-core K.M.T. who are maintaining a base from which one day they hope to 'liberate' China, and the more undisciplined fringe elements who live by ambush and looting. A fairly regular source of income to these latter are the convoys which travel from Kengtung to the Burma-Thai border village of Tachilek. The following extracts are from the Rangoon newspaper *The Nation*, and they appeared about the time we were in Burma.

Kengtung, December 17. Marauding K.M.T. bands committed another vicious crime when they captured and slew a R.C. priest, Father Ferranto, an Italian scholar in Hkun Shan language, who had spent a considerable number of years among the Shans.[14]

Kengtung, December 17. Reports reaching this town reveal that about 1,000 Nationalist Chinese troops are concentrating at Mong Hpong, 110 miles south of Kengtung and 10 miles east of Tachilek. The K.M.T. are reported to have informed the villagers that they intend to 'liberate' mainland China and that they do not wish to harm the villagers nor do battle with the Burmese armed forces. They added, however, that as long as China is not 'liberated' they would be compelled to remain in Burmese territory. It is also reported that patrols of this K.M.T. concentration have reached within three miles of Tachilek, the village on the Thai-frontier and the terminus of the road from Kengtung.

Kengtung, January 7. Four R.C. nuns were fired upon by K.M.T. soldiers when the truck in which they were travelling was ambushed on January 2 on the road between Mong Ling and Mon Pyak.

In addition to these incidents, there had been a number of jeep-burnings, and, only a fortnight before our arrival in Kengtung, the K.M.T. had shot up a convoy travelling to the Thailand frontier, looting five trucks and killing three men. However, according to various people in Kengtung, this unfortunate incident was very much to the Expedition's advantage, for now that the K.M.T. were well stocked with rice—for which they had attacked the trucks—they would not ambush another convoy until they had eaten their fill. As the five trucks had been carrying several tons of rice, we were cheerfully assured that traffic would not be molested for several more weeks. Nevertheless, we might have been excused a feeling of apprehension, for, although the British Embassy in Rangoon knew of our plans, the decision to proceed was entirely up to us. Maybe we were rather sticking our necks out, but there was little point in getting cold feet at this late stage, and, anyway, one cannot achieve much without taking a chance now and then.

Ⓟ

As the convoy was due to leave at daybreak we had breakfast by lantern-light, and then drove down to the assembly point by the police station. Sure enough there were three or four broken-winded trucks piled high with goods and people waiting to set off. One of the lorry-drivers proudly told us that his lorry had been shot up in the attack of a few weeks before, and he showed us the bullet-holes in his windscreen by way of proof. We waited for an hour, but it seemed that the escort were still trying to get their jeep started.

Presently Sao Kun Suik (alias Prince War Lord, Lord C.B.W.) appeared, to wish us well on the journey. As by now the sun was high in the sky, we asked him about the delay. "Punctuality," he replied pontifically, "is quite unknown in the East—you must be patient." Then, thinking of a catch-phrase much used by Burmese politicians, he smiled wryly and added, "Anyway, this is Burma—the Land of To-morrow." Eventually, however, the jeep was started, and the nine policemen clambered aboard, legs and rifles sticking out all round like the petals of a flower, and about as effective.

A good deal of cranking, and clouds of black smoke mingling with the dust—then away we went; four trucks, a motor-cyclist, our two Land Rovers, and the escorting jeep. After an hour we had covered almost fourteen miles, and the escort pulled up in a small village to have a self-congratulatory lunch. Two of the trucks had broken down, and did not show up for an hour and a half. Then there was a further delay while the thirty dust-clad passengers disentangled themselves and had their midday rice. They ate as if they had all the time in the world, and merely looked sympathetic at our impatience. As B.B. aptly put it, "How unhurried can you get in the Land of To-morrow?"

Abandoning hope for one of the trucks, which had still not appeared, we set off again. We did not see the escort for the next twenty miles because, except when their jeep broke down, they raced on ahead so that they might have a good rest at the next stop while waiting for the convoy to catch up. Meanwhile we were stuck behind one of the lorries, which paused at every stream to refill its leaking radiator.

The road was unsurfaced, very narrow and very twisting. It elbowed its way through steep jungle-clad hills with a cliff on one side and gorge on the other. Ten miles an hour was the maximum speed, and ambush conditions were ideal. One could not help wondering what might lie round the next corner. If two terrorists, armed with nothing more than rifles and common sense, had wanted to hold up the convoy there was nothing to stop them.

There were three or four stretches where the K.M.T. were known to cross the road frequently. It was near these that the ambushes usually occurred, so that the loot could be more easily carried away. Needless to say, the escort jeep or one of the lorries chose to break down right in the middle of these danger-spots. But, while Henry and Nigel carried out some hurried repairs, the rest of us took our minds off the situation by recording the farce on film.

Towards evening the road led into a sort of Dead Man's Gulch, with high cliffs on either side. But by now we were becoming rather fatalistic about the whole business, and merely took the precaution of getting the tow-rope ready to give the escort a quick pull to some place farther up the road where the expected repairs might be carried out in relative safety. However, the jeep managed to get through without stopping, and, equally fortunately, the K.M.T. were evidently busy elsewhere on this particular day.

It was quite obvious that we should never reach the frontier by dark, so, having covered only sixty miles in the day, we stopped in a small village for the night. By now we were the only people left in the convoy. What had become of the lorries and the motor-cycle no one seemed to know, or, for that matter, seemed to care. Perhaps they had given up, broken down, or turned back to Kengtung.

That night the Expedition's navigator (Pat) reported that our position was exactly a hundred degrees east of Greenwich. The occasion was celebrated after supper with spoonfuls of neat lemonade powder and medicinal brandy.

In the morning it was some hours before our mechanics had thoroughly checked the escort jeep, and deemed it fit to travel. The precaution of this overhaul proved to be more than worth while, for the jeep ran with unprecedented goodwill, and gave us no further trouble for the rest of the journey. Nevertheless, by the time we eventually reached the frontier village of Tachilek we had taken the greater part of two days to drive the 105 miles from Kengtung.

As we came into the village we realized that the most dangerous part of our journey was past. Now that we were safely through the K.M.T. area, it did not occur to any of us to think too deeply of our continued good fortune. But it is interesting to note that a Land Rover belonging to the Burmese Government was ambushed and burnt to a cinder less than a fortnight later.

After some very informal Customs formalities we went down to the frontier river. As the only bridge had been bombed by the R.A.F. twelve years before, we prepared to ford. It was the deepest river we had yet tackled, but we were feeling rather pleased with ourselves, and quickly stripped to our underpants in anticipation of some fun. The entire village turned out to enjoy the show, but to every one's surprise (including our own) the cars surged through—with water flowing in one door and out the other—as if that sort of thing was exactly what they had been designed for.

On the far bank we were in a new country, our fifteenth. Yet it was with relief tinged by regret that we climbed aboard again and motored away from the close hills of Burma towards the open paddy-fields of Thailand.

⊛

A day and two hundred miles later we were approaching Chiang Mai, the second city and northern capital of Thailand. It was dark when we stopped at a cross-roads on the edge of the town to ask the way to the British Consulate, where, in a letter some months earlier, we had been invited to stay. A jeep came by and I waved it down. Inside were two American sergeants (members of the United States Military Mission to Thailand) and when they heard that we were looking for the Consulate they offered to lead us. "Yep, just follow on and we'll take you."

A little later we turned into the Consulate compound, passed a little statue of Queen Victoria, and pulled up at the end of the drive. While the others went to find the Consul I went across to thank our guides.

"Oh, it was a pleasure," said the driver. Then he asked, in a puzzled tone, "Say, where you guys from?"

"Well," I replied, "to-day we've come from Chiang Rai—you know, about 150 miles north."

"Yep, but where you based? Bangkok?"

"No, originally from London."

"Yeh, I know you're Britishers," he said, missing the point and getting slightly annoyed at my apparent evasiveness. "But where's your outfit located?"

"We're not exactly 'located' anywhere. We've driven overland from London."

"You've what? You've driv . . . London? London—England? No!"

I nodded. I was really enjoying this.

His face went dead-pan in utter disbelief, he turned to his companion, he switched off the jeep's engine, and then suddenly seemed to explode in amazement. "H—oly mackerel, Mac, did ya hear that! These guys just driven in from London. From London—England. H—oly mackerel. M—an!"

It was so very spontaneous, and, when they had grasped what I had told them, their enthusiasm knew no bounds. They wanted to meet the others, they wanted to shake our hands, they wanted to see the cars, they wanted to know everything. In answer to what we told them all they seemed to be able to mutter was, "H—oly mackerel—that's good. Hey, Mac, d'you hear that? My, but that's good."

To be given such a sincere and impromptu welcome was most flattering. They could have gone on congratulating us all night. Maybe my diary for that day got a little swollen-headed, for I notice the entry concludes, "Well, after all, holy mackerel and all that—it *is* pretty good, London to Chiang Mai."

14.

Mishaps, Bangkok, and a Problem

AMONG the letters waiting for us at the Consulate was one from the Rover agent in Bangkok requesting that "in the unlikely event of your being ahead of schedule I suggest that you should not arrive in Bangkok until after the Chinese New Year (February 13), as every one will be on holiday." Strangely enough, we were ahead of schedule, so we gladly accepted the Consul's invitation to stay on in Chiang Mai for a couple of days.

The Watlings (or Mr and Mrs Consul, as I once absent-mindedly called them) did far more than merely provide a roof and a total of eighteen meals a day for six itinerant British subjects—an overwhelming enough task in itself! But, though I could catalogue their hospitality for several pages, I should particularly like to mention just one thing; it was typical. My red sweater, a most valued possession, had lately developed several large holes, and, unknown to me, these had caught the eye of our hostess. In fact, I had not even noticed the sweater's disappearance when Mrs Watling returned it to me with each hole carefully and most beautifully mended. The job must have taken all day. I jokingly promised that I would mention this in the book I hoped to write. That promise I can now keep. Thank you again, Mrs Watling—those darns are still much admired!

Throughout our journey we had been extraordinarily lucky where accidents were concerned. We had had none. But it seemed too much to expect that this good fortune should continue indefinitely. Sure enough, on the afternoon we left Chiang Mai the spell broke—four times.

It had been raining quite heavily for a couple of days, and the unmetalled road was a deep slush. Both cars were therefore driving very carefully, but, despite this precaution, Cambridge got into a very bad skid, and after sliding sideways for some yards ended the evolution rocking right on the edge of a deep embankment. Winching her back on to the road was tricky, for unless the pull was applied from exactly the right angle there was a real danger of her swivelling round and going over altogether.

However, after a considerable amount of juggling we got her clear and motored on. Then, half an hour later, we met a lorry loaded with two huge teak-logs coming round a corner. The lorry was almost past when her tail slid round and crashed into Oxford. The damage was not great, but it was most annoying—one side of the car was stove in, and a window broken. The lorry pulled up; the driver got out and looked sheepish. But, concluding that it was just one of those things, we knocked out the broken glass and resumed the journey. So far nothing serious.

By the time it was dark the road had improved greatly, and had a good dry surface. Cambridge had taken over the lead, and was about half a mile ahead. Unexpectedly, we in Oxford came on to a slippery patch. B.B., who was driving, braked gently, and then things started happening—in slow motion. The car swerved, went into a bad skid, spun round, and ended the manœuvre pointing in the wrong direction. When she had almost stopped she leaned a bit, made up her mind, and toppled right over. Everything that was normally horizontal became vertical. Our immediate reaction was Petrol—Fire. Fortunately, B.B. had switched off the ignition as the car went over, but nevertheless there were forty gallons aboard, and the exhaust pipe was obviously very hot. Nigel and I were out pretty smartly, and wasted no time in getting the fire-extinguisher off its clip. B.B. took a little longer to get out, as the car had gone over on the driver's side; consequently, he had to hoist himself vertically up to the passenger's door. Moreover, he had hurt his arm, so Nigel and I hopped up on to the side of the car to give him a hand.

Fire was still a risk, as by now petrol was spilling out of the tanks. So we sluiced the car's underside with water out of the jerry-cans in order to cool the exhaust-pipe. Then, as soon as the flap was over, we sat down on the roadside and talked it over. B.B. had not, as first thought, broken his arm, but merely gashed it rather badly. Nigel and I bandaged it up, and then waited for the other car to return.

Sure enough, Cambridge were back in a few minutes. Missing our head-lights, they had turned round to see what was wrong. As soon as they saw that we were all right they stood around and looked superior. "Typical—just typical" was their unjustified comment. But it was in good humour, and when they had had their joke we all set about rigging the Cambridge winch to pull Oxford back on to her wheels. However, just when the cable was in position, a bus came along. It was crowded with Thais, who, full of the joys of their New Year festivities, swarmed out and gathered round the crashed car. Then, with one well-directed heave, they had her upright in less time than it takes to tell.

We restowed the kit, dried out the spilt petrol, started the engine, and thanked our helpers profusely. It was found that the skid had been caused because the near-side tyres had been running over slippery mud, while the off-side had been on a much drier patch. Consequently, when the brakes had been touched the car started to swerve.

The final accident of the day occurred twenty miles farther on. A bus had skidded right off the road into a broad ditch, and, as we approached, the passengers ran forward to ask if we could help. The task of pulling the bus back looked almost hopeless, but, having had our own share of misfortunes that day, we were sympathetic to those of others. So we set to work. A winch cable was run out, threaded through a pulley which we had fixed to the front axle of the bus, and then led back to a crowbar hammered into the ground. Thus we had a double purchase. Pat, "like a clot" (as he admitted afterwards), pulled against the top of the crowbar to give it extra support. Winching commenced. Everything was going very well, and the bus was beginning to move, when suddenly the strain became too great. The crowbar bent, the hook at the end of the cable shot up in a shower of sparks and whipped past Pat's hand. It tore open the end of a finger. He took off down the road yelling blue murder. But, though it must have been extremely painful, he had been very lucky—the hook had been moving with quite enough force to have smashed his forearm.

As B.B. (the Doc) was himself a casualty, Adrian and I got out the medical kit and deputized for him. For the second time that evening a hand was dressed and put in a sling. Meanwhile, Henry and Nigel continued with the recovery of the bus; it was another two hours' work, and long past midnight, before we finally dragged her clear. The passengers were extremely grateful, and, had it not been for Pat's injury, the trouble would have been well worth it.

The Expedition had suffered four mishaps in four hours. It never rains but it pours! And that night it did so literally—the tent went up for the first time since Turkey.

⊛

Two days and four hundred miles later we were met just outside Bangkok by Mr Burt, the Rover agent. He took us to lunch at Don Maung airport. There was something deeply satisfactory in knowing that another long leg of the journey was over. The feeling was emphasized as we sat on the veranda, beer in hand, and watched the aircraft coming and going to airports all over the world. A group of business-men at the bar had left London Airport less than forty eight hours before; it seemed almost incredible, and yet faintly ridiculous. There at Don Maung, with our two dust-stained cars parked outside, one could truly appreciate the fantastic speed of air travel. Forty-eight hours earlier, when we were already well south of Chiang Mai, those business-men had not even left London!

After lunch we drove into Bangkok. It must be one of the most rapidly changing cities in the world. Lying seventy miles up the rice-growing delta of the Menam, the old capital of Siam has become a sprawling metropolis of neon-lit pagodas and reinforced concrete, of seventeen radio stations and an atomic pile. The American influence is almost complete, and, like Kansas City, Bangkok "has gone about as fur as she kin go."

We moved into the Y.M.C.A.; two to a room and, most things considered, this was a convenient arrangement. The other occupants of the building were thirty young Thais, students at one or other of Bangkok's five universities. They were a pleasant crowd, but, with thirty different wireless sets tuned to seventeen different radio stations from dawn until midnight, sleep was almost impossible. The other menace was the mosquitoes; they swarmed in packs a thousand strong. Fortunately, they were not malarial, but, on the other hand, they were of the latest armour-piercing pattern, and merely regarded a net as a challenge to be overcome. Nevertheless, these two things—radios and mosquitoes—were our only complaints of Bangkok.

It was the original intention to stay only a few days—long enough to have Pat and B.B. patched up, to have the cars overhauled, to answer our mail, and to make inquiries about the final one thousand miles to Singapore. But we found so many new-found friends in the British colony were pushing the boat out on our behalf that our plans went to the wind.

We were invited to the races, to cocktail parties, to night-clubs, to luncheon, to radio interviews, to dances—in short, the Expedition's head became vastly enlarged. To the Thais the Expedition was evidently some kind of official goodwill mission. This mistake had sometimes happened before, but, none the less, it could be embarrassing to be asked, as Nigel was during a T.V. interview, to comment on the cultural affinities between Britain and Thailand. His answer, "just splendid," hardly fitted the bill.

But besides enjoying ourselves—and there was plenty of that—we had a more serious task. It was now, in Bangkok, that we came up against the final difficulty of the journey. We had known from letters received many months earlier that, after the crossing from Assam to Burma, the greatest remaining problem would be met in Southern Thailand. From Bangkok to Singapore was not much more than one thousand miles; by air the journey took a morning. But by land no one knew. The facts, as we saw them in Bangkok, were simple: there was no motorable route all the way through to Malaya. To be more exact, half-way down the Kra Isthmus there was a roadless stretch of over one hundred miles. We already knew that, in the previous year, this barrier of hill and jungle had defeated a Land Rover expedition endeavouring to drive north from Malaya. After three fruitless weeks trying to hack out a path they were forced to give up and turn back.

Set against these almost final facts were two possibilities. Our maps showed a railway-line running down the eastern coast of the isthmus. If necessary we determined to bump down that—providing, of course, that the trains ran according to the published timetable, which in Thailand would be doubtful! We had already practised driving over sleepers in India, and we reckoned on averaging about twenty miles a day. Alternatively, and also on the map, was a line marked "elephant track." The chances of using this as a route were increased when we heard that it had recently been chosen as the alignment for a future road. Indeed, our informant even suggested that the road might have been started. We hastened to the Thai Highways Department for confirmation of the rumour. They, however, looked quite blank, and said that they knew nothing about it at all. (Why should they know about roads? After all, they were only the Highways Department. It is this sort of non-committal informality that adds such charm to Thailand.)

Most people reckoned that we could not overland any farther. They pessimistically advised us to take a ship for the missing one hundred miles. But we were fairly determined; overlanding had become something of an obsession with us. After all, we had come this far by land, and it would be a great pity if we now had to give it up. There was another reason, too. We had recently heard of a Frenchman who, it was alleged, had driven overland from Paris to Saigon in 1938. But it was known that he had had to take a ship down the Burmese coast, for in those days there had been no road from India to Burma. This news made us more determined than ever not to go by sea—not even for a short distance. If we did we would really be doing little more than had been done years before. No, nothing short of overland all the way was enough.

It was in this slightly belligerent mood of "let's have a bash at the elephant track" that we prepared to pack up our kit and drive south. But, the evening before we were due to leave, Pat (as Navigator) received a mysterious summons to call at the American Embassy. News of our search for information about a motorable route had evidently filtered through to one of the American attachés. He told Pat that he himself had recently returned from Southern Thailand, and had, in fact, spent a week walking down the so-called elephant track. He thought that construction of a proper road might have already begun. He advised us to try it.

This was just the news we had been waiting for. So, with unfounded confidence, we set off on the last leg.

15.

Eighteen Thousand—Plus

A LONG and dusty day's driving took us south across the plains from Bangkok. It was hot, it was dry, and the dust was everywhere. It got in one's hair, up one's nose, and it dried on the sweat of one's face. Hot dust has a smell, too, something between looking gas and stale rags. But by the end of the day it was not so bad; the featureless paddy-fields had been left behind, and the road was threading its way down long avenues of palms. The evening was cooler, too, and as usual driving was altogether more pleasant after the heat of the afternoon. One could put away one's dark glasses and enjoy the draught of night air blowing in through the roof-hatch and windows; the engine ran with a more satisfied note after dark, and once again, as the miles hummed away from the tyres, it seemed good to be back on the road.

We were just thinking about making camp when, through the trees, we saw the distant shine of the sea; it was something we had not seen for some time. Without more ado the cars hit top speed, turned off at the next sidetrack, and bumped their way down to the beach. We stripped, and ran over the warm sand to the surf. This was the Pacific—and our first swim since Karachi. The water was warm, the sea breeze rustled the palms, and the soft sand—still cooling from the sun—almost glowed in the moonlight. This was truly the tropics. It was nearly midnight before we finally dragged ourselves from the breakers, unrolled our sleeping-bags, and lay down to sleep with the sky and the stars for a blanket. The Pacific was everything we had ever heard it to be.

The early morning brought a group of villagers, who squatted down and, in silence, eyed us curiously. However, both sides were soon at their ease, for, as so often happened, after a few jocular preliminaries one could have long conversations full of good-natured banter with these people, despite the fact that neither side understood a word. They took a lively interest in all that we did, and as there were several village maidens dressed in pleasantly uninhibited costumes we could hardly help returning the compliment. Then, after breakfast and more swimming, we pushed on.

The road followed the palm-fringed coast as far south as Chumporn; there it turned inland. This was the narrowest part of the Kra Isthmus. In fact, on the good road, we crossed over from the Pacific to the Indian Ocean in barely three hours. The road may have been good, but the dust was worse than ever, and, in order to save the following car the discomfort of driving in the other's wake, both cars billowed along side by side. We also hit on another idea which, though it seems an illogical remedy, definitely kept the dust and heat down. We kept soaking the floor-mats with water. This became standard practice thereafter.

It was at the tin-mining town of Renong, reached in the evening, that the road officially came to an end. From here we should have to find a way through to a place called Takua Pa, about one hundred miles to the south. There, according to the map, it was possible to pick up a road which would eventually lead to the Malayan border. That one hundred miles was virtually all that now stood between us and Singapore; so we really had to get through.

Inquiries were made about the rumoured new road. Yes, it had been started. Our hopes rose. No, it had not been cut more than a third of the way. Our hopes fell. Nevertheless, it seemed reasonable to suppose that beyond the thirty miles which had already been cleared there would be some kind of path up which the engineers would be going to survey the farther alignment. There might even be a bulldozer track along which the building equipment would be brought to the scene of operations. Anyway, our prospects looked fairly good, and the following note appears in my diary: "To-morrow's road to Takua Pa—rather like throwing the 'six'— good luck and we're 'home.'"

The next morning we left Renong and followed the line of construction towards the south. At first the way was reasonable, and, threading past the bulldozers and piles of earth, we made good progress. But after a few hours the road had been cut no farther, and we turned away from the dust and sun into the dark shade of the jungle. From the end of the road there led the narrow track for which we had been hoping. It followed the old elephant trail. In bottom gear, and four-wheel drive, the cars growled along the twisting path as it wormed its way through the bamboos and creepers.

It was very slow going. Driving at a really low speed for hour after hour can be very tiring to all concerned, not only to the driver. For one thing, the passengers have time to see the obstacle ahead, and form their own opinion as to how it should best be tackled. Which gear? Slowly or with some speed? Straight or at an angle? He'd better change down pretty smartly if he isn't going to fluff it. Oh. the fool! Anyone could have told him that was going to happen. . . . Back-seat driving was rigorously barred, but, nevertheless, if the driver's solution differed from the passengers', and was unsuccessful into the bargain, there was a definite tension in the car. The passengers, inwardly drumming their fingers, would have to force themselves to look out of the window as if quietly admiring the view! Each person had his own particular driving faults, which his companions had grown to know only too well. I was bad over bumps. In fact, for a given bump, I could almost guarantee to get the car farther into the air than anyone else. This must have been particularly aggravating to Nigel, for he was primarily responsible for repairs; when I was driving over rough ground Nigel was on tenterhooks for his springs and shock absorbers. He himself was a good cross-country driver, but, on the other hand, was not nearly so good in traffic. Neither was he neat on his gear-changes— particularly second. This might seem a trifling fault, but it was surprising how it could grow in annoyance after a few months. B.B. was rather erratic, usually good, occasionally bad. He had one particular habit which still makes me bubble whenever I think of it: he would drive for mile after mile in the dust of the car in front, when, by dropping back only a little farther, we could have been clear. But this did not seem to worry Nigel at all, and that only made me more annoyed—"bloody fools, both of them." I have a 'thing' about dust—as may have been gathered!

However, all this is rather off the point.

All afternoon and evening the cars bucked and thrashed, twisting and turning, always on hard lock one way or the other. There was one very hilly stretch where the track was little more than a footpath, and we were down to walking speed for hours on end. Most of the rivers were shallow, but there was one ford where the track disappeared, and we could not see where it climbed out on the farther bank. Despite the possibility that we might have called it a day and delayed finding a way through till the morning, general opinion seemed to be of the "press on to-night" variety.

So Oxford—fan-belt removed—was sent in to drive up the river-bed on a reconnaissance. I stood on the bonnet to point out the rocks, the snags, and the other navigational hazards to Nigel, who was driving. It was tricky work, for if the car went too deep and the engine got flooded we were well beyond the reach of the Cambridge winch cable. Eventually, however, after driving up-stream for quite a way we found a place where the bank shelved, and it looked as if the cars might climb out. But it was steep, and the car had lost some power by now. Nigel stopped in midstream and roared the engine in an endeavour to dry it out. There was the obvious risk that if we stayed there too long the water would eventually reach something vital, and then we would stop altogether. However, at a rush, we surged out of the river and slithered up to the top of the bank, where the car seemed to pant gently like some well-behaved dog. Cambridge, with the advantage of knowing where to go, followed shortly afterwards.

As the jungle shade became deeper, and then dark with the night, we stopped and took stock. There was probably another forty miles to go—if the track went that far. Every one was impatient to find out, and so, switching on the head-lamps and searchlights, we pushed on. The track was very indistinct—so much so that several times we lost it altogether, and ended up facing a wall of trees, bamboos, and matted creepers. Fearing lest this really was the end of the way, we hunted about with torch and searchlight until we found the track once more. In the dark tree-stumps and logs were a constant menace. Each person only drove for a short time, but even so Oxford hit a hidden tree-root with a crash that sent her skewing off the track and into the trees. Inspection showed a broken spring, a bent shock-absorber, a buckled wheel, and a bunch of somewhat roughened tempers. We changed the wheel and drove on.

It was a little later that Cambridge's dynamo packed up—for some reason best known to itself. It seemed that we would have to camp and look for the trouble in daylight. However, the mechanics put their heads together, and the problem was temporarily solved by swapping the batteries between the two cars, then swapping them back again after every half-hour. In this way Oxford's dynamo could at least keep each battery partially charged. This seems a good example of our advantage in having two cars, for if Cambridge had been travelling alone, and her dynamo had broken beyond the limits of running repairs (as we discovered later it had), the situation could have been most awkward. Some one might have had to walk the better part of fifty miles carrying the broken dynamo. The delay could have been weeks rather than days—whereas, with two cars, it was only a few minutes.

At about midnight we realized that the track was rapidly getting better, and that the cars were travelling faster. Our lights lit up an occasional bulldozer. It was almost too good to be true. Then, through the thinning jungle, a dim red light appeared in front. We motored down the track towards it, and found that it was the tail light of a lorry which picked up speed and drove slowly ahead.

Several times there were small bridges to cross, for the road seemed to have come nearer the coast, and the rivers were wider. These bridges had been made by throwing two parallel sets of logs across, but the gap between the logs had been measured for the wider wheel track of lorries such as the one ahead—for our narrow Land Rovers the crossings were a delicate business. However, with some one on foot guiding carefully by torch, the cars were eased over—though, on at least two occasions, the inside edges of all four tyres were unsupported. The lorry stopped on these occasions, and seemed to take a paternal interest in the proceedings. It occurred to us that it might have been sent to look for the Expedition, though we had no idea who had sent it or why. The driver spoke no English, but his benevolent smile and his offer of a cigarette seemed to confirm him as our guide.

"Takua Pa?" I asked him, pointing down the track. "How far?"

He looked as if he'd never heard of the place. But experience had taught us that one must pronounce a place name in precisely the way that a local inhabitant would say it himself, otherwise one might as well ask him for the Woolwich Ferry. The combination of cadences has to be absolutely exact—no mere approximation will do.

"Tak-you-arper?" I tried.

"Tarkuah Pah?"

"T'kua Pah?"

With the last his face lit up like a pin-table. He held up both his hands twice.

"Charlie says there're twenty kilometres to go," I called to the others, who were guiding one of the cars across a log bridge.

"Huh," B.B. replied pessimistically, "he probably means that there are twenty more bridges like this one."

An hour later we came down to a broad river. Our maps and milometers showed that this should be the end of the road; but we were too tired to try the crossing by night, and, anyway, it looked much too deep. So, neglecting supper, we were just unrolling our sleeping-bags when the lorry-driver started to flash his headlights on to the river. We watched, curious to see what would happen. A moment later a diesel motor was heard throbbing across the water, and then an unlit ferry loomed out of the darkness. We were bidden aboard. Shortly afterwards the cars rolled ashore in the little town of Takua Pa.

In fourteen hours of continuous driving we had crossed the hundred-mile gap. We were through.

The mysterious fairy godfather who had dispatched the lorry to look for us turned out to be the Mobilgas agent from Penang. Mr Fong Loong had journeyed three hundred miles north to meet us, and now, as he stood there in his pyjamas at three o'clock in the morning, he gave us our first advance welcome from Malaya. Apparently his office in Penang had cabled their opposite numbers in Bangkok a few days earlier to get our schedule. Bangkok were under the impression that we had left a couple of days before we really did, and they had cabled back accordingly. Mr Fong Loong had therefore been waiting two days for us, and, thinking we must be stuck, he had sent one of the road-works' lorries to search.

There was only an hour or so left of the night by the time we finally made camp on a near-by beach. In the morning no one got up before they felt like it—even B.B. lay in bed. Every one took their time; we ate breakfast, swam, and lazed in the sun with determined ease. B.B. started painting a sign on the back door of each car: "London—Singapore, First Overland." I am afraid that there was nothing modest about us; on the contrary, we were very pleased with ourselves. With only another eight hundred miles to go, with roads all the way, we had thrown the six, and were savouring the pleasure of it.

Later that day we reluctantly drove off the beach and headed onward down the Isthmus. Speed had to be reduced owing to Oxford's broken spring and shock-absorber, but this, if anything gave us more time to enjoy the scenery. There was nothing particularly new to us now about the almost cloudless skies, the emerald green of the jungle, or the dazzling whiteness of the road, but, nevertheless, one could never really grow tired of watching the slowly changing landscape, for there always seemed to be something different. On that day we passed the occasional plantations of rubber-trees which we had not seen before; there were the people, who now seemed more Malay than Thai; and there were the sheer-sided limestone hills which, poking out of the plain for a thousand feet or more, looked like mysterious fairy mountains. The geographers and geologists among us went into long-winded discussions on these curious features, but failed to reach agreement on even the relevant terminology

This would seem an appropriate point, with six months behind us, at which to make some remarks on a topic which we have often been asked about since, To wit: how did we all get on with each other? In some ways I have already answered the question by the very fact that it has not been necessary to introduce it before. Nevertheless, I do not think that this book would be complete without a few remarks on such an important aspect of the Expedition's day-to-day life. The six of us were never separated for long, and, travelling day after day in the limited space of a car, a degree of compatibility became absolutely essential if the Expedition was to stay in one piece. In fact, it was the very obviousness of this fact which helped, for, like it or not, we simply had to get on with each other. Each person realized this, and consequently made a conscious effort towards it. But I would emphasize that it certainly did require an effort at times. Occasionally it proved too much, and some one blew up. Every one exploded at some time or other, but B.B. and I were probably the worst offenders.

It is paradoxical but not altogether illogical that the smaller things could annoy the most—though they rarely seemed small at the time. A good straight argument could always be thrashed out and forgotten, but many of the smaller things were recurrent. It was not necessarily the thing itself which got under one's skin so much as the accumulated irritation of the same thing happening for the umpteenth time; it might be a mannerism, a particular driving habit, an unusual method of doing something, or even some one else's annoyance about some matter on which you yourself thought he had no cause to be fractious. B.B.'s never-failing insistence on knowing exactly what time we were going to get up the next morning; Pat's reluctance to get up at all; my own habit of packing the Oxford car with over-zealous neatness; Nigel's customary delay in the mornings while he tinkered unnecessarily with the engine—these are only some of the small things which became increasingly irritating as one grew to expect them. But I must not imply that we were all quivering psychopaths. On the contrary, I don't think we possessed a twitch or neurosis between us. It was just that things sometimes got on one's nerves!

Each person had his merits, each had his faults. But, at the same time, it was often just because of his faults that the individual was good at his job. For example, B.B. was meticulous to a degree about anything which he considered his department; this was accompanied by a bustling efficiency which was quite intolerant of any half-measures from the rest of us. Delay or procrastination were a complete anathema to him. These things could be most annoying to those of us who were not always prepared to turn the Expedition into the precision instrument that B.B. desired. But, when applied to precautions for our health, it was precisely because of this rigidity and almost unnecessary discipline that we had no illness throughout the journey. That, I think, was a remarkable record, and the credit is B.B.'s entirely. Perhaps if he had been more easy-going the story would not be the same. Pat was extremely good at his job of looking after our route information, petrol-requirements, and schedule. But, at the same time, just because he had all the facts at his fingertips and could tell you exactly how far it was from here to there, he was inclined to be rather a pundit and expert. This, given enough of it, could become rather tedious, and it was not helped by the fact that he was invariably right. Adrian was quite convinced that he was the only person really capable of handling our business affairs. If he had made up his mind about what should be done he would get on with it, reluctant to tell anybody else for fear that we might meddle and disturb his well-laid plans. We would sometimes find ourselves presented with a *fait accompli*. It was not that the *fait accompli* was unsuccessful, but rather that we had not been consulted beforehand which annoyed. But here again, the credit for keeping the Expedition financially sound—a considerable task—must go to Adrian. In fact, who is to say that he was not right in thinking himself the only person capable of doing it? My thesis is obvious: that apparent faults were often really valuable attributes in disguise—though it was not always easy to recognize them as such at the time! Unfortunately, this theory does not seem to hold good for Henry or myself. Henry seemed to have no faults to compensate for his excellence as a mechanic, while, on the other hand, I cannot think of any particular attributes to compensate for my faults. When roused I was a champion grumbler; I could, to quote Pat, "drip like a tap."

I would not pretend that there were never any full-scale arguments. There were quite a number, but as time went on they became rarer—because we knew each other better, and because we could no longer be bothered to argue. The more important the problem, the more dispassionately it was discussed. In any case, I do not remember any disagreement which lasted over-night. And that, I think, really answers the question with which I started this subject.

With the surprisingly easy stretch between Kenong and Takua Pa now behind us, we found that we had time up our sleeves. So, travelling by fairly easy stages, it was a week after leaving Bangkok that we eventually drew up at the border station on the southern frontier of Thailand. Passports were stamped, the barrier was swung open, and the cars accelerated away down the road to Malaya. We had gone about half-way across the few miles of jungle no-man's land which lies between the two countries when, rounding a corner, we were unexpectedly waved down by a group of Malay policemen standing by an armoured lorry. We slowed to a stop beside a British police officer carrying a Sten gun and clad in immaculate khaki. "Welcome to Malaya. Had a good trip?" was his formal greeting as he reached through the window to shake our hands. "The superintendent thought we'd better do the job properly, so he sent out this escort to bring you in." Then he looked at his watch and added, with a reproaching twinkle in his eye, "But do you realize that you're half an hour late? I've been waiting here since ten o'clock."

We had, it was true, telegraphed the Malayan frontier with an approximate time of arrival, but, as Pat replied, "Well, hell, what's half an hour in six months? This isn't a bloody bus service, you know!"

"I'm only pulling your leg," said the police officer, thinking his joke had misfired. "Let's go. Follow on behind my truck. Chen Ping and his boys are around—it'd be a pity if you got shot-up right on the doorstep." It would have been a pity indeed. But, in fact, this part of the country was a favourite haunt of Communist terrorists, and it was not far away that Chen Ping, the leader of Malaya's Communists, had come out of the jungle a few months before for the celebrated but fruitless Baling peace talks.

The convoy picked up speed, and in only a few minutes we drove into Malaya. Customs and passports were quickly dealt with, and then we were on our way again. Not since Germany had there been such good roads, and the cars lengthened their stride accordingly as they sped through the rubber down the smooth tarmac highway to the south.

At the first big town in Malaya, Alor Star, we were led to the Rest House by a police officer who gave us a sumptuous lunch. This, he said, was being paid for by the Automobile Association of Malaya as a welcoming gesture. It was more than generous in view of the trouble which the Association had already taken in answering our numerous letters of inquiry over earlier months.

FROM THE DIARY

After lunch we were taken down to the police station to be introduced to the chief-of-police for the district. He sat us down in the briefing room and said he would give us "a brief résumé to put you all in the picture about the Emergency set-up." At least, that is how it started, but it soon seemed to be a justification for all British policy in Malaya. It was clear that he had been instructed by some one higher up the administrative chain to make sure that we knew the official 'line,' in order that we should not say anything wrong in the interviews we might later have with the Malayan Press. This was a pity. I, at any rate, had done my National Service in the country and did not think that the British record in Malaya needed any justification; it speaks for itself. It therefore rather worried me to see the others growing sceptical as the pep-talk continued. They felt that their intelligence was being a little underestimated.

Perhaps in quoting this extract I am making a mountain out of a mole-hill, but I remember thinking, at the time, that the lecture tended to destroy the very impression it was meant to build up.

That night we reached Penang, where we were met by a group of reporters. What did we think of Malaya? they asked, with pencils and notebooks at the ready. We had only been in the country eight hours, but were already expected to have a whole host of newsworthy comments. So we said it was hot, and we'd seen lots of rubber-trees, and everybody seemed very nice, and we were glad to have arrived, and that Penang looked a beautiful city, and so on and so on. They were still not satisfied, and asked, among other irrelevancies, for our views on Communism and democracy. "One's good, the other's bad," replied Pat, with the terse diplomacy of eighteen thousand miles behind him. I think it was Adrian who gave them the tip that I had been in Malaya before. Anyway, in the paper the next morning there was a large photograph of us all with the heading in thick black print "Bandit-hunter Returns." I got ribbed a good deal about that!

The following day we headed on southward to Ipoh. This 150-mile stretch was familiar ground to me, for it was the area in which I had served almost four years before. Though, looking back, some times had seemed more comfortable than others, I had very much enjoyed my National Service in Malaya, and now it gave me quite a kick to be driving down that road once more, to see half-remembered places along the way suddenly swing back into clear reality. The others must have been bored by my reminiscences, but they pretended to be interested, and even asked some of the questions which I was bursting to answer.

FROM THE DIARY

Over the pass at Bukit Berapit where Jerry M.'s patrol had sat on a bandit path every night for a week without seeing a thing; but the long-waited bandits—eight of them—came down the path the night after the patrol gave up. Through Padang Rengas where they used to take pot shots at the night-express. Then into Kuala Kangsar itself. I dumped the others in the Idris Club while I drove up to the camp for a quick look-see. The 1st Federation Regt. in occupation now, and very easy and peacetime everything looked too. Even the sentries were unarmed and dressed in khaki—whither the jungle greens? The old Officers' Mess had been taken over by the Sergeants; I invited myself in. They were a decent crowd, gave me a drink, and seemed quite interested to hear tales of 'the good old days'—in fact, they asked almost as many questions as I asked them. (I felt the real old soldier!) They laughed when I recounted how the emergency patrol used to be called out two or three times each week. No, they said, they hadn't had an incident in the area for nearly three months. Ops were so slack around K.K. that all the officers went home for lunch! As for walking into the jungle— helicopters saved them the trouble. I really enjoyed myself.

Back to the Club to meet up with the others, then out of K.K., across the Perak river and down the road to Ipoh. Away to the east, as usual, the rich green of the Cameron Highlands rolled up into the clouds. Then, as we motored quickly through the fierce sunlight towards Sungei Siput (where the Emergency started nearly eight years ago), there was that wonderful dirty white of an afternoon storm brewing ahead. We ran underneath it just outside Ipoh and, suddenly, the whole sky burst. For nearly an hour, the black clouds thundered and the rain roared until one had to shout to make oneself heard. The headlights were necessary to penetrate the fog of spray but even so we had to slow right down because the windscreen-wipers couldn't cope with the downpour. Slowly the storm passed over and then, abruptly, died away. Within ten minutes we were splashing along the flooded road in bright sunshine. The air hung still and cool; it smelt of damp earth. Typical Malaya.

We stayed the night in the Y.M.C.A., and went on to Kuala Lumpur the next day. Normally we avoided any suggestion of travelling to a schedule, but for once, in the case of our final arrival in Singapore, we had agreed to fit in with arrangements made by the Singapore representatives of those British firms which had helped us. Apparently they were laying things on, and did not want us to arrive in Singapore for another three days. This meant that we had to forego the pleasure of a glorious helter-skelter over the last four hundred miles and instead mark time for a couple of days in

Kuala Lumpur. The delay would have been tantalizing had it not been for the wonderful hospitality of every one we met, who seemed determined to make us think that the real terminus of our journey was Kuala Lumpur, not Singapore (and if we had availed ourselves of every drink that seemed available it might have been too!).

Before setting off from Kuala Lumpur for the last night's stop at a Dunlop rubber-plantation in Johore we were asked by the police to make sure that we had no food aboard. This, a rigid regulation enforced by numerous police checks, was primarily designed to prevent lorry-drivers from carrying food (either by chance or intent) which might find its way into the hands of terrorists, who, in Johore particularly, were still sometimes encountered on the highway. We haughtily pointed out that this warning was quite unnecessary, as we had hardly "driven all this way just to come and give food away to your bandits"; we got smartly rapped over the knuckles for our cheek. It so happened that the last tins had been eaten some days before, but, all the same, I'm afraid we were getting a little bumptious.

It was an afternoon's drive from Kuala Lumpur to the rubber estate where we were invited to stay the last night. Then, the next morning, we were up at six and away—at last.

FROM THE DIARY

There were 130 miles to go by ten o'clock; the cars fairly flew down that road—the last day of the journey. The needle went up to 62 m.p.h. and hung there almost continuously for mile after mile. Only an occasional slackening as the road zigzagged between the barbed wire barriers at either end of a village; then, foot down and away again. Through the flat rubber-lands of Johore, through Segamat, Yong Peng, and Ayer Hitam, the milestones going by one a minute and Singapore getting closer all the while. We were on top of the world, even the cars seemed alive as they gulped down the decreasing miles. Singapore, here we come!

The cars, a hundred yards apart, with the dragon pennant of Kengtung flapping from their aerials, raced eagerly down the sweeping curves and level reaches of the highway. The jungle and the rubber swept swiftly by until, a few miles outside Johore Bahru (the town at the mainland end of the famous Singapore causeway), a shirt-sleeved figure standing beside a Rover saloon waved us down. It was Tom Wall, the Far Eastern representative of the Rover Company, a person who as much as anyone else had helped us in planning the journey. We had last seen him in Lahore, and, although we had always kept in fairly constant touch, it was very good to see him again. Then on into Johore Bahru itself, where we were met by a couple of motor-cycle policemen and a gathering of the Singapore Auto Club who, as we came past, hooted on their horns and then hopped into their cars to follow on behind.

We paused briefly just before the causeway, so that Nigel and Henry could take over the driving of Oxford and Cambridge respectively. They were the mechanics, the maintenance of the cars had been their responsibility throughout, and now it seemed right that they should have the reward of taking their charges into the finish, over the final fifteen miles to Singapore itself. Turning on to the causeway, right on time, and with an escorting entourage of cars strung out behind, Oxford mischievously pulled a fast one and slipped in front of Cambridge, thus reversing the long tradition of Cambridge leading the way and also establishing us, the Oxford crew, as the holders of the newly-invented London-Singapore land record! Cambridge were forced to pretend that they were above such a childish prank.

As the Land Rovers sped over the mile-long causeway the journey was almost over. The crossing of that causeway was a moment we had talked about in our Cambridge rooms before we left England, nearly a year earlier. It was a moment which we had talked about throughout the journey—sometimes hopefully, and sometimes as if it were on the other side of the world. And, after all, in the early stages it was on the other side of the world. But now it was right underneath us, rolling away under the tyres as if there had never been any doubt about it at all. One's mind flashed back over the long road which had brought us there, to Anatolia, to the deserts of Persia, to India's Grand Trunk Road, to Ledo, to the Salween and Kengtung, to Takua Pa and a dozen other places. It seemed wonderfully worth while.

They gave us quite a welcome as the two cars crossed the City Limits and, when we finally pulled in and turned off the engines at the Rover garage in Orchard Road, they opened the champagne. Cameras clicked and whirred, flash-bulbs popped, reporters buzzed about, and we were the centre of attention. It would be sheer false modesty to pretend we did not enjoy it, for, as I have said before, we were not a modest lot. When some one offered us some more champagne we did not hesitate or hang back. After all, it had been a long drive—six months, six days, and nearly nineteen thousand miles. We had reached the far end of Asia, and, by land, we could go no farther. As an American journalist opined, "I guess you boys have run plumb outta road." We guessed we had.

And it was most satisfactory.

Epilogue—Four Months Later

Based on the Diary Entry for June 17, 1956

CALCUTTA is two weeks behind; England is eight weeks ahead. And we've been on the road ten months.

Five days ago we left Peshawar, in Pakistan, and headed away towards the hills of the North-West Frontier. The road ran out across the bare and empty plain until, quite suddenly, it rose in straggling curves up to the Khyber Pass. The plains of Pakistan and India were finished—broken at those ragged hills as if at the sea. The Grand Trunk Road which trailed away behind, straight and level into the morning sun, back for fifteen hundred miles to Calcutta and the Bay of Bengal, was ended. Our field-work was over; the cars were together again after two months apart in India and Burma. At last we were on our way home.

To-day we're heading slowly west through Afghanistan. Slowly, because this road is just an endless strip of corduroy, of rocks and holes and dust. In the noise of thrashing tyres, flying stones, and droning engine there's not much point in trying to talk. So one just sits and, sometimes, thinks. Out of the window it all looks the same as it did ten minutes ago; the desert and the sky are so huge that we might hardly be moving at all. The other car is miles ahead, a little speck creeping along with a dust-plume rolling out high behind her. Far away, beyond the edge of the plain, there's a range of wrinkled mountains crouching under the glaring sun. On the outward journey, when everything was new, I could look for hours at this slowly changing loneliness. But now—well, I'm a little tired. Perhaps we all are.

B.B., who has been driving for the last three hours, must keep his eyes constantly on the road. I glance at the dashboard—oil-pressure, water-temperature, 26 gallons in the tanks, speed about 30 m.p.h., milometer reading 26,906 miles.

The other car is slowing down, seems to be stopping—probably changing tanks. There's a wadi just ahead. He brakes, and changes hurriedly into third. We slam shut the windows, as the car slides down through the rocks, rolling and skidding in her dust. He took it too late and too fast. (But the passengers always think they can do better than the driver. They can't.) The car picks a way across the bottom, and then the engine gives a deeper roar as she accelerates up the other side. I'll never be car-sick after this journey—even my grandchildren will be immune.

Cambridge is off again; it must have been a petrol-change. But we're catching her up, and are getting her dust. B.B. slows down to give her time to draw away. The evening sun doesn't help, either; on this, the homeward run, we're driving west, and always into the sunset. The slanting glare and the dust are very tiring.

The road tapers away to the mountains; soon we'll climb away from this plain, twist through a pass, and then run down on to another plain—we've done it a dozen times in the last six hundred miles, so we know the pattern. The other car has already disappeared into the hills, though her wake of dust still wisps behind her.

The sun is going.

We motor up the slope from the plain, and cross into the deep shadow of the mountains. The surface improves, and the car picks up speed. The faster the better—we might make three hundred miles in the day. We've only passed one other vehicle since last night—a diesel lorry going the other way; it must be hundreds of miles behind now.

We're swinging up through the curves of the pass, dropping through the gears as we go. Away behind, across the amber desert, I can just see the mountains over which we came earlier in the day. Mountains and desert, desert and mountains—that's Afghanistan. We're at the top; the road kinks through the rocks. B.B. looks at his watch; he slows and stops. "Time for a change?" We get out to stretch. On this side of the pass we're in the last of the evening light, and can see the other car winding her way down on to the next plain. It's quiet—no noise at all, except for the rush of the tyres, which still seems to sing in my ears.

A quick drink from the water-bag, and we climb aboard. Now it's Nigel's turn to drive, and mine in the back. The doors slam shut; we're off again. He pushes her quickly through second to third, then holds her in third to steady the run downhill.

Roll on the Bosporus—and Hyde Park Corner.

NOTES

1. Our title should not be taken to imply that we were in any way sponsored by our Universities. It is not the policy of either University to sponsor expeditions, but, in so far as the members of an expedition are members of the Universities, the powers-that-be raise no serious objection to the use of their names.
2. These opinions and comments were made almost exactly a year before Israel's raid into Sinai.
3. The names have, of course, been changed!
4. Microclimatology being the study of climate on a very precise scale (e.g., the differences between temperatures or wind speeds at ground-level and those at an elevation of say three feet). It is particularly important in agricultural research.
5. Pronounced, believe it or not, Mitch-in-ah.
6. Nevertheless, we did carry supplies of waterproof tape. Also exhaust-pipe extensions. But these measures were only intended for extreme emergency, as it would have been a long job to fit them, and of doubtful success.
7. Together with "The Wild Green Earth," this is an incomparable account of the Chindits. Both books are by Brigadier Bernard Fergusson, D.S.O.
8. The other verses were more robust but less printable.
9. In Bhamo we once again crossed the path of Marco Polo. The last time had been nearly ten thousand miles behind in Persia.
10. B.B. kept a special bag of 'photographic sweets' for children—woe betide any member of the Expedition who was caught filching them.
11. W.H.O.=World Health Organization, one of the United Nations agencies.
12. Inspection Bungalow.
13. The other car (Cambridge) would return by sea to India in order to complete the irrigation work started on the outward journey. When both cars had finished their work they would meet in India, and then drive back to England. This was the plan, anyway!

14. There is a certain amount of R.C. missionary work in the Kengtung area. This particular missionary had been shot because he had repeatedly urged one of his villages not to co-operate with the K.M.T.

Appendix A

Medical Notes
by B.B.

The diseases that may be met during the course of a trip like ours are so many and diverse that it is impossible to guard against all of them. Even the precautions which can reasonably be taken are not certain safeguards, but that does not mean that all precautions are futile. We managed to maintain almost perfect health throughout—in the course of a year not one day was lost due to illness. This was mainly good luck, but our precautions undoubtedly had something to do with it. Some of the rules listed below may seem elementary, but, in fact, that is just my point; they are so elementary that one is apt to forget them—particularly at the end of a tiring day.

1. Boil all drinking-water, or at least add a stiff quota of sterilizing tablets.
2. Eat no lettuce or uncooked green vegetables (except cucumber). Wash all thin-skinned fruit (grapes, tomatoes, etc.). Inspect melons for cut or bruised skins before buying.
3. Always wash hands before eating or preparing food. The 'always' cannot be stressed too strongly.
4. Take one tablet of Paludrin daily (anti-malarial).
5. Wash feet regularly, and dust, when necessary, with anti-fungal powder.
6. Apply antiseptic cream (Cetavlex is excellent) immediately to all cuts and sores, however small.
7. Wear dark glasses, especially when driving. Optone is an excellent eye-soother after dust-irritation.
8. Use proper toilet-paper (and burn or bury afterwards to stop it blowing about).
9. Salt tablets are invaluable in counteracting the enervating effect of hot climates.
10. One person should be appointed i/c health; his word should be final.

Dysentery and malaria are, potentially, the most serious complaints. Dysentery is combated by rules 1-3, especially 1. In order to build up resistance to malaria it is necessary to take Paludrin for three weeks before entering a malarial area; this usually means starting in England, since the disease is still endemic in parts of Turkey. A daily dose, though perhaps overdoing it, is easier to remember than a 'thrice weekly,' and is therefore safer. We also took vitamin pills each day (quantity depending on current diet). The common cold and sore throats are prevalent everywhere; a supply of throat sweets is most desirable.

If there is an accident—we had several—triangular bandages are more useful in the emergency than normal roll bandages. Five or six will be needed to secure a splint, apart from the dressing of the wound. Twelve should be a minimum supply.

We had inoculations against smallpox, typhoid (TAB), typhus, cholera, plague, yellow fever, and tetanus. These should be well spaced, or the effect, just before departure, is likely to be devastating! Certificates of these inoculations are required at some frontiers.

Besides having a full medical chest, it is also very useful to have a small 'ready-use' box, which is kept in the glove pocket or on the front seat. This, containing a few pieces of Elastoplast and antiseptic cream, and easily available at all times, encourages people to treat their own minor cuts immediately, whereas the heavier medical chest is sometimes too much trouble to get out, unless the cut is a fairly large one. In other words, it should be made as easy as possible to treat all cuts and sores, no matter how small.

The following medicaments were taken, and found useful, or are considered in the light of our experience to be advisable to take on such a journey. Quantities are omitted for obvious reasons.

Acriflex	*for* Burns
Cetavlex or Propamidine cream	General antisepsis
Anthisan	Antihistamine cream
Dimp	Insect-repellant
Golden Eye Ointment	Styes
Optone	Sore eyes
Dettol or T.C.P.	Disinfectant

Surgical spirit
Marzine   *for* Travel sickness
Thalazole   Bacillary dysentery
Nivembin   Amœbic dysentery
Sulphatriad   Boils, septicæmia
Paludrin or Daraprim   Malaria (prevention)
Nivaquin   Malaria (cure)
Morphia   Major emergencies
Disprin   Headaches
Veganin   Malaise
Bisodol   Hangover
Cascara   Constipation
Nicorbin   Vitamin pills
Phytodermine   Athlete's foot, etc.
DDT.   Lice
Cough Sweets

The following items are also necessary:

Safety pins   Gauze
Scissors   Lint
Razor blades   Cotton wool
Needles   Elastoplast
Thermometer   Zinc oxide plaster
Tourniquet   Bandages
Crepe bandage   Triangular bandages
Tweezers   (at least 12)

Useful books are:
Red Cross First-Aid Manual
Health and Disease in the Tropics (Wilcocks).

Appendix B

Mechanical Notes
by Henry Nott

ON most motorized expeditions there will be some one who has the job of mechanic. There will be a confident few who already know all the answers. But for those who don't I have compiled the following list of comments, which, I hope, may be of some use.

1. Local mechanics, outside Europe, often know very little about cars, and can cause considerable damage during their operations. When a car is taken out of garage after repairs it should be carefully inspected. (Nevertheless, these mechanics should not be despised; their aptitude for improvisation is very considerable.)
2. Sometimes there are *no* garages. In view of this, it is wise to be able to maintain and repair one's vehicle. A manufacturer's workshop manual is invaluable.
3. Among other tools should be: high-quality spanners, a heavy hammer, a 'mole' wrench, a hand drill, a feeler gauge, and a small set of tools for electrical work.
4. Oil-levels and tyre-pressures should be checked daily. An oil-pressure gauge on the dashboard increases mechanical safety. Tyre-pressures should not be let down when they build up in the heat of the day. (If you don't believe this, ask a tyre-manufacturer.)
5. In hot climates radiator and battery water-levels should be checked every 2 or 3 days. It is common practice to remove the thermostat in the water system in order to improve the reliability of flow.
6. When travelling over rough ground the suspension should be inspected every day for spring leaf fractures. Inspection all round the car for loose bolts (particularly in the steering system) is essential.
7. Under great heat—110°F. in the shade—petrol tends to vaporize in the fuel pump and leads, causing fuel-starvation. This is particularly so in those countries where large percentages of alcohol are added

to the petrol. To prevent this many drivers change the position of the fuel pump, putting it in a cooler place than the engine. In the case of mechanical pumps (they are especially prone to vaporization) an auxiliary electrical system can be fitted. Alternatively, the pump can be wrapped in damp rags to keep it cool.

8. Hot, self-vulcanizing, puncture-repair patches are invaluable for their reliability and ease of application. (They can be obtained on the Continent, but are not easy to find in Britain.)

9. An hydraulic jack (as opposed to the mechanical 'screw-up' type) is well worth its price.

10. It is a good thing to stick to one grade of oil, and preferably the same make. (In our case it was Mobiloil A—obtainable in almost every country.) Always carry a spare can of oil—this cannot be over-emphasized.

11. Spark-plugs should be cleaned regularly. Our Lodge plugs were checked weekly; they gave us over 30,000 miles of trouble-free service.

12. Loud horns, preferably French, are very worth while. English manufacturers don't know what loud is!

13. Track-grip tyres are not good for a long journey, as they wear quickly, and then skid easily. A tyre like the Dunlop RK3 (for Land Rovers), which combines track-grip with road-holding qualities, is an ideal compromise, and can be used in both mud and sand.

14. When driving off the limit of normal roads a winch can save hours of work if one gets stuck in mud or sand. Where there are no rocks or trees to winch against, a 'sand anchor' (a large piece of canvas, spare tyre, or matting dug into the ground) or three crowbars chained together can do the job almost as well. When winching another vehicle out, the winch wire can be run through a pulley attached to the vehicle, and then to a tree—thus the winching force is nearly doubled. A drum winch is the strongest and easiest to manage, but its high cost and heavy weight on the front suspension make it uneconomical unless a lot of winching is expected. (In any case, on the overland drive to India, as long as one sticks to the roads a winch is unnecessary.)

15. When fording rivers the fan belt should be removed. A length of rubber hose with which to make an exhaust-pipe extension is useful. (Not necessary on the road to India.)

16. Trailers are best avoided; they restrict mobility. But, worse than this, the driver of the towing vehicle cannot tell (unless he stops every few minutes) when a trailer tyre has been punctured. Consequently, he drives blissfully on. Owing to this problem a recent expedition ruined a dozen tyres in 9000 miles—a costly business.

17. It is possible to keep a car quite cool in desert areas by soaking the floor in water, or by hanging wet cloths over the open windows. As the wind blows through the car it absorbs the moisture, and the temperature drops.

18. One hopes that one will never need a fire-extinguisher, but it is better to take one than to be sorry.

19. It is impossible to anticipate every mechanical failure. Improvisation will take one a long way—and it will take one even farther when it has to. But the possession of the following spares may well save a great deal of trouble: a fan belt, a set of gaskets, a patrol pump (complete), a half shaft, an inner tube (beside the one in the spare tyre), a spring leaf, radiator hosing, spark-plugs, head-light bulbs and fuses, tyre valves, a tow-rope, a distributor, dynamo brushes, and a set of coils and condensers. (I take no responsibility for the incompleteness of this list!)

20. Lastly, the mechanic does not wash up breakfast—he maintains his vehicle.

Appendix C

Navigation and Route
by Pat Murphy

THE job of expedition navigator is not just one of collecting maps or merely of knowing where petrol and water points are to be found. It consists also of knowing the average annual temperature in Upper Assam (this the photographer requires for some unknown scientific purpose); how long it takes to get from Peshawar to Istanbul (making due allowance for fifteen punctures, two broken springs, and a sudden expeditional whim to divert to the Caspian); precisely where the sun will rise the following morning, so that all ranks can continue to sleep in the shade; and whether the Indian word *Hah* means "Yes, this is the road to Jopigophaghat," "No, it isn't," "I haven't the slightest idea," or "Anything you say, sahib."

Small wonder that one tended to give an immediate answer and work out the reasons later.

Languages are also the navigator's department, but those with no linguistic ability need not worry—English will get them through (though the tendency merely to shout louder when misunderstood should be resisted). French is, however, useful in Europe and the Middle East, while German doctors and engineers seem to be found everywhere. From Aleppo to Amritsar milestones are in pukka Arabic, so it is as well to become familiar with the numerals in that script. But, apart from this slight concession to foreign ways, it is not necessary to know much more than the local words for bread, water, petrol, and a few numbers. After all, one's main requests concern which road to take to a given place, and this can be confirmed by repeating the name of that place (with every possible permutation of cadences) until it is at last understood. Anyway, in Asia there is usually only one road, and if you're not on it you're in the desert—and first-class honours in Uzbeki won't help you.

Basic to everything are maps and itineraries—the tools of a navigator's trade. It is best to get them in Europe. A compass has its uses, and, besides this, it looks good.

1. Bartholomew's maps of India and the Middle East on the scale of 1:4 million are the best generally available. The Survey of Pakistan publishes good maps, but road maps of India are unobtainable in that country.

2. The Mobil Oil Company publish road maps of Greece, Turkey (particularly useful), and the Middle East, while their associates, the Standard-Vacuum Oil Company, perform the same service for Thailand and Malaya.

3. The Burmah Oil Company published a booklet in 1948 entitled *The Motor Roads of Burma*, which is still very useful.

4. The War Office G.S.G.S. maps on 1:1 million are invaluable.

5. Alliance Internationale de Tourisme, 9 rue Pierre-Fatio, Geneva, publish an excellent itinerary for their Geneva-Bombay rallies, which no overlander should be without.

6. Visas should be obtained in reverse. In other words, if you want to drive from London to Pakistan start by getting the Persian transit visa (ensuring it is still valid for the time you get there), and work back from there.

The trip from London to Calcutta has been done many times, the all-time record being a round-the-clock fortnight. A month's daylight driving would be very good time, but to do it in comfort and see the sights on the way one should reckon on two to three months.

The seasonal hazards consist of winter mud and rain in Southern Europe and Turkey, and snow-blocked passes in Persia between November and April. Autumn is undoubtedly the best time of year to leave Europe.

The longest stretches without petrol in the Middle East are about 200 miles, but from Zahidan (near the Persia-Pakistan border) to Quetta there are probably no supplies for 450 miles, unless there are now outlets at Nushki or Dalbandin. But it is not necessary to carry jerricans up to this capacity, since petrol is sold in four-gallon tins which can be abandoned when empty.

The routes are given in the following pages:

Stage	Road Condition	Stage Mileage	Driving-time (in hrs.)	Total Mileage
London to Belgrade	Excellent (via Milan or Vienna)	1470	—	1470
Belgrade to Nis	Good asphalt or gravel	162	5	1632
Nis to the Greek border	Generally bad asphalt or gravel	225	6 $^1/_2$	1857
Greek border to Alexandropolis	Good asphalt (via Salonika)	260	7 $^1/_2$	2117
Alexandropolis to Istanbul	Very poor to Edirne then good	233	7 $^1/_2$	2350
Istanbul to Ankara	Good asphalt or gravel	291	9	2641
Ankara to Aleppo	Good asphalt or gravel (via Iskenderum)	549	16	3190
Aleppo to Beirut	Fair asphalt (via Homs)	242	6 $^1/_2$	3432
Beirut to Damascus	Good asphalt	72	2	3504
Damascus to Mafraq	Fair asphalt (improves in Jordan)	99	3	3603
Mafraq to Ramadi	Fair asphalt along pipe-line	450	14	4053
Ramadi to Baghdad	Appalling pot-holed earth	65	3 $^1/_2$	4118
Baghdad to Kermanshah	Asphalt to Persia, then hilly, bumpy gravel	230	8 $^1/_2$	4348
Kermanshah to Qazvin	Very hilly (8,600 ft.) and bumpy	278	9$^1/_2$	4626
Qazvin to Teheran	Worn asphalt (usually fair)	87	2$^1/_2$	4713
Teheran to Isfahan	Asphalt to Qum, then good gravel	258	7$^1/_2$	4971
Isfahan to Kerman	Fair corrugated gravel	547	11	5518
Kerman to Bam	Fair corrugated gravel, also sand	118	3 $^1/_2$	5636
Bam to Zahidan	Fair gravel and sand. (Load petrol)	214	6	5850
Zahidan to Persian frontier	Poor gravel. Difficult sand at frontier	53	2	5903
Persian frontier to Quetta	Good gravel and asphalt	398	9	6301
Quetta to Sukkur	Good asphalt. Through Bolan Pass	253	8	6554
Sukkur to Multan	Asphalt or brick. Some double strip	305	8	6859
Multan to Lahore	Good asphalt. Along L.B.D.Canal	210	5	7069
Lahore to Delhi	Good asphalt. Grand Trunk Road	307	9	7376
Delhi to Cawnpore	G.T. Road. Via Aligarh (Agra is off route)	267	7	7643
Cawnpore to Dehri-on-Sone	G.T. Road. Rail across river at Dehri-on-Sone	284	7 $^1/_2$	7927
Dehri to Calcutta	G.T. Road. Last stretch congested	337	8 $^1/_2$	8264

ALTERNATIVE ROUTES

1. Through Eastern Turkey direct to Teheran (recommended)

Stage	Road Condition	Stage Mileage	Driving -time (in hrs.)	Total Mileage
Ankara to Erzurum	Good or fair gravel (via Sivas and Erzincan)	641	2 days	641
Erzurum to Persian frontier	Good gravel. (Military permit required)	195	$5^1/_2$ hrs.	836
Persian frontier to Tabriz	Narrow and hilly, then good gravel	187	5 hrs.	1023
Tabriz to Teheran	Good to fair asphalt or gravel	387	11 hrs.	1410

2. Through Afghanistan to Lahore (not recommended)

Stage	Road Condition	Stage Mileage	Driving -time (in hrs.)	Total Mileage
Teheran to Meshed	Mostly rough corrugated gravel	586	$17^1/_2$	586
Meshed to Herat	Reasonable gravel	235	$8^1/_2$	821
Herat to Farah	Bad bumpy gravel. Deep ford at Farah	177	8	998
Farah to Kandahar	Bad bumpy gravel with some good stretches	233	9	1231
Kandahar to Kabul	Fair to bad corrugated gravel	312	12	1543
Kabul to Jalalabad	Abominable gravel and rocks	102	6	1645
Jalalabad to Peshawar	Fair gravel to Khyber, then good asphalt	80	4	1725
Peshawar to Lahore	G.T. Road (Attock Bridge closed at sunset)	270	8	1995

3. Quetta to Lahore (crossing Indus via Dera–Ghazi–Khan)

Stage	Road Condition	Stage Mileage	Driving -time (in hrs.)	Total Mileage
Quetta to Rakhni	Narrow mountain road (via Loralai)	234	1 day	234
Rakhni to Dera–Ghazi–Khan	Good asphalt	61	2 hrs.	295
Dera-Ghazi-Khan to Ghazi Ghat	Indus. Boat bridge October–April, ferry May–September	18	—	313
Ghazi Ghat to Multan	Good asphalt (via Muzaffargarh)	42	11/2 hrs.	355
Multan to Lahore	Good asphalt. Along L.B.D. Canal	210	5 hrs.	565

Note. All driving-times are those done in a Land Rover travelling fast. A normal car would take longer, except on good-surfaced roads, as in Western Europe. Times do not include frontier formalities or any stops.

From Teheran to Quetta is virtually desert, and therefore devoid of amenities or supplies, apart from occasional petrol, water, and food. Petrol-consumption in this kind of country is apt to be fairly high (the price is, however, low), since the best policy for corrugated gravel is speed.

This book will have pointed out the difficulties of motoring beyond Calcutta and through Burma. The following notes are therefore more of academic interest. They refer to dry-season conditions, and times depend very much on ferry availability and escorts' speed and maintenance,

Stage	Road Condition	Stage Mileage	Driving -time (in hrs.)	Total Mileage
Calcutta to Dhulian Ghat	Fair asphalt. Three ferries	207	$8^1/_2$ hrs.	207
Dhulian Ghat to Khajuria Ghat	Ganges ferry (3 hrs.) three times a day	—	—	—
Khajuria Ghat to Siliguri	Earth or asphalt. Three ferries or boat bridges	216	7 hrs.	423
Siliguri to Jopighopa Ghat	Assam Trunk Road, asphalt. Temporary bridges	267	8 hrs.	690
Jopighopa Ghat to Goalpara	Brahmaputra ferry ($1^1/_2$ hrs.) three times a day	—	—	—
Goalpara to Dibrugarh	Assam Trunk (via Gauhati and Jorhat)	358	10 hrs.	1048
Dibrugarh to Ledo	Asphalt to Digboi, then earth and gravel	68	3 hrs.	1116
Ledo to Myitkyina	Stilwell Road. Jungle. (G/Capt. Townsend took one week)	272	3–7 days	1388
Myitkyina to Muse	Very hilly gravel or earth (via Bhamo)	202	1 day	1590
Muse to Lashio	Burma Road. Undulating asphalt	110	4 hrs.	1700
Lashio to Loilem (for Taunggyi)	Fair. Mostly gravel or laterite. Escort necessary	185	1 day	1885
Loilem to Takaw	Fair to bad gravel or earth. Escort. Salween ferry	111	1 day	1996
Takaw to Kengtung	Mostly bad. Very hilly and narrow. Escort	114	$1^1/_2$ days	2110
Kengtung to Tachilek	Mostly bad. Very hilly and narrow. Escort	104	$1^1/_2$ days	2214
Tachilek to Chiang Rai	Good wide gravel or laterite	31	1 hr.	2245
Chiang Rai to Muang Fang	One-way earth mountain road. Road construction	53	$3^1/_2$ hrs.	2298
Muang Fang to Chiang Mai	Good wide gravel or asphalt	91	$2^1/_2$ hrs.	2389
Chiang Mai to Bangkok	Good wide gravel, then asphalt (via Tak)	450	16 hrs.	2839

Stage	Road Condition	Stage Mileage	Driving -time (in hrs.)	Total Mileage
Bangkok to Chumporn	Asphalt to Hua Hin, then good laterite	312	8¹/₂ hrs.	3151
Chumporn to Renong	Good laterite or gravel	76	2 hrs.	3227
Renong to Takuapa	Road under construction. Jungle	108	1 day	3335
Takuapa to Sadau	Good laterite (via Trang and Haadyai)	366	13 hrs.	3701
Sadau to Singapore	Good asphalt (via Butterworth and Kuala Lumpur)	600	1¹/₂ days	4301

Note. The south-west monsoon breaks in Burma at the beginning of May, and a little later on the west coast of the Kra Isthmus, in Southern Thailand. This monsoon does not reach the east coast of the Kra Isthmus, which receives its rain from the north-east monsoon breaking about October. Motoring in this part of the world should be planned to avoid the monsoons. Malaya is non-monsoonal—it just rains!

Appendix D

Photographic Notes
by B.B.

ON the journey I was responsible for three types of photographic work. First, black-and-white stills; second, colour stills; third, cine film. (Other members of the Expedition, I believe, took 'snapshots' from time to time!) Before I left England people told me I couldn't possibly hope to operate both cine and still cameras, but I argued that in most cases the choice of which to use would be obvious. And so it turned out. I usually gave priority to the cine, as there was most money in it, and the gaps would be more noticeable. When, for instance, the cars were fording a deep river the cine camera was obviously called for, and I would give the still cameras to one of the others and tell him what I wanted. At other times it was possible to use first one, then the other.

Between some remote places I found interesting differences in the reactions of human subjects. Some didn't mind the Leica but were afraid of the Rolleiflex because of its 'two eyes.' Others fled before the 'pointing finger' of the Leica, but ignored the non-directional Rolleiflex. I usually found that it paid to let the children look through the view-finder, as a means of inspiring confidence among both them and their elders. In the Middle East one has to be careful with cameras. Serious Muslims have strong objections to representations of living things—and this includes photography. The police are another snag. In Syria and Persia, for example, there used to be laws forbidding photography without a permit. These have been repealed years ago, but no one has thought of telling the police. If one applies for a permit one is told that it is 'not necessary,' nor will they issue a note to dispense with a permit. So one just gets arrested!

Now to some more technical points:

Camera Equipment. Undoubtedly it pays to take the best possible apparatus, not so much for its optical performance as for its reliability under adverse conditions, and ease of operation. Cheap cameras tend to become clogged by dust very rapidly, and cheap shutters fail to operate in extremes of heat and cold. Of cine cameras, only the Bell and Howell 70 is robust enough to withstand being dropped—which it certainly will be at least once. Its competitors are more versatile in the studio, but their refinements make them too delicate—and are unnecessary for newsreeling work. Of still cameras, the Rolleiflex is ideal for general black-and-white work; the Leica M3 is perfect for colour, superbly easy to operate, dust-proof, and its lenses are quickly interchangeable (not so in the case of earlier Leicas). The rigid 9 cm. Elmar lens is not recommended (too clumsy), but the collapsible Elmar is invaluable.

Accessories. Lens-hoods for all lenses are essential. An orange filter is the most useful for black-and-white, as it eliminates some haze, and gives excellent skies. For those who must have an exposure meter, the Weston cine model is the simplest to operate for both still and cine. Our Schiansky tripod gave excellent service, and its pan-and-tilt head is unbeatable. Although a large quantity of flash gear was carried, only the Rolleiflash and the Chico were handy enough to be useful. The Chico gives correct flash fill-in for colour portraits in sunlight at 6 feet (9 cm. Elmar) with a Sylvania FP26B, at f/5.6 and 1/100 sec.

Film. Ilford HP3 and HPS were used throughout for black-and-white pictures. Standard exposure outdoors was 1/125 at f/16, with an orange filter for HP3. HPS two stops less. Kodachrome Rochester Stock was used for colour, both still and cine. Standard exposure 1/100 sec. at f/6.3, or 24 fps. at f/9.

Processing. Black-and-white film was processed by me as occasion arose, usually in batches of twelve, developed three at a time in a Tribox tank. There was often uneven development, whatever precautions were taken. Ice was usually necessary to get the solutions down to 20 degrees C. A tin of D76 was made up in a polythene bottle for each batch, and then discarded. Amfix packs were used similarly. When possible still colour film was sent direct to Washington, and colour cine to London. Customs and censorship difficulties are often insuperable; in general, post is easier than air freight.

Replacements. Film is always obtainable in Lebanon, India, Thailand, and Malaya; elsewhere in Asia supplies are more difficult. Supplies sent from abroad will almost certainly cause days—perhaps weeks—of frustration and wrangling with Customs.

Points to Note. Dust is a constant problem. Lens-caps are essential, a lens brush even more so—use the fountain-pen type, not the lipstick pattern. Use a half-inch paint-brush for dusting camera bodies. Use lens-cleaning tissue *after* initial brushing, then brush again. For carrying all the numerous bits and pieces which are part of a photographer's trade I found it very useful to have extra pockets sewn on both trouser legs in front.

A handful of sweets is invaluable; grown-ups tend to trust those who make friends with children. A few cigarettes are also needed as bribes or rewards. A magnifying mirror is always a big attraction to all ages.

With cine film it is advisable to take plenty of cutaways, and then more. Leave long-focus cine lens off for general use—fill the mount with a blank cap, and cover both ends of lens when not in use.

Finally, always take a picture when you see it—the opportunity will not return.

The equipment which I used regularly was:
- Leica M3:35 mm. Summaron, 50 mm. Summicron; 90 mm. Elmar (collapsible); 2 Lens-hoods. Chico flash-gun.
- Rolleiflex: Orange filter, Lens-hood; Rolleiflash, Rolleigrid.
- Voigtlander Vitessa (reserve). Lens-hood, UV filter.
- Bell & Howell 70 DL 16 mm. TTH, 25 mm. TTH, 75 mm. Yvar.
- Schiansky 141 tripod, with 142 head.
- Weston Master II cine meter.
- Tribox tank. D 76. Amfix. Photoflo. 2 thermometers.
- 6 film clips. 2 Polythene Winchesters.

Appendix E

Quartermastering
by Nigel Newbery

THE selection and subsequent packing of kit for a journey is always a problem—be the journey just an afternoon picnic or a trans-continental drive. I hope that the following suggestions may help.

1. Lamps and stoves which run on ordinary car petrol make for a considerable saving in weight, since they obviate the necessity of carrying an extra container of paraffin. But, when opening the car's tank to refill such stoves, strict precautions against fire must obviously be taken.
2. Rubber pads, clips, and elastic straps (the latter can be made from lengths of tyre inner-tubing) are very useful in stowing the smaller items of kit. Take a spare strip of sorbo rubber with which to eliminate chafing, rattling, and banging—which really only develop after the first two thousand miles.
3. Polythene containers of all kinds (boxes, bottles, buckets, and bags) are very useful, for polythene does not rattle, and is almost unbreakable. On the rare occasions when it cracks it can easily be soldered up again with a red-hot screwdriver.
4. Melmex is excellent material for cups and plates. It is an unbreakable, highly glossed, and scratch-resisting plastic which does not retain the dirt.
5. Terylene socks are the complete answer to an all-male prayer. They wash easily, dry quickly, and never need darning. We had six pairs a head, and, after a year, out of these seventy-two socks, only one had a hole. A pair of 'social' trousers made of Terylene are a good investment; after being squashed up at the bottom of a case for a couple of weeks they keep the right creases and lose the wrong ones.
6. The desert can be extremely cold at night, and, in addition to one's sleeping-bag, an extra blanket is advisable. In any case, blankets are better than sleeping-bags should some one be ill.
7. "Tensile" camp-beds are not only most comfortable but pack up very small. We had some small fittings whereby a camp bed could be put inside our Land Rovers—thus converting them into emergency ambulances.
8. A tray (particularly the Silva, made of laminated wood) is useful. It can be used as a dip tray for nuts and bolts during mechanical 'goings-on,' for food, washing-up, or for laying out medical kit.
9. It is impossible to keep dish-cloths hygienic. If they are not to smell they require frequent washing, and then there is the problem of how to dry them.

Furthermore, they are perfect germ-carriers. Paper towels are undoubtedly the answer; they can be thrown away after use. We carried 20,000 on leaving London; we still had 2000 when we returned!

10. A convenient (but not perfect) way of washing clothes is to put them in a leak-proof container in the back of the car with a suitable amount of soap-flakes and water added. Two hundred miles of Eastern roads should do the trick. (In Afghanistan only a hundred miles are needed.)

11. An electric razor running off the car battery is the obvious answer for those who intend to shave (Remingtons make a dual 12v/220v model). Tim, our one unbearded member, used to plug in to the dashboard every morning—often while the car was travelling at speed.

12. If each person carries his personal baggage in a miniature trunk or a strong wooden box these containers can also be used as seats, lamp-stands, or tables when camping. This is more useful than it sounds.

13. Extensive Thermos capacity is essential for carrying cooked meals, cold drinks, or tea (and, as one has got to boil all one's water anyway, one might just as well make it into tea.) It is a good idea to have a Thermos fitted within reach of the car seats—for drinks on the move.

14. A canvas water bag hung outside the car will keep drinking-water cool (but don't forget the sterilizing tablets!) However, until the bag is broken in, it will lose a good deal of water owing to leakage and evaporation. The best treatment is to soak it in water for a couple of days, and then rub it in the dirt.

Appendix F

Cookery
by Pat Murphy

BESIDES being the navigator, I was also the chef. This combination of jobs was not so strange as it might seem; the connexion may have been subtle, but it was none the less important. Where, for instance, lies the frontier 'twixt lard and olive oil? How long will it take, and will it be worth the attempt, to convert an expedition on to Greek oil, which, to say the least, has plenty of body in it? (The answer to this one is, "Definitely no." We carried a gallon of the stuff 20,000 miles before we found some Hellenophiles willing to accept it.) How many thousands of miles can one go on chicken noodle soup before a change is absolutely necessary?

Although all our expeditional cookery seemed to consist of either 'boil-up' or 'fry-up,' there still remained the problem of 'what?' and 'for how long?' This can only be answered by research. To this end I entered into correspondence with Elizabeth David, of the *Sunday Times*, who was quick to point out that her published recipe for *saucisses à la salade de pommes de terre froides* (bangers and cold spuds) was not the panacea I hoped it might be, since in Muslim countries there would be no *saucisses*! Even with a geographical training, one is apt to forget these points.

In the event, 'boil-up' consisted of tinned steak and local vegetables. 'Fry-up' included peppers, onions, tomatoes, and eggs, which, by the addition of a tin of corned beef and a bouillon cube (French for Oxo), could quickly be converted into *ragoût*.

Post-prandial drinks were always under what the Army calls 'individual arrangements,' and some pretty fantastic concoctions resulted. Billy tea was, however, the staple tipple, and its manufacture therefore calls for some description.

The billy—never a 'billy can'—is an empty and semi-sacred four-pound jam tin with a wire handle. After the water has boiled two handfuls of Brooke Bond (none other will do) are thrown in. The side of the billy is meticulously tapped with a tin-opener or boot. This, they say, does something to the molecules, and is an essential part of the proceedings. The brew is then put back on to the fire to 'jazz up.' When the molecules have been rearranged to satisfaction the tea is poured into mugs and sugar is lifted in. Limes may be added to taste.

Since in hot climates liquid consumption is likely to be ten pints per man per day, it is well worth brewing vast quantities of this beverage.

Lastly, a word on rice. There are over a thousand varieties of this grain, only one of which does not form itself into a thick, glutinous mass on cooking. This variety is not to be found on the London-Singapore route.

Other points which may be of use are as follows:

1. Take a sieve. It may solve the glutinous rice problem.
2. A pressure cooker must have a good burner or burners under it. Pressure burners are the best, but avoid the cheaper makes—they will let you down.
3. You will need at least three burners to prepare a meal; therefore take four.
4. Sugar and jam are consumed in vast quantities. 1-1b tins of jam are the most practical.
5. Polythene containers are good for dry foods, but not wet, since they impart a taste.
6. Lemon or other fruit crystals make a welcome change from tea.
7. Drinking-chocolate and Nescafé are 'musts.' The latter is rare, expensive, and much sought after in many countries; so keep stocked up.
8. The best places in which to stock up with European tinned foods are Beirut, Baghdad, India (though there it is now getting more expensive), and Singapore.
9. The cook must have a chair.
10. The cook does not wash up.
11. When in doubt about what else to do, boil water.

Appendix G

On Money
by Adrian Cowell

"WHAT do you do about money?" It's a natural question, and we were often asked it on our way to Singapore. It came from the governor's wife, delicately, to keep the conversation going; from students, worded casually—too casually to be anything but an attempt to get in on what they believed to be a 'racket'; and once from a nightclub hostess, who had her motive too.

"We just use lots and lots of American dollars" was the usual reply, frivolous, and designed to turn the conversation. Seldom did we explain that, entered into our account book, there was a little money from academic grants and not much from our own pockets; that we were financed by what we could earn as an 'Expedition'; and that we had left England with enough money to get to Singapore, but that we had to earn enough to get back again. Furthermore, once home there would be commitments to fulfil and debts to pay off. We were, in fact, something of a gamble on wheels.

A few startled newsvendors must have noticed two highly painted Land Rovers debouch their disreputable passengers to study with quite unusual interest the magazine *Newsweek*, which compares the official and not so official exchange rates throughout the world. And occasional curious locals must have watched the foreigners conspicuously disguised in beards and dark glasses trying to exchange a few pounds—for an illegal profit so small that it could only be assessed by the minutest of calculations—in Turkish mosques, Afghan caravanserais, and Burmese opium-houses.

Onlookers in Asia certainly saw that we cooked our own food instead of going to restaurants; that we camped on the roadside, in garages, stadiums, or schools in preference to an hotel; but few associated it with anything more than a foreign whim; and fewer still noticed the limpet eye with which each of us, like Russian woman commissars in a Paris hat-shop, watched the others spending.

Some people may have noticed the articles, photographs in illustrated magazines, and television programmes which emanated from the Expedition, but only a few could have realized that 10,000 feet of film, 3000 photos, and eighty articles were the product of a year's almost unceasing effort to break in on a highly competitive and most unco-operative market.

But what really made the journey possible in the first place was the generosity of the eighty-three firms which supplied the Expedition with camping gear, foodstuffs, and petrol—about £8000 worth of equipment. We thank them.

It is a delicate question as to how far an expedition of proverbially penniless students should commit themselves to accepting items of equipment in return for services of varying usefulness that they might offer. I think the answer depends on whether that expedition has the time, means, and intention of doing what it offers to do—be that taking part in some local sales drive or merely taking photographs of a tribesman enjoying a Puff Puff cigarette for the Puff Puff House Magazine. We had the intention, but, more important, we had the time. There are many other expeditions who, having to confine their journeys to the four months' summer vacation, are not so fortunate.

To give advice to other travellers is likely to be considered patronizing. But, accepting that risk, I finish with a few random tips which do not depend so much on common sense as on experience. For this reason, then, the following comments may be useful.

1.   The American magazine *Newsweek* carries a table which gives both the official and unofficial exchange rate in almost every country in the world. As there is sometimes a considerable difference between the two rates, this is an invaluable guide when dealing with money-changers.

2.   If you intend to ship your car (and to accompany it) endeavour to get it entered on the various shipping documents as your 'personal baggage.' If it travels on the 'ship's manifest' (the more normal way for cargo) there are likely to be frustrating and time-consuming complications at the other end.

3.   Letters of credit are the safest way of carrying a large amount of money. But they can only be changed at comparatively few banks, and, therefore, traveller's cheques are more useful for smaller sums. American dollar notes are invaluable in out-of-the-way places where cheques are difficult to cash. The Indian rupee is negotiable throughout the Far East, and, likewise, the

Lebanese pound in the Middle East. Foreign currency is best purchased in Switzerland or Lebanon, where there are free markets.

4.   The major oil companies provide information about relative petrol prices in different countries.

5.   Cigarettes, as always, are the most negotiable currency in the world.

6.   Certain insurance companies will issue a policy 'at a very reasonable premium' which allows any member of the party—should he be seriously injured—to be flown to the nearest fully equipped hospital. Likewise, policies can be prepared allowing any member to fly back to Britain in the event of a near relative (specified before-hand) becoming seriously ill. These policies are, perhaps, most worth while for the peace of mind they bring.

7.   Lastly, if you must take a financial risk, make sure it comes off! But if you should go bust, then get unbust—don't expect the nearest British Embassy to do it for you. It isn't their job, and, anyway, they've heard your story dozens of times.

Appendix H

A Summary of the Expedition's Return Journey

IT had never been the Expedition's intention to try both outward and homeward journeys wholly by land; once overland was reckoned to be enough. But, apart from this, there were other reasons which made a wholly overland return impossible. First, the monsoon would have already broken in Northern Burma, thus almost certainly making the Stilwell Road impassable. Second, it was extremely doubtful whether we should ever have got political permission to make the journey back through Burma to India. In any case, owing to our field-work programme, we certainly had not time to spare in trying.

At the beginning of April—after three weeks enjoying itself and organizing the return journey—the Expedition boarded the M.V. *Sangola*. At Rangoon, the ship's first port of call, the Expedition split: Oxford disembarked, while Cambridge sailed on to Calcutta.

Cambridge, on arrival in Calcutta, drove up to the Punjab. There, based first on Delhi and then Lahore, they spent six weeks studying the effects of Partition on the Punjab's irrigation network, and, in particular, India's Bhakra Nangal project. A return visit of three weeks to Thal completed their field-work, after which they left the furnace of the Indus plain for the cool of the Himalayan valley of Swat.

Oxford spent seven weeks in Burma carrying out field-work on mineral development in the Shan States. This involved 3000 miles of motoring, and it took the car as far north as Lashio, to the Burma Corporation mines at Bawdwin, to the zinc and manganese deposits of the Taunggyi area, and to the oil-fields at Chauk. On returning to Rangoon, three weeks were spent in and out of Government and commercial offices on 'follow-up' work. Oxford then shipped out of Rangoon to Calcutta, whence they drove across India and Pakistan to the North-West Frontier. Shade temperatures were above 112 degrees F. throughout this 1500-mile drive, and—as the only shade seemed to be directly beneath the thermometer—Oxford also went up to Swat, in the Himalayas, for refreshment. There, at Kalam, surrounded by snow, the two cars joined company. Three days were spent in the mountains, then the Expedition returned to the North-West Frontier town of Peshawar preparatory to beginning the journey home.

In Peshawar the captain of a United States military aircraft offered the Expedition a flight back to Britain. He was quite sincere, his plane (a Fairchild Packet) was more than capable of lifting the two Land Rovers, and it was leaving Peshawar the next day to return to its British base—in Cambridgeshire! The Expedition refused. The captain thought the Expedition was mad. The Expedition thought likewise.

Leaving Peshawar on June 12, the cars drove through the Khyber Pass to Afghanistan. Thence, by way of Kabul, Kandahar, and Herat to Persia. A brief halt was made in the holy city of Meshed before continuing on to Teheran. After a week in Teheran, the Expedition went north through the Elburz mountains to the Caspian Sea for a swim. From the Caspian the route led through Tabriz, across the steppes of Persian Azerbaijan, past Mount Ararat, and into Turkey. In the seven-day drive from Teheran to the Turkish town of Erzurum the Expedition suffered seventeen punctures.

From Erzurum the Expedition diverted north once more—to Trabzon (Trebizond), on the Black Sea. A lazy week was spent idling along the Black Sea coast as far west as Sinop. Then all speed was made for the Bosporus. The journey across Europe was straightforward, and led via Greece and Yugoslavia to northern Italy and Switzerland. Monaco was taken in, to make the twenty-first country.

On the morning of August 21 the cars crossed the Channel and drove up the Dover Road. At noon exactly they pulled up outside the Royal Automobile Club in Pall Mall. The journey was over.

Acknowledgments

1. The most difficult task is to thank all those people who made us their personal friends, and who went out of their way—almost inevitably at inconvenience to themselves—to help us. Some we knew for only a few hours, or even a few minutes, some we never met at all, and some took us into their homes and looked after us for several weeks (as did our hosts in Singapore and Rangoon). There are so many different people—at least three hundred—who befriended us in so many different ways that it is, quite literally, very hard to know where to begin, and even harder to know where to end. For this reason, then, we have decided against listing each person by name. Such a list would have some formal value, but we might leave some one out by mistake, and perhaps thereby cause some slight offence. Anyway, our friends know who they are, and we, the Expedition, assure them that we know full well the debt we owe. It is a debt which we cannot repay—but none the less real because of it. Merely to say 'thank you' is enormously inadequate. But—and we hope these people will understand—there is nothing else we can say.

2. We acknowledge with gratitude the help, interest, facilities, advice, or funds with which the following organizations helped us on our way.

Aitchison College, Lahore
Albert Reckitt Trust Fund
Assam Oil Company
British Broadcasting Corporation
British India Steam Navigation Company
British Missionary Society's hospitals at Isfahan, Shiraz, and Sukkur
Burma Corporation, Ltd
Burma Foreign Office
Burmah Oil Company
Cambridge University Explorers' and Travellers' Club
The Charles Henry Foyle Trust
Departments of Geography at Cambridge and Lahore Universities

Department of Irrigation, Lahore
Dewar's Garage, Calcutta
Edgar Brothers, Ltd, Bangkok
Gonville and Caius College, Cambridge
High Commission for India
High Commission for Pakistan
H.M. Board of Trade
H.M. Commonwealth Relations Office and High Commissions
H.M. Foreign Office and Embassies
Lahore Autos, Ltd, Lahore
Merchant Taylors' Company
Ministry of Agriculture, Pakistan
M.R.D.C, Burma
N.E.F.A., Shillong
Royal Geographical Society, London
Shan States Government, Taunggyi
St Catharine's College, Cambridge
Steel Brothers, Ltd, Rangoon
Thal Development Authority
UNESCO
Worts Fund

3.   The Expedition thanks the following firms for the loan or gift of equipment. Just why these firms should have helped us we do not really know, but, without any doubt whatsoever, their generosity was the thing that made the journey possible. Without it we could never have left England.

Aladdin Industries, Ltd
Army & Navy Stores, Ltd
Atkins, E., Ltd
Barrow, Hepburn & Gale, Ltd
Bedford, John, & Sons, Ltd
Brettle, George, & Co., Ltd
British American Optical Co., Ltd
British Patent Perforated Paper Co., Ltd

British Ropes, Ltd
Cascelloid Division of British
Xylonite Co., Ltd
Ceag, Ltd
Cellular Clothing Co., Ltd
Coleman Quick Lite & *Co.,* Ltd
Condrup, Ltd
Dunlop Rubber Co., Ltd
Eden, Robert, & Co., Ltd
Eversure Accessories, Ltd
Fleming, J. & R., Ltd
Flint, Howard, Ltd
Halex Division of British Xylonite Co., Ltd
Hawley, T., & Co. (Walsall), Ltd
Holt, Douglas, Ltd
I.C.I. Terylene Council
Johnson & Johnson, Ltd
Lodge Plugs, Ltd
Lowe & Fletcher, Ltd
Lucas, Joseph, Ltd
Lyle & Scott, Ltd
Lyonite Specialities, Ltd
Mackinnon Mackenzie, Ltd
Maclellan, George & Co., Ltd
Mobil Oil Co., Ltd
National Fire Protection Co., Ltd
National Pressure Cooker Co., Ltd
Nuway Manufacturing Co., Ltd
Osborn Manufacturing Co., Ltd.
Parramore & Sons, Ltd
Pye Radio, Ltd
Remington Rand, Ltd (Dry Shaver Division)
Remington Rand, Ltd (Typewriter Division)
Rover Co., Ltd
Schrader, A., & Son, Ltd
Silver City Airways, Ltd

Smith's English Clocks, Ltd
Stanley Works (G.B.), Ltd
Stein, S., & Sons, Ltd
Streetly Manufacturing Co., Ltd
Tebbutt Taylor, Ltd
Thermos (1925), Ltd
Tootal Broadhurst Lee Co., Ltd
Turner, William, (Kismet) Ltd
Standard Vacuum Oil Co., Ltd
Weathershields, Ltd

CONSUMABLE GOODS

Ardath Tobacco Co., Ltd
Beecham Foods, Ltd
British-American Tobacco Co., Ltd
Brooke Bond & Co., Ltd
Dewar, John, & Sons, Ltd
Findlater, Mackie Todd, & Co., Ltd
Gilbey, Mark, & Co.
Gilbey, W. & A., Ltd
Giordano, Ltd
Graham's Trading Co., Ltd (Calcutta)
Great Eastern Stores (Calcutta)
Guthries, Ltd (Singapore)
Imperial Tobacco Co., Ltd
Nestlé Co., Ltd
Schweppes, Ltd
Spinneys (1948), Iraq, Ltd
Twiss & Browning & Hallowes, Ltd
Unilever, Ltd
Waugh, Henry, & Co., Ltd (Singapore)
Watney, Combe, Reid & Co., Ltd
West Indian Sugar Producers   Association

CAMERA & RECORDING EQUIPMENT

Bell & Howell Co., Ltd
Franke and Heidecke
Grundig (Great Britain), Ltd
Pullin Optical Co., Ltd
Sangamo Weston, Ltd
Valradio, Ltd

MEDICAL STORES

Burroughs Wellcome & Co., Ltd
Glaxo Laboratories, Ltd
May & Baker, Ltd
Optrex, Ltd
University Health Service